File >
New >
Presentation

Presentation skills for software developers
and other technical professionals

Simon Guest

ISBN: 978-0615910451

Acknowledgements

Writing a book is never the job of only one person. Behind any single author is always a team of reviewers and other people who have been influential in building the content. This book is no exception to the rule, and as a result, I'd like to highlight some of the people who have made it what it is today.

From a presentation skills perspective, I owe great gratitude for many of the tips and recommendations to Richard Klees of Communication Power. Richard was my presentation mentor during my time at Microsoft, and although he never sugarcoated his words, he always gave incredibly valuable advice about how I could improve on stage. If you ever get the opportunity to work with Richard, or any of his team, I thoroughly recommend it! In addition to Richard's advice, much of this book comes as a reward from listening to others present, tell their stories, and share their experiences. While there have been too many influential presenters to name individually, I did want to make a special mention to David Chappell, Don Box, Chris Sells, Gurpreet Pall, Ian Phillips, Kirill Gavrylyuk, Miha Kralj, Pat Helland, Scott Hanselman, Shy Cohen, and Ted Neward—many of whom have influenced the stories told within.

With any book, a review team plays a big part. To that end, I would especially like to recognize Aaron Weissberger, Robert Altland, Shantanu Sarkar, and Steve Muise for their continued feedback, particularly with the early chapters. I would also like to call out Erin Shapley for all her incredible work while editing the book, and Glen Edelstein for the excellent cover design you see in front of you.

Finally, a personal commitment such as writing a book takes a lot of devotion from those closest to you. For this, my heartfelt thanks goes to my wife, Mako, and my two sons, Kylen and Kendan, for their continued support and love.

Table of Contents

Chapter 1: "Excuse Me, Mr. Guest!" - 7
   Why I wrote this book - 10
   My background - 12
   Who should read this book - 13
   How this book is structured - 14
Chapter 2: Who Is Your Audience? - 17
   What is a persona, and how can it help my presentation? - - - - - - - 18
   Where are we? - 38
Chapter 3: Structuring Your Presentation - - - - - - - - - - - - - - - - - - 41
   The presentation mind map - 41
   Introducing the 10/85/5 structure - 48
   Choosing a title and abstract for your presentation - - - - - - - - - - 84
   Time for your first rehearsal! - 97
   Where are we? - 99
Chapter 4: Your Slide Canvas—The Pencil Sketch - - - - - - - - - - - - 101
   Layers - 104
   Choosing a tool for your canvas: Microsoft PowerPoint... - - - - - - 106
   First Layer: Your pencil sketch - 109
   Your second rehearsal - 145
   Where are we? - 161
Chapter 5: Your Slide Canvas—Composition - - - - - - - - - - - - - - - 163
   Backgrounds - 163
   Acquiring and selecting images - 181
   Applying background templates to sections - - - - - - - - - - - - - - 196
   Fonts - 208
   Colors - 218
   Standalone images - 227
   Videos - 235
   Where are we? - 238
Chapter 6: Your Slide Canvas—Fine Details - - - - - - - - - - - - - - - - 241
   Diagrams - 241
   Screenshots - 256
   References and quotes - 267
   Animations - 270
   Packaging the deck - 278
   Where are we? - 284

Chapter 7: Rehearsing _____ 285
    Opening your presentation_____ 286
    Humor_____ 292
    In-room rehearsal_____ 294
    Additional rehearsal techniques_____ 302
    Where are we?_____ 305
Chapter 8: Demos_____ 307
    How many demos should I have?_____ 308
    Demo gods_____ 309
    Separate demo machine_____ 316
    Demo script_____ 317
    Secrets to a smooth demo_____ 320
    Where are we?_____ 329
Chapter 9: Your Big Day_____ 331
    Preparation_____ 333
    And you're on!_____ 341
    Interacting with the audience_____ 345
    At the podium after the presentation_____ 354
    Written feedback from the audience_____ 355
    Where are we?_____ 357
Chapter 10: Variations _____ 359
    Presenting in other countries_____ 359
    Presenting to online audiences_____ 365
    Presenting 1:1 to executives_____ 369
    Where are we?_____ 370
Chapter 11: Anti-Patterns for Presentations_____ 373
    Never offend the audience_____ 373
    Never inflate your ego_____ 374
    Never mention politics or religion in your presentation_____ 375
    Never swear or include profanity_____ 376
    Never present someone else's presentation_____ 376
    Never present from someone else's machine_____ 377
    Never let anyone else give your slides a "makeover"_____ 378
    Never move room or location_____ 379
    Never mess with the A/V equipment_____ 379
    Never use "Next slide, please!"_____ 380
    Conclusion_____ 381

CHAPTER 1: "Excuse Me, Mr. Guest!"

* * *

The stage lights went down, which was my cue to begin. I tapped my lapel microphone to make sure that it was on, and started my introduction. "Good morning everyone, and welcome to Microsoft TechEd in Orlando. My name is Simon Guest, and I'm here today to talk about Web Services." I hit the button on my presentation remote to move forward to the agenda slide, and proceeded to give the audience an overview of what they could expect in the next hour.

Halfway through reading the list of six bullets of my agenda, my focus was drawn to someone in the audience who had approached one of the microphones normally reserved for Q&A at the end of the talk. Before I could get to my next bullet point, I heard "Excuse me, Mr. Guest!" amplified around the room in a strong Indian accent. Everyone turned towards the man behind the microphone.

The man, wearing a turban and what appeared to be a faded T-shirt from a developer conference held far too long ago, continued. "Excuse me, Mr. Guest. I haven't come all the way from Bangalore just to hear things that I could have read on the web. Could you please share some real case studies with us?"

This wasn't a dream. This was my worst nightmare, and it was unfolding before my very eyes. I wasn't even past the agenda slide, and I was being heckled by the audience. I decided to take the high road.

"Thank you for your comment, sir. I'll definitely be saving some time at the end for questions. Now, let's move on with the agenda…"

I was able to read the next line of my agenda slide before I heard the all too familiar voice again.

"Excuse me, Mr. Guest. I'm not sure you heard me correctly. I really am very interested in any real case studies that you might have on this subject."

More people in the audience turned to look at my heckler, and I could hear a few giggles from the front rows. With a goal of moving on quickly, I replied a little more sternly.

"Thank you, sir. I appreciate your question, but we do have a full room, and I really must get on with the scheduled presentation now."

Hoping that this was now put to rest, I continued with the final couple of bullet points from my agenda. I was almost through the slide, and it had felt like an eternity.

"Excuse me, Mr. Guest. I must insist—"

I cut him off before he could continue. Now I was mad! Who was this guy, anyway? More audience members broke into laughter, which wasn't helping my cause.

"Please, sir. You must understand that we have three hundred people in the room who would like to hear the presentation. Would you like to do this presentation instead of me?" I challenged.

As soon as those words left my mouth I felt a twinge of regret. Surely he was going to back down on this one and return to his seat so that I could continue?

"Oh yes, Mr. Guest! I would love to do that!"

Before I could say anything else, the individual had left his position behind the microphone and was making his way down the center aisle towards the stage. Complete with attendee badge and what looked to be an overly full backpack, all the eyes in the audience followed him as he made his way to the front. Aside from a few whispers and an occasional laugh, the room was silent as he climbed the stairs onto the raised platform beside me. I murmured something I won't repeat in this book. The ground could have opened up beneath my feet and taken me to a different place—any place—and it would have been just fine with me.

Now standing next to me on stage, he made a quick introduction.

"Hello. My name is Gurpreet Pall."

"Hello, Gurpreet," I replied with a slightly sarcastic tone. Pointing to an area of the stage just to our left, I added, "Why don't you just stand there, and let's get on with the presentation." Using my remote, I clicked on the button to advance to the next slide.

Suddenly, out of nowhere, the slide changed from the blue theme of the Microsoft presentation template to a full-size picture of the Taj Mahal.

"What in the heck is this?" I exclaimed, turning to my new co-presenter.

"Why, Mr. Guest. That is my office!" said Gurpreet, smiling. "Well, not the big, white building, of course…We have a smaller office just outside the photo."

I remained temporarily confused.

"But how did this picture get into my slide deck?" I quizzed.

Gurpreet replied, "Ah! Yesterday, I attended a session on hacking. It was very good!"

As I'm sure it has for you, this is the moment that the penny dropped for the audience. This was, of course, all a setup, designed to add a little more flavor into what was a somewhat dry and boring topic. We continued the skit throughout the rest of the presentation, and instead of focusing on the original, fake agenda, completely changed the presentation to focus on case studies from Gurpreet's fictitious company in India.

The result of the following hour was an engaged audience who were able to get a lot of value out of the information, and were still talking about the presentation for many days during the remainder of the conference.

Why I wrote this book

Although this example was created specifically for one conference, took a lot of rehearsal, and even more coordination with the audio guys, it was designed to do one thing: Stand out. That, in itself, is my one hope for you as you read this book. My goal is to provide content and recommendations that will help you rethink the way that you plan, create, and deliver presentations to ensure that they stand out from others.

This hope comes from experiencing far too many presentations in the IT industry that, in my opinion, still fail to connect with the audience and never achieve what they set out to do. Presentations that are a complete disconnect for the audience in the room. Presentations that reel off facts, yet don't tell a story. Presentations that are overwhelmed with pages of text and bullet points. Presentations that show diagrams that no one understands. Presentations that go well under- or well overtime, and are clearly not rehearsed. Presentations where demos routinely fail in front of packed crowds. All delivered by presenters who make numerous mistakes while they are on stage.

For me, one of the indicators of a good presenter, especially for larger audiences, is how many hours of preparation they have put into a presentation relative to how many hours of time has been invested by the audience. Let me explain. Let's say that you are presenting a 60-minute session as part of your company's upcoming annual conference. You don't know the exact audience size, but you are expecting a fairly large group of 250 people. If you happen to get 250 people in attendance for your hour-long session, mathematically the time invested by the audience is six and a quarter man-weeks (as 250 hours equates to 6.25 x 40-hour working weeks). Now, if the audience is cumulatively going to spend over six weeks of their time listening to you on stage, is it not prudent that you put some effort in in order to pay back their investment?

Although it's not a perfect equation, nothing infuriates me more than a presenter who, given the same situation, will spend at most a couple of hours stealing slides from other people's decks, in order to "wing it." It is my hope that not only does this book provide valuable content for structuring and creating your presentations, but it also encourages you to invest this additional time such that you can justify the investment that the audience is making for you.

As I'm sure you know, this is not the only book on delivering presentations. In recent years, books such as *PresentationZen* (Reynolds, 2008) and *Beyond Bullet Points* (Atkinson, 2005) have motivated presenters towards moving away from text-heavy, bullet point approaches to expressing their presentation through visual images. While I applaud this approach, I have witnessed some struggle with the transition. For many people, the pendulum often swings completely the other way, and the result is decks that used to be filled with bullet points now replaced with arbitrary pictures of animals, sunsets, pictures of the world from space, and anything else that tries to loosely connect a beautiful looking picture to a speaking point. The result is a beautiful set of images, but often a presentation that fails to connect intellectually with the audience, especially executives, and is often not reusable outside being delivered by the original author. As you will discover when we investigate slide composition in more detail in Chapters 4, 5, and 6, the goal of this book is to attain a balance between the two. The goal will be to explore the use of visuals, imagery, and other effects to enhance a presentation, but not lose sight of the fact that the presentation should also stand alone in many circumstances.

Finally, and related to the previous point, it is my intention with this book to cover more than just slide creation. The skills required to put together a great looking slide deck are an important factor, but a great presentation is more than just a set of slides. Knowing your audience, planning the structure of your talk, rehearsing, delivering demos, preparation, and what you do behind the podium are as important (if not more so) than the slide deck that you end up showing on the screen. It is the intention of this book to build upon this balance of creating a great presentation, and arm you with everything else required in order to deliver it well.

My background

I will never lay claim to be the best presenter ever, however, I've been fortunate to have had a career with many opportunities to present in different circumstances, as well as listen and learn from many other wonderful presenters.

My experience has run the gamut from 1:1 presentations with Bill Gates to onstage talks to many thousands of people, and almost everything in between. I've delivered presentations where I've been awarded the best speaker, including twice inducted to Sun Microsystem's Speaker Wall of Fame, through to presentations that I now conceal in a far corner of my memory because they went so horribly wrong.

My presentation experience isn't limited to the United States, either. I've had the opportunity to speak in countries covering almost every continent across the world, having to learn how to modify my presentations for different cultures, and often having to deliver presentations together with simultaneous translators for non-English-speaking audiences.

When I've not been presenting, I've been fortunate to witness some of the best speakers in the industry—stories from whom will be retold within this book. This, together with many years of coaching from Richard Klees, President of Communication Power, whom I would argue is one of the best speaker coaches ever, has given me great insight into what works well and how to tailor my own talks to better connect with the audience.

Finally, I've also seen presentations through the eyes of conference organizers. My team at Microsoft was responsible for organizing and running one of the tracks for a worldwide conference between 2006 and 2008. During these three years, we had to select topics, mentor speakers through presentation creation, conduct literally hundreds of dry runs and rehearsals, and deal with virtually every incident or request imaginable from speakers during the week of the conference. It was all worth it, however, and we were able to take the track from almost last place in 2006, to the highest-rated and most well-attended track in the 2008 conference.

Who should read this book

There are many different types of presentations, ranging from small group presentations to an online audience to standing in front of thousands of people in a crowded theater. While it would be difficult, if not impossible, to cover every possible situation imaginable, I wanted to spend some time covering the types of presenters that this book has been written for:

- **You are a software developer or professional in the IT industry.** Being in software development for many years, this book has primarily been written to appeal to an audience of similar background. Many of the terms and structures that we'll use within the book will relate to those who are delivering presentations in the software field. With that said, many topics in the book are generic enough to be used for other roles within IT, and even for technical presenters who work in different industries.

- **You want to improve your storytelling.** The content found within this book, especially Chapters 2 and 3, is aimed towards presenters who want to "tell a story." This, of course, can vary dramatically, and might range from sharing an idea or knowledge of a particular subject with your team to pitching a product or vision to a large customer in the corporate world. During Chapter 3, we will investigate three types of presentation story and the audience types that support these. Although storytelling can, and arguably should, apply to all presentations, there are certain types of delivery—such as audience facilitation or continual audience participation—that we will not be covering here.

- **You plan to use slides for your presentation.** For the majority of this book, the guidance and recommendations outlined within will assume that you will be using some form of slides (created using

Microsoft PowerPoint or similar) to support the delivery of your message. While there are many presentation scenarios that don't use slides, such as in-person workshops performed with only a whiteboard, this book is skewed towards presentations that try to maintain a balance between the presenter's narrative and the visuals shown to the audience.

- **You will be presenting your content to an in-person audience.** This book, especially Chapter 9 that focuses on delivery, assumes that you are conducting your presentation in person to your audience. In Chapter 10, we will discuss some variations, which do include online presentations and webcasts. However, the style of presentations that you will end up creating as a result of this book will likely be better suited towards an in-person setting.

- **You don't want to be Steve Jobs!** There are other books that have been written to try and make your presentation skills similar to Steve Jobs, and by design, this is not one of them. While Steve was an awe-inspiring presenter, his presentations were designed for specific situations (namely, product launches to a worldwide audience). As I suspect that few readers will be in the same position as Steve, the goal with this book is to provide you the tools, tips, and recommendations to help develop your own unique presentation style rather than simply try and copy something that was attributed to someone else.

How this book is structured

Now that we've covered who should read this book, I want to spend a little time covering the structure of many of the chapters.

As mentioned previously, there are many aspects to planning, creating, and delivering a presentation beyond just creating slides. To support this idea, this book is structured chronologically, taking you step-by-step from planning your presentation and putting the slides together, to the big day and ultimately creating a feedback loop so that you can incorporate learnings into future talks to make you a better presenter.

The book starts with Chapter 2 and covers defining your audience, one of the most important things to do before starting any presentation. In this chapter, you'll learn about personas—especially how to develop a set of them that will work for your presentation.

Next, Chapter 3 will cover the structure of your presentation. Taking the personas forward you'll use a tool called a "mind map" to create a structure for your presentation following a set of proven rules. You'll also choose a title and abstract for your session as well as undertake your first rehearsal.

Chapter 4 introduces the concept of a slide canvas, which is the presentation that you'll be creating. You'll start by defining a "pencil sketch" by importing the details from the mind map, creating sections, lists, content placeholders, and templates. At the end of this you'll also do your second rehearsal.

The following chapter, Chapter 5, continues the process of creating the slide canvas by adding backgrounds, images, fonts, colors, and other composition elements. By now your presentation is starting to take real shape and, as you might have guessed, you'll be doing some more rehearsing!

Chapter 6 adds the fine details to your canvas, including diagrams, screenshots, and animations. Here, you'll be learning how to put the final touches on your presentation.

In Chapter 7, you will take everything that you've done so far and focus on rehearsals. You'll learn how to open your presentation, think about humor, discover how to set up the room correctly, and learn techniques for dealing with common presentation mistakes.

Many developer-related presentations have need for demos, and this is something that we'll be covering in detail throughout Chapter 8. You'll learn about demo gods and what it takes to avoid them, plus how to put together a demo script to ensure everything goes as planned.

With your big day approaching, Chapter 9 will cover everything that you need to think about on the day, including combatting presentation nerves, setting up at the podium, and interacting with the audience before, during, and after your presentation.

Chapter 10 is where you'll take everything you've learned and understand how to apply it for various situations. This will include presenting in other countries, presenting to an online audience, and presenting 1:1 with executives.

Finally we wrap everything up in Chapter 11 where we will cover anti-patterns for your presentation. You'll learn ten things that you should never, ever do in any presentation!

CHAPTER 2: Who Is Your Audience?

* * *

You've been asked to present at an upcoming conference. It's exciting! This will be your big chance to win over the crowd and deliver a presentation that knocks them off their feet.

First step in creating your presentation: Launch Microsoft PowerPoint, and select New Presentation from the File menu?

Absolutely not!

While it might be tempting to think that the first step in creating a presentation is to start with a new PowerPoint file, this is exactly what you should never do. By doing this, you are skipping over the most vital parts of planning and structuring your presentation.

An analogy can be drawn between creating a presentation and creating a movie. Do you think that the first thing a movie director does is to load a camera with film and start shooting scenes? Of course not. The same is also true for writing. As any successful novelist will tell you, the idea that a writer loads a blank sheet of paper into a typewriter and starts drawing upon their inner muse is a complete fantasy. The same should be taken for developing a presentation, and starting by opening Microsoft PowerPoint to begin creating slides will likely lead to disaster.

As with movie directors and writers, there is one question that needs to be answered first when embarking on a journey to create a new presentation:

Who is the audience?

One of the most common reasons that presentations are poorly received is due to a disconnect between what the audience needs or wants and the content that the presenter is delivering. If you've ever been in the audience, you've probably witnessed this on several occasions. Some of the conversations I've overheard as people have left the room have included:

"It was a nice looking presentation, but all that information was already covered in the keynote. It wasn't really worth my time to hear that again."

"I was hoping the speaker was going to talk about issues related to today's product, but instead they just talked about the future roadmap."

"I had no idea what the speaker was talking about. I thought this was supposed to be an introductory talk!"

Again, we ask the question: Who is the audience?

On the surface, this appears to be a simple question to answer. Maybe the audience is your team at work. Maybe it's a customer. Maybe it's a group of industry peers at a conference. While this might be true, it doesn't fully answer the question. To have any hope of understanding and connecting with your audience you first need to build up a persona—or, in many cases, a set of personas—that represent the likely attendees who will come to your presentation.

What is a persona, and how can it help my presentation?

A persona is a fictional role or character, often used to give a face and a name to a broad set of individuals sharing common characteristics and goals. Personas are frequently used in software development, and as a developer you may have used them in your own projects, especially if the project has focused on a lot of user interaction. For those who haven't run across personas before, we can start by taking a look at an example in order to understand how they are created.

When designing software to address a particular need or market, a development team will likely create a set of personas that represent the users who are going to be interacting with the software. These personas will focus on the background, characteristics, and goals of a set of individuals that represent the user.

For example, let's imagine that a software team was developing a new website designed to sell books online. Based on previous analysis and research, they may end up representing potential customers through these three personas:

- **Corrie the Casual Browser.** Corrie, 27, runs a flower shop in her local town. She is single and rents her own apartment close to work. She was encouraged by her parents to read, and now enjoys reading romantic fiction. She has access to the Internet through her smartphone and a PC at home. Although she has purchased books from other online retailers, Corrie is very cost conscious. She will often browse the reviews of books from an online store only to then check them out at the library in order to save money. Her goal is to find a couple of books that she knows she will enjoy for her upcoming vacation.

- **Pete the Professional.** Pete, 42, is an intellectual property lawyer working in a major metropolitan area. He is divorced with two children, who he sees regularly. Coming from an affluent background, Pete is also a keen investor and spends a lot of his spare time day trading in the stock market. He is technically very savvy, and uses the Internet for all his trading. Pete is always ordering books online, especially about trading and other financial topics of interest. He is often not concerned about the cost of a book, but as time is money for him, he instead values books being delivered as quickly as possible, preferably within two days. His goal is to order the new book that he's just read a review about in the Wall St. Journal.

- **Iva the Institutional Buyer.** Iva, 56, is the manager of a bookstore specializing in educational materials. Her bookstore has several contracts with the local university to supply reference books in bulk. Iva comes from an academic background herself and, during her career, has been an associate professor and head librarian. Iva is comfortable ordering goods online, but values personal relationships and support as part of the process. She sometimes gets stuck (especially with some of the complicated orders), and appreciates having access to someone that she can call if needed. With the next semester quickly approaching, her goal is to place a large bulk order to fulfill the needs of the university.

The above characters are fictional by design, but are given an identity, background, set of characteristics, and one or more goals. If you've ever purchased a book online, you might be able to relate to one or more of them. Moreover, they represent a segment of the potential customer base for the online bookstore, which enables the software development team to ensure that they are addressing the needs of customers uniquely.

For example, if the software development team is thinking about the checkout process for the online store, instead of asking a generic question, such as "What would the user want here?" they can ask the same question to each persona instead.

What would Corrie want? Probably the ability to find out return information and price guarantee information.

What would Pete want? A quick checkout process with multiple delivery options.

What would Iva want? Access to either live chat or a telephone helpline in case she has questions when placing her large order.

As you can probably tell, the answers given on a persona-by-persona basis are much more powerful than just wondering what a generic "user" would want to do.

This concept of personas can also work wonders in helping you develop your presentation. Instead of asking yourself the question, "What would my audience want to hear?" a set of personas enables you to answer the question in far greater detail and with much more context. In addition, a set of personas can live with you during the creation of your presentation. When you come across questions or decisions that need to be made during editing or rehearsing your presentation, personas can help bring a sense of clarity and perspective.

Questions to develop your own personas

Although it is tempting, personas shouldn't be created from thin air. Instead, you will need to research many aspects of the potential audience. While there is extensive study into the area of persona development,[1] for the purpose of providing you with a starting point in this book, I've found that answering the following seven questions can be very effective.

Q1: Will your audience be internal or external?

A great question to start developing your own personas is to first ask whether your audience will be internal to your organization. By internal, I'm referring to employees or colleagues, whereas an external audience would be customers or business partners. This might seem like an obvious question to ask, but it's amazing how many presenters overlook tuning their presentation for either an internal or external audience.

Not only will the answer help you define your personas, but it can also offer a lot of guidance on how you should approach the structure and delivery of the presentation.

For example, it's often a common mistake to think that presenting to an internal group might be easier than delivering a presentation to external customers. While there might be different circumstances for both audiences, I've personally experienced (and also witnessed through others) that internal audiences can be much more difficult to present to. In fact, I'll go so far to say that sometimes they can be downright evil! I remember vividly one of my first presentations at Microsoft. I had been with the company only a couple of months, and my manager had recommended holding an informal "brown bag" lunchtime presentation based on some C++ development I was working on at the time. Although there were only about ten of my peers in the room, I got eaten alive. I was well prepared on the topic, but I completely misunderstood the audience in the room, the questions they would likely ask, and their expectations for my presentation. Although it was harsh at the time, it proved to be an invaluable lesson for future presentations to internal teams.

✧✧✧✧✧✧✧✧✧

Why are internal audiences more difficult to present to?

An internal audience will often be more critical, especially if the topic of your presentation threatens their project, position, or group in any way. Throughout my career, I've been involved in multiple presentations on topics and products that were in direct conflict with other people in the room. While all of the presentations were held with a great deal of mutual respect, the approach of an internal audience can be far more critical than an external audience. This tends to show itself in three different ways.

Firstly, there is a good chance that an internal audience will know the domain much better than an external audience would. They will likely expect a deeper level of content, and their questions will get down into the weeds much faster than an external audience who is new to the topic. Moreover, they will likely come prepared with a preconceived idea of your presentation and the questions they are likely to raise before you've even started the first slide!

Secondly, an internal audience will be less afraid to ask questions. Being part of the same team, department, or organization makes people much more comfortable with each other. Where an external audience may have waited until the designated Q&A slot at the end of your presentation, an internal audience will likely interrupt halfway through before you've even reached the majority of the topic you are trying to get to.

Finally, an internal audience will often go beyond barriers that an external audience would not. Where an external audience may have been polite in not revealing what they think of your presentation or product, an internal audience will likely not hold back in letting you know exactly what they think!

As a presenter, this will mean that you need to be more prepared than you otherwise would have been if presenting to an external audience, including getting to the main parts of your presentation quicker, being much more prepared to answer the dreaded "You may be covering this in the next slides, but…" question, and other things thrown at you from left field. While we will be covering many of these topics when we discuss handling feedback in Chapter 9, hopefully this gives you an early appreciation of the differences between internal and external facing audiences, and why they matter for defining your personas.

Q2: Will you know your audience members personally?

Similar to the internal vs. external makeup of your audience, knowing members of your audience will have an impact on the personas that you create, and of course your resulting presentation.

The answer to this question will likely be a sliding scale. If you are putting together a presentation for your team of five employees, you'll will more than likely know 100% of your audience personally. If you are presenting a product to a new customer you have never met before, there's a chance that you won't know anyone in the room. In certain circumstances, the answer might be in the middle. Maybe you are presenting at a conference, with some familiar faces that you see every year, in which case you might know 20% of the audience.

The reason this is important is that the more you know about your audience personally, the more personalized and tailored you can make your presentation, and the more positively it will be received.

This personalization might range from including stories or events that you were both involved with to previous conversations and needs. For example, your presentation might include a story about how you worked together using a previous product that was inferior, and how the actions that you had to take to overcome this, led to the development of a new product.

In addition, knowing the audience personally can also give you a sense of how they will react to your presentation. Based on previous presentations to them, do they like to get to the point quickly? That might influence the timing of your presentation. Did they really enjoy the last presentation? In which case, are there things that you can take across to the new one?

Q3: Are there primary segments or categories that your audience will likely represent?

In the previous examples of personas for the online bookstore, it was clear to see how each persona represented a particular customer segment. In the case of Corrie, it was the more cautious customer. For Pete, it was the more impatient customer, who was interested in getting books delivered as quickly as possible. In real life, although people have these traits, it can be difficult to tease them out, especially when thinking about the audience for your presentation. There are a number of things you can potentially look at to identify different segmentation or categories for your audience.

For example, if you are presenting a topic to an internal audience, you might be able to predict which departments or groups will be interested in the topic. Maybe your presentation will be interesting to the accounting and HR departments. Each of these departments represent a different segmentation that is likely going to demand different things from your presentation.

Another good segmentation I've seen, especially for larger presentations, is job title or function. Many conferences bring together people based on theme, but often it's possible to construct personas for your presentation based on the role of the audience who is likely to attend. For example, if you are planning a presentation where you are showing your latest code to a sales audience, there's a good chance you are going to have a mix of people with job functions such as account executives and business development managers that you may be able to derive personas from.

Q4: What will be the goal of the audience?

Although in the middle of the list, this is arguably the most important question to ask when defining a set of personas for your audience. What is the goal of the audience? What are they trying to achieve?

When thinking of the answer to this, segmentation of the audience can play a big role. It is likely that audience members that fit within different segmentations will have differing goals. For example, for a presentation on a new and improved product, an audience member from the support group might have a goal of "understanding the new features of the product in order to support the customers." For the same presentation, an audience member from the sales group might have an orthogonal goal of "understanding the new features of the product so that they can more effectively sell against the competition." This is also what makes the persona approach more powerful as you will end up creating goals for each persona in your audience instead of trying to assess a common goal for everyone in the room.

More than often, I see presenters lose sight of not only understanding the goal of the audience, but even letting this slip out in the first sentence of a presentation. A common example of this, and a popular opening line for presentations, is: "I'm here today to talk to you about X." In this one sentence, the presenter is inadvertently communicating that they are not here to address the needs or goals of the audience, which can be a bad way to start. While we will cover your presentation opening in more detail during Chapter 7, know that personas can help focus you on the goals of the audience right from the start.

Let me restate the point for clarity: If you are able to address the underlying goals of the audience in the room, your presentation is already in great shape. Everything else—the slides, the fonts, images, low volume, walking around like a caged animal on stage—all these take a backseat to fundamentally addressing the goal of an audience in a presentation.

Q5: What are your goals?

Even for presenters who think about the goals of the audience, this is a question that is often overlooked. What are your goals? Why are you here? As the presenter, what do you hope to get out of the presentation?

While these might sound like they are going to take you down a crazy path of finding yourself spiritually, they are very effective questions to ask.

Maybe your goal is to sell more of a product. Maybe it's to educate a group of people to reduce support calls for your company. Maybe it's to share your opinions and ideas on a programming language that you truly believe could change the world.

While everyone's answers to this will be different, a fascinating exercise—and one that will ultimately make your presentation more effective—is to take your goal and see how it matches up with the goals of your personas.

Sometimes there will be close alignment. For example, let's imagine that you plan on delivering a presentation on tips to further the sales of a piece of software. You have a goal of selling more software. If your audience has a goal of learning how to sell more software, these goals are in alignment. Assuming the content is useful for the audience, this could be a great presentation.

Sometimes there won't be an alignment whatsoever. For example, imagine that you are planning on delivering a presentation that covers the next version or roadmap for your software product. You have a goal of sharing information about a topic you are passionate about. If your audience has a goal of learning how to troubleshoot the current version, while both goals are related to your software product, they are not in alignment. Even if the content contains the best information ever released, if the goals don't match, many people in the audience could walk away disappointed.

Often the goals will align, but the level of the goals will be different. For example, let's say that you are planning a presentation on maximizing the use of a SDK (Software Development Kit) to a room of developers at a conference. You have a goal of educating the audience on some of the more advanced techniques of the SDK. If the goal of the audience is to learn the fundamentals of using your SDK, the goals are technically the same—learn how to use the SDK—but the level of the presentation will likely be a complete mismatch. As a result, the content of the presentation might be top class, but the audience will walk out of the room completely overwhelmed with what they've just heard. We'll cover more detail on setting the expectation and level for your presentations in Chapter 3.

Finally, is your goal genuine? This might sound like a strange question, but I have witnessed many presenters where the goal of the presenter is just to look smart. I've fallen victim to this several times as this often comes about innocently. On several occasions, I've been asked to present on a topic that I'm unfamiliar with, possibly covering for a colleague who is out at the time. Someone will say, "Simon is smart. He can present on this topic." While this might be the case, my goal as a presenter ends up as "to look smart" or "to cover for Joe while he's out of town" or "to not let the side down." It's not a genuine goal for me as a presenter. The consequence of this is that it often bleeds through into the preparation and my enthusiasm when delivering the talk, and I find the presentation isn't as effective as it should have been.

If you are ever placed in such a position where you are asked to present a topic that is outside your normal realm, my recommendation is to revisit this question in particular to try and refactor the presentation to one where you can discover a genuine goal for you as a presenter.

Q6: What might the audience already know?

If you understand what the audience knows, you'll more easily be able to build upon this knowledge, while at the same time avoiding repeating things that they may already know.

With many audiences however it can be difficult to guess what this knowledge might be, but there are several approaches that can help add clarity.

For example, if you have been asked by your company to present to a potential new customer, there are questions you might ask beforehand. Has anyone presented to this customer before? What did they present? What did they think? How many previous meetings have we had with this new customer? How much does this potential new customer know about our company?

Asking and getting answers to these questions can help educate you on the background knowledge that a customer will be walking into the room with. As one example, if they have already had multiple meetings and a couple of presentations from other people, there's probably a good chance that they know about your company. If they know about your company, you may want to spend less time explaining the company as part of the presentation.

Secondly, if your presentation is to be held on the same day as other presentations, it's also important to find out where you stand in the agenda. If your presentation is following three others, who are the other speakers and what are they talking about? This can help you build upon the topics that have already been covered, and also avoid repeating some of the information that will likely have already been presented in the previous sessions. The result of this is a strong foundation for your presentation that flows and connects with information that the audience has heard that day.

This also holds true if you are speaking in a developer conference, especially if your presentation covers anything that was mentioned in the keynote. Nothing is more infuriating for an attendee than to sit through a two-hour keynote only to then go to a "deep dive coding" session that is a complete repeat of what they heard before. By understanding what will be talked about in the keynote, and at what level, you already know the knowledge that the audience members will be walking in with. Understanding this will enable you to do a quick recap of the keynote before presenting new information that will be valuable to the audience.

Q7: What is their background?

The final question in the list focuses on background information about the audience that might be relevant for your presentation. This is less about the background of a particular individual, as this would have been covered in Question 2, but instead refers to the collective audience as a whole.

One common background question is to try and determine where the audience is coming from. Are they local? Are they specific to a region, state, or country? Are you expecting an international audience? The answers to these can help frame information in your presentation that might provide a connection point with the audience. As an example, during one of my previous presentations, I knew beforehand that the audience would be coming from Canada. This was a Canadian customer who was traveling to meet with several groups at the company. As a result, I did a quick search on Google, found out some of the recent headlines and stories around the hockey scene in Canada, and was able to interject a "Hey, did anyone see the Calgary Flames last weekend?" question in to my opening remarks. Although I didn't know the slightest thing about Canadian hockey teams, it provided an instant connection with the audience even before I started the presentation.

Ironically, this same connection can be made even if the data you have is completely wrong. On one occasion, I had a brutal schedule where I was flying from Seattle to Amsterdam, only to be picked up after my 10-hour flight and driven directly to a customer site to give a presentation to a hundred or so developers. I felt proud that I remembered a few facts from my last trip to Amsterdam I could repeat to the audience. Although the facts were correct, one audience member quickly informed me that we weren't actually in Amsterdam, but instead were in Utrecht, about 30km due southeast. Although I had completely messed up on the facts, I was able to inject a humorous line about jet lag, which later became a theme that I built upon during the rest of the presentation.

How big will your audience be?

Now that we have covered the questions that can help create a set of personas, you may be asking how many personas you should end up creating. This answer can vary greatly depending on the potential size of your audience. If you only have one person coming to your presentation, unless they are Dr. Jekyll and Mr. Hyde, chances are that you wouldn't want to create more than one persona. However, with an audience of a hundred people, one persona for each audience member is not going to work, either. Before you can decide on a number of personas, it's first important to understand the different sizes of audiences that you might encounter.

As you can imagine, audience sizes can vary dramatically, ranging from one person to a room full of thousands. Despite this great variability, I've found that audience sizes generally fall into one of five categories:

- **1:1.** Believe it or not, you can have an audience of one! This is actually more common than you may think. Maybe you are responsible for presenting to a CEO, CTO, or founder of a company. Maybe you need to make a presentation to an influential venture capitalist. With this type of presentation, there may be other people in the room, but throughout you are directing the presentation (and your focus) to this one person. As this one person can more easily dictate the flow of your presentation, there is a dedicated section at the end of Chapter 10 for some of the modifications that you can make.

- **Small group (2–15 people).** The second category of audience is the small group, ranging from 2 to 15 audience members. This is a fairly intimate setting, normally held in a small conference room or equivalent. For the smaller end of this group size, you may present directly from your screen or an external monitor. For the larger end, you'll likely be using a small projector.

- **Medium group (15–40 people).** A medium audience group is anywhere between 15 and 40 people. This group size doesn't have the intimate feel of the small group, but is still manageable. As a result, presentations of this size are normally held in a large conference room or area. If you are presenting in the exposition hall at a trade show, this can be a typical size for some of the talks. You'll definitely be using a small projector for this group size, and a microphone may be required if the surroundings are noisy.

- **Large group (40–150 people).** A large group ranges from 40 to 150 audience members. Due to the increased size, presentations of this size will normally be held in a dedicated room or small auditorium, and you will likely be speaking behind a podium or equivalent. Talks of this size require the speaker to use a large projector, and a microphone will certainly be required to reach the people at the back of the room.

- **Theater (150 people and above).** A theater presentation is defined as any audience with over 150 members. This setting will require a larger, dedicated presentation room, or auditorium, often with a well-lit, raised stage and podium to enable everyone in the room to clearly see you. Depending on the size, the room may also have multiple screens connected to the projector, with screens typically located either side of the podium. A microphone will be a necessity in this environment, and there will often be multiple audio speakers to carry your voice throughout the room.

We'll be using these five categories throughout the book, so it's a great idea to memorize these or bookmark this section to make it easy to refer back to this section. You may ask why we don't have categories for over 150. Maybe a category for 300? 500? How about over 1000?

In my experience, and I've found other presenters generally agree, there tends to be little difference presenting to a 150-person audience compared to a 700-person audience. Yes, there are more faces in the audience, and there may be additional screens or audio speakers to accommodate the room, but the fundamentals of the presentation style and content are generally the same. Moreover, with the types of lighting used in larger presentation rooms, often you can't see beyond 150 people, anyway. There may be more faces, but they will all be hidden in the shadows when the lights go down.

The rules do change however as you reach over 2,500. At this size, you are likely to be in a concert hall or stadium, and you'll need to take into account subtleties such as a greenroom and dedicated A/V (audio/visual) team to help with the environment. Given that these presentations are few and far between, and at this size you'll probably be working with a dedicated speaker coach,, it is safe to say that this is probably outside the scope of this book.

How big will your audience be? Great question! There is no exact science to tell how many people will turn up to your presentation, but there are certainly a few indicators that can help narrow down the range.

Firstly, you can ask questions. If your presentation is going to be held at a customer site, it might sound obvious, but you can ask how many people are likely to be coming to the meeting. Often an account representative will already have a good guess based on the response to their invitation.

Secondly, if you are speaking with others at a conference, gut feel can be a good indicator. How many people are going to talks of similar subject or complexity? Are you talking about a popular topic? Is the title of your talk very focused, which might result in a smaller crowd interested in this niche subject—or is it a generic title, which could attract a wider audience? Often you can use a lot of these indicators to get a good sense of how many people will be in the room. We'll talk more about how you can also change the title of a session to influence audience size in Chapter 3.

Finally, if you are at a large conference, you might consider visiting the organizers ahead of time. Ask which room you'll be in and how many people that room seats. Often the conference room organizers will pre-assign rooms based on early interest and registration numbers. For example, if they have assigned you to room B302, and that room has a maximum capacity of 350 seats, you are somewhat guaranteed to have between 0 and 350 people show up! Of course, if the organizers have placed you in such a room, they have probably done it for a reason, so there's a good chance they are expecting a good crowd. In this case, a range of 150 to 300 might be more accurate.

How many personas should you create?

With a better sense of the audience size, you can now determine how many personas make sense for your presentation. As a general rule of thumb, I would recommend the following:

Firstly, if you are conducting a 1:1 presentation, you should create one persona based on the previous questions and your knowledge of who you will be presenting to. Even though it might seem academic, the process of collecting this information and building this persona will prove invaluable for delivering a great presentation for this person.

For the small and medium audience groups, I would recommend two or three personas. The segmentation of the audience will likely be such that one persona doesn't make sense, yet anything over three personas will probably result in too much overlap.

Finally, for the large and theater audience groups, I would recommend anywhere between three and five personas. I've often found that the segmentation of these larger groups means that if you are using any fewer than three, you are probably still thinking about the audience in generic terms, which will defeat the purpose of using personas. In this instance, all you are doing is giving your collective audience a nice name. Conversely, if you are finding that you are developing more than five personas, it's possible that you might be overanalyzing each of the roles or functions which could lead to a presentation that heads in too many different directions. More importantly, as you take your personas throughout the creation of your presentation, having more than five can also become quickly confusing.

An example of creating personas

Using the answers from the seven questions, together with an understanding of the audience size, let's now look at how you can construct personas for your own presentation. To achieve this, we are going to introduce a fictitious example. Imagine that I am playing the role of a lead software developer for a large organization, which specializes in GPS navigation devices, particularly the portable devices used in cars. I have been asked to speak at the company's upcoming all-hands meeting, where I will be revealing the details of my group's new product, a next generation GPS device, which we have been working on for the past 12 months.

To start, I have answered the seven questions to help me develop the personas, specific to this example:

- **Question 1: Will your audience be internal or external?** This is a company all-hands meeting, so the audience will be internal employees.

- **Question 2: Will you know your audience members personally?** The company has many thousands of employees coming to the conference, so there's a good chance that I will only know a handful of people that come to my session.

- **Question 3: Are there primary segments or categories that your audience will likely represent?** The audience will likely be made up of people in the room who are eager to find out about the next version of the product. I was able to ask one of our seasoned product managers, and based on previous launches, I found that there are probably going to be three main segments:

  Engineering: Other engineers around the company that are working on related software and products.

  Sales: Various sales representatives from around the company.

  Support: We may get a number of folks from the support organization.

  In terms of percentages, I would take a rough guess at 25% engineering, 60% sales, and 15% support. This mix might include some roles outside these three groups, but these will likely be in the minority. For the sales representatives that come to the session, about half will be account executives representing large distributors and online retailers, whereas the other half will be account representatives for more targeted sales, such as rental car companies.

- **Question 4: What will be the goal of the audience?** The engineering attendees will be most interested in how the product works, especially the underlying software and SDKs. Their goal will be to find out if and how their product can work well with ours. Representatives from the sales force will want to know how to sell the product after launch. Their goal will be to understand the selling points of the product, and how it differs from our previous version and our competitors. Finally, the support organization will be keen to support customers after launch. Their primary goal will likely be to understand the differences between the previous and new versions of the product so that they can train their staff.

- **Question 5: What are your goals?** My goal is to ensure that the product is successful. This is a key product launch for my group, and the fate of the company—and likely my career—rests on it. What does success mean? It means the product sells a lot of units, and customers are very satisfied with their purchase.

- **Question 6: What might the audience already know?** Firstly, I know that there will be a section about the product in the keynote of the conference. Our CEO will be talking about the new launch, what it means to customers, and showing one of the first demos of the GPS unit in front of most of the company. For most people in the room, this will be the first time that they've seen anything about the product.

The exception to the rule will be some of the engineering group. Many have had access to an early set of prototypes and drops of the SDK before launch, so there will be a subset of the engineering team in the audience that has already has some experience of prior use.

- **Question 7: What is their background?** Our company has many offices across multiple countries, so I'm expecting an international audience. Of note is the support group, who are based in our offshore facilities in Bangalore and Hyderabad. All attendees will be full-time employees of the company, however the company has been hiring many new employees recently, so I'm expecting that several will be new hires. These new hires will likely have little to no previous experience of our products.

Based on the answers to these questions, and our belief that we are going to see around 150 or so people in the theater, we've created the following personas:

- **Eddie the Equipment Engineer.** Eddie, 39, is a lead engineer working in a sister product group within the company that specializes in devices that connect to the GPS device, such as speakers, headsets, and other Bluetooth devices. He has a master's degree in science, and deeply enjoys tinkering with new products and making other products better. Eddie has had the opportunity to play with a prototype over the past few months, and has already been vocal with some of the early feedback. Eddie's goal of coming to the presentation is to find out how the final product will be different from the early prototypes, and how his product should integrate with it.

- **Oliver the Online Retail Salesperson.** Oliver, 46, works in the enterprise sales group within the organization. Oliver has been with the company for 20 years, rising through the ranks, and is now responsible for online retail sales, which accounts for the company's largest source of revenue. Oliver has been very successful in selling previous products and is looking forward to sharing information about the new release with his largest customers. Oliver's goal of coming to the presentation will be to find out enough information that he can develop a sales presentation of his own to present at the launch.

- **Rita the Rental Car Evangelist.** Rita, 27, is a recent hire to the organization, and works with rental car companies across the world, evangelizing the company's product. Although Rita has a smaller revenue target than Oliver for this year, she is chartered with getting rental car companies to adopt the GPS product in their cars. Research has shown that if a rental car consumer has a great experience with a GPS unit, they are more likely to buy the same unit for their own personal car. After learning about the new product in the keynote, Rita's goal of coming to the presentation will likely be to learn about the new features that will resonate with her customers, and especially how they compare with competitive offerings from similar companies approaching the same market.

- **Sanjay the Support Professional.** Sanjay, 32, is one of the top performing support professionals in the company's offshore office in Hyderabad. Sanjay leads a small team of support staff who operate the front line support desk for customers who call in with issues or questions around the product. Due to the success of the offshore support team last year, Sanjay and a number of other people from his team are being flown over to attend the annual conference. Although very comfortable with current products, Sanjay is looking forward to learning as much as he can about the new product so that the support team will be ready at launch.

Although persona creation is never an exact science, I hope the above examples start to show you how the answers to the questions influenced the development of the four personas. Given that this is an internal audience, the personas are largely based on the departmental segmentation. Eddie represents the engineering department. Not only will he have a different perspective, but he's also the only one to have seen the new product. As we develop the presentation, Eddie's persona will make sure that we won't look past that fact. The sales segmentation is represented by Oliver and Rita. Both have different motivations and goals, which more naturally leads to two separate personas. Even though we are estimating online retail sales as being over 60% of our audience, if we had simply two different sales groups with identical goals, we may have chosen to keep this as one persona. Finally, Sanjay represents our additional segment, the support organization, and also introduces an international and cultural component because of his location.

All of the personas are internal facing, and as a result, the characteristics of the personas try to echo this. For example, all of the personas are eager to learn and are likely positive about the product. If we had done this exercise for a set of external customers, we may have introduced an element of caution or questioning as part of their characteristics.

Finally, due to the number of attendees who are going to be present at the conference, there is little chance that I will know more than a handful of people in the audience, and the personas reflect this. If I was expecting a personal connection with one or more of the personas, then the characteristics could have been changed to reflect this.

Where are we?

In this chapter, we've covered the importance of understanding your audience, introduced the concept of personas, and created four personas that we can take forward and use as a foundation for creating our presentation. You'll notice that the personas each have unique names, such as "Eddie the Equipment Engineer" or "Oliver the Online Retail Salesperson." This is purely a way of remembering the personas as we move forward. You are free to name your personas however you like (after all, these are fictitious people), but I would recommend doing so in a way that makes them easy to remember. As you go through putting your presentation together, it is often useful to pause and think, "Is this what Eddie would want?" or "Would Oliver find this valuable?"

Even if you've heard of the concept of personas before reading this chapter, I'm hoping that the information you've found within has been useful in demonstrating their power and value, especially when using them for presentations.

If you find yourself getting stuck or becoming anxious over the details, remember that a persona is not meant to be 100% accurate, and the intention is to use them as a guide for creating your presentation. Rather than focusing on the exact attributes, it's more important that you feel you can relate to your personas. The goal is to imagine these fictitious people coming to your presentation and representing the audience. If you can feel positive that this is the case, then chances are you have a great set of personas that will help you move forward.

A useful exercise at this point in the book is to spend some time creating your own personas, especially if you have an upcoming presentation that you are planning for. Once you have your personas, you can take them with you into the next chapter as we start looking at structuring your presentation.

---

1. If you are interested in further exploring persona development, I thoroughly recommend the *Persona Lifecycle* (Pruitt/Adlin, 2010). It's one of the most comprehensive guides on persona development, together with multiple real life case studies and examples. http://www.amazon.com/The-Essential-Persona-Lifecycle-ebook/dp/B0048EJW6C

CHAPTER 3: Structuring Your Presentation

✳ ✳ ✳

In the previous chapter, we covered the needs of the audience and defining personas for your presentation. In this chapter, we are going to build on this topic by creating the structure of your presentation. Investing time in creating the structure of a presentation is important as it allows a presenter to not only brainstorm ideas, but makes it easy to make changes early on. Putting everything in Microsoft PowerPoint at this stage would be shortsighted as it would be difficult to get an overview of the whole presentation, and any changes would be very expensive, involving moving large parts of the deck around.

To start things off, we are going to investigate creating a "presentation mind map" to form structure and provide a platform where your presentation and story can evolve.

The presentation mind map

The presentation mind map is a map of all the topics that could possibly go into your presentation. Why do we do this? There's a good chance that you probably know the domain for your presentation very well. For example, if you have been asked to put together a presentation on mobile operating systems, chances are that the reason you've been asked is that you are seen or known as an expert in that area. One of the side effects of just opening Microsoft PowerPoint and working on the presentation at this stage is that you'll likely focus on one area, and will potentially miss other areas that are important to include. The goal of creating a mind map is to first avoid this by capturing all of the topics that could possibly be included in your presentation. There is a good chance that not everything will be, and that you'll end up making cuts or deciding not to include pieces, but going through this process will force you to capture all of the possible areas ahead of time. Moreover, cutting pieces from a mind map at this stage is a lot easier than going back and retrofitting content to a finished presentation!

What is a mind map?

A mind map is a way of visually outlining information, typically in a hierarchical fashion. A mind map tends to follow a "hub and spoke" model, originating from a single topic in the center and branching out to different topics. Popularized by BBC TV personality Tony Buzan, mind maps are used across multiple domains and industries in order to help capture ideas and brainstorm topics. The visual aspect of the mind map makes them suitable for discussing interrelated topics, and lend themselves well for moving parts of the mind map around as you formulate your ideas.

To put all of this into perspective, let's take a quick look at a simple mind map:

Figure 3.1 - Example mind map showing thoughts for an upcoming vacation.

Figure 3.1 shows a mind map outlining some ideas for an upcoming vacation. As you can see from the map, there are three branches: "Things not to forget," "Must do before leaving," and "Possible activities." Underneath each of these branches are additional items that are related to the parent topic. Although this is a very simple example, we can use it to outline some terms that will be used in this chapter.

- **Nodes.** Any item on the map, whether it is a parent or child is known as a node. The top level "My Vacation" is often known as the root node of the map.

- **Parent/Child.** As you can see in the map, there are several parent/child relationships. "Buy new luggage" is a child of "Must do before leaving" and "Possible activities" is a parent of "Golf at Waikoloa."

- **Levels.** In a mind map, each represented branch is also known by using a level. For example, "Things not to forget" is called a 1st level node, whereas "Beach umbrella" is referred to as a 2nd level node.

- **Collapsing and Expanding.** As you can imagine, as the mind map grows larger, it's often useful to be able to collapse and expand different nodes to help you work with the large amount of data. Many mind mapping tools support this today, an example of which is shown in Figure 3.2. The diagram shows how the "Possible activities" and "Must do before leaving" nodes have been collapsed from view. The data still exists in the branches, but has just been hidden to make it easier to work with other parts of the map.

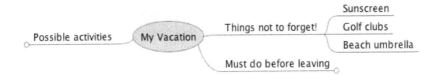

Figure 3.2 - Example of collapsed nodes in a mind map.

- **Moving Nodes.** Finally, most mind mapping software supports the moving of nodes from one place in the mind map to another. Figure 3.3 shows how nodes can be moved with our example map.

Here, the "Must do before leaving" node has been moved from being a 1st level node to being a child node of "Things not to forget."

Figure 3.3 - Example of moving a node.

You should now be in a position to understand some of the basic features of mind mapping. If you haven't used mind mapping software before, there are many applications to choose from. My personal favorites include a commercial product called Mindjet (http://mindjet.com), an open source alternative called Freemind (http://freemind.sourceforge.net), and an iPad tool called iThoughtsHD (http://www.ithoughts.co.uk). Of course, if you don't go the software route, a large piece of paper and pencil can also be effective. Whatever tool you do choose, the goal is to be able to capture your thoughts in a mind map hierarchy and be able to quickly rearrange them and group them visually.

Creating your presentation mind map

Once you've chosen your mind map tool, I would recommend bringing in the personas that you defined from the last chapter, together with a placeholder for title and abstract. We won't be finalizing the title and abstract until the end of the chapter, but having a place on the map can be useful in case any potential titles come to mind during the brainstorming process.

To do this, create a new mind map with three nodes. The first node should be for your personas, the second for the structure, and a third for potential titles and abstracts. Figure 3.4 shows what this might look like using the example personas that were created for the fictitious GPS product example in the previous chapter.

Figure 3.4 - An initial presentation mind map for our GPS product presentation.

Now comes the fun bit! Underneath the "Structure" node, simply brainstorm all of the topics that you believe could go into your presentation. Don't worry about whether they are the right or wrong topics for now. Don't worry about order or priority. Don't worry about what level they should be in the map. Just empty your mind. The only goal here is to do a "brain dump" of as much as you can.

Creating a complete mind map of everything that could go into your presentation will take some time. What I often find is that the first few topics come really quickly, often within the first few minutes of starting the map. These tend to be the obvious topics that I've been thinking about for some time. As the map starts to increase in size, however, the number of new topics will start to trickle out a little more slowly. This is to be expected, and time can play a great part here. If possible, try to give yourself a couple of days during this process. What I commonly find is that I'll be in a meeting, or driving the car, or sometimes even in the shower, when a good topic for the presentation will come to mind. As soon as I remember it, I make sure I capture it on the mind map.

During this process, it can also be useful to include the viewpoint of the personas. While you are creating new topics, go through each of the personas in turn and ask yourself the question, "What are the subjects that Eddie, Oliver, Rita, or Sanjay would want to see in the presentation?"

Often this can raise new topics that you may not have thought about, which is exactly the reason that the personas exist.

As you approach the end of your brainstorming, you'll likely see a few patterns emerge. This might include topics that really are subtopics for another category, or topics that seem to be related to each other. Feel free to move and group things around as you go to create some sense of hierarchy. This will help start to make sense of everything in your map, although try not to over think the structure of the presentation at this stage.

After some time, you should start to see a complete map of potential topics for your presentation start to emerge.

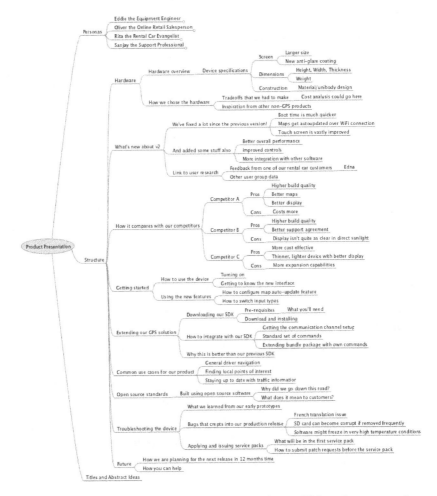

Figure 3.5 - An example presentation mind map for our GPS product presentation.

Figure 3.5 shows this for our example scenario. As you can see in this map, the map contains nine different topic areas related to what should be in the presentation, albeit in no exact order. As you construct your own mind map, you should certainly feel free to develop the branches with as much information as you feel is needed for the presentation. It's always better to have too much information, as cutting topics and branches is a lot easier than thinking of more content to add later on.

In addition, when you add nodes to the map, try to do so using single sentences rather than paragraphs of text. Think about the sentences as being reminders or prompts rather than verbose lines of text that you'll need to read. Somewhat related, as you are adding these sentences, try to include ones that bring back memories of any personal stories or experiences. There doesn't have to be a story for each sentence, but scattering such memories and experiences throughout the map will help make the map more personal to you.

Once you reach a point where are you feel that you are doing more rearranging and grouping as opposed to adding new content, it's time to move on and think about how you are going to structure the content you've collected.

Introducing the 10/85/5 structure

If you've watched a lot of speakers present, you'll likely know that the structure of presentations can vary greatly. The way that speakers bring an audience into a presentation and then dissect the information to be told can be done in many different ways.

This book is going to introduce a structure where a presentation is divided into three logical sections. I call this the 10/85/5 rule. The numbers stand for the percentage of time allocated for each part, with the parts being the opening story, the main content, and the related conclusion. For the rest of this chapter, we'll be examining each of these parts in detail, using our example GPS presentation to show how each of these could work.

This, of course, isn't the only way of structuring a presentation, and over time you will likely develop a presentation structure that suits the types of topics and talks that you give. With that said, I have found the 10/85/5 rule to be very effective in many presentations that I have both given and watched, and hope that this gives you a good starting point for your own presentations.

Opening story

The opening story is arguably the most powerful piece of your presentation's structure. How you open your presentation will determine how the audience interprets the problem or issue that you are trying to address. In the first few minutes of your presentation, your audience is also going to create a mental picture of what the rest of the presentation content will be like. A strong opening will therefore setup the rest of the presentation for success.

Successful opening stories tend to have three qualities:

Firstly, the opening story is, as its name implies, a story. It should have a main character—known as a protagonist—and must be told in their voice. As we'll discover shortly, the protagonist could be you (the presenter), it could be one of the personas, or could even be the audience themselves.

Secondly, the goal of the opening story is to lead the audience into the main narrative of the presentation without necessarily revealing all of its parts. The opening story is not a replacement for an agenda slide, and instead should gradually pull the audience in to the topic.

Finally, the opening story must be based around a challenge, problem, or issue, to which the audience can relate. Ideally, the audience should be able to put themselves in the shoes of the protagonist and feel what they are experiencing. Moreover, once the challenge, problem, or issue has been described, the opening story must end on a positive note or upbeat tone.

To put all of this into perspective, let's look at how an opening story can be constructed for your own presentation. A good place to start is to review the mind map you have created. If you've gone through the brainstorming exercises, chances are good that you'll have multiple topics and stories. The goal is to extract the opening story from within the mind map. To do this, you should look for one topic or point that personifies your presentation. Ask yourself about the one thing that stands out as the foundation of everything you will be talking about, and has some connection to the other topics. Is there a topic or subject within the mind map that can act as a raison d'être [a reason for existence] for your presentation?

To show an example, let's return to the GPS product presentation that we are building. As you may recall, we created a mind map for a presentation unveiling a new GPS device to our company. When we were going through the presentation mind map, you may remember seeing this section, as shown in Figure 3.6.

Figure 3.6 - Mind map node of the features in new version of GPS.

During the brainstorming for our example, we included a piece of user research that was performed for our previous product. This research was performed in conjunction with one of our rental car customers, and involved observing how drivers used the previous version of the GPS in real life scenarios. The research reported on driver's experiences, and there was one particular customer called Edna, who was having a really hard time coming to grips with the device, struggling with how slow the device was (an outdated set of map data), and frustrated that she couldn't use the touchscreen correctly.

This particular element in the mind map could be a great opening story. We have a protagonist, a story, a set of issues that were faced, and topics that underpin a lot of the rest of the presentation. We don't even need to mention that this revolved around the user research. The goal is to simply extract and develop a story around this point.

How might this work? Let's forget that this is a presentation for the time being, and instead imagine a script of what an opening story might look like:

I'd like to share a story about Edna. Edna is one of the many customers that we've been working with since last year. When we met Edna, she had just landed in Colorado. She was visiting a friend, who lived about 25 miles from the airport. Because of the journey, she hired a rental car from the airport. At the rental car facility, Edna picked up her car which was equipped with our current model, the GPS-1000.[1] Although she was initially pleased with GPS, her experience didn't start well.

Firstly, the device took a long time to start. Edna waited for up to 5 minutes before the GPS loaded all of the maps from memory and was able to get a good satellite lock. When the device did finally acquire a signal, Edna had issues using the keyboard. Every time she tried to enter the city in the address, the touchscreen keyboard seemed to freeze. And to make matters worse, once she did get going, she discovered that the unit was loaded with an old set of maps. Because her friend lived in a new residential development, the GPS was unable to locate her house accurately.

As you can imagine, Edna didn't have a great experience with our GPS device. She did get to her destination eventually, but using the product wasn't as smooth as it should have been. Being part of the product team, we are keen that this experience doesn't happen for Edna again. In fact, we've learned a lot since then, and today I'm very proud to announce our next product—the GPS-2000.

We now have the basis for our opening story. While this particular story about Edna and GPS devices is very specific to the example we are building throughout the book, I hope that this has demonstrated the power of an opening story.

Compare this opening story with a more "traditional" way of opening a presentation:

Today I'm going to talk about the GPS-2000. Based on our user research, we've found that users are having issues with previous devices. Specifically, I'll be covering three functions…

I'm hoping that you'll agree the concept of an opening story provides an immediate connection with the audience that stretches well beyond a simple agenda slide.

Variations

There are, of course, many variations on the opening story, and I encourage you to experiment. One variation can be to change the protagonist. Although we chose Edna in our previous example, if the presentation topic is something that you personally were involved with, then you should consider yourself as the protagonist. Telling the opening story as something you personally experienced will come across as the most genuine to the audience. In previous presentations I have also used stories about other people in my industry, and even fictitious people that were designed to represent my personas. The opening story told right at the start of Chapter 1 with Gurpreet invading the stage is a good example of this, and was even played out in front of the audience!

In addition, I encourage you to go back and watch some of your favorite presentations. Look for how other presenters use opening stories to bring the audience into the main part of the presentation. If you are looking for a good set of examples, I find that a lot of the TED[2] presentations use the power of the opening story very effectively.

A key part of the opening story is how you transition from the challenge, issue, or problem to the positive note for the audience. This is very important as you want to enter the main portion of the presentation with the audience feeling hopeful that things are going to change for the better.

One example of this is a presentation that I created in late 2009. At that time, the product team that I was working with was facing a lot of competitive challenges. One particular competing software product was stealing marketshare at a dramatic rate with a business model that was radically different to ours. I chose to present the opening story through the lens of one of two customers—one using our product, and one using our competitor's. This proved to be very effective as it was immediately clear to the audience how easy it was to use the competing product compared to our own. Together with an animation showing losing marketshare, the opening story painted a picture of near defeat.

As stated, however, I had to end on a positive, uplifting note. The last slide of my opening story was simply a picture of Yogi Berra, the former baseball catcher, outfielder, and manager. In 1973, Berra's team, the New York Mets, were trailing the Chicago Cubs by 9 1/2 games. When asked about the fate of the season, Berra famously said, "It ain't over till it's over," and ironically the Mets ended up winning the division title on the last day of the season. In my presentation, I used this quote, and a theme of baseball, to transition the audience from what could have been defeat to the main part of the presentation, focused on how the next version of the product was going to be superior.

Adding the opening story to your mind map

Once you have settled on an opening story and structure, it's important that you capture everything in the mind map.

Figure 3.7 - Our opening story in the format of the mind map.

To do this for your presentation, create a new node called "Opening Story" in the "Structure" section. Under here, capture the main talking points of your opening story. As you can see in Figure 3.7 for our example, we've put together the eight main talking points for the story.

Also, note how each of the elements are just one or two sentences long. Instead of writing a long paragraph of text about Edna's frustration with entering in the address on the device, we captured "Lots of issues using the keyboard." It's really important that you don't write the opening story in full. You are not going to read this word by word, so all you really need are words and sentences that remind you about the story.

How long should your opening story be?

I've experimented with this on several occasions and, per the 10/85/5 model, would recommend that the opening story accounts for approximately 10% of your total presentation time. Assuming that you are planning a 60-minute presentation, this translates to approximately 6 minutes in length. This isn't a perfect equation, and both shorter and longer opening stories can be very effective.

One thing you should do however is be careful that your opening story doesn't last for too long. I've found that anything over 15% (around 10 minutes for a 60-minute presentation) may not be received well. Not only are you eating into the time of your main portion of content, but you may also be faced with an audience who start to wonder where your presentation is going!

Main content

With the opening story in hand, it's now time to start structuring the main content of your presentation. If you've been following along by creating your own presentation mind map, then you'll likely have a lot of brainstormed topics, but at this stage there will likely not be any order or flow to them yet. This is the point where we add this structure. To start, let's look at the rule of three.

The rule of three

Inherently, people are more likely to remember things if they are in sets of three. If you've not seen this before, it's amazing to see how prevalent the rule of three is across many areas of our lives. In storytelling and theater, many stories are divided into a series of three acts. In the art world, the "rule of thirds" makes for more interesting pictures or photographs. In marketing, many advertising slogans rely on the power of three to be memorable. For example:

Just do it.

Finger-lickin' good.

Taste the rainbow.

Next time you are reading a story, watching a movie, or even looking at a commercial, I would encourage you to see if you can spot these patterns.

It should come as no surprise, therefore, that the rule of three can also be applied to the structure of your presentation. By doing so, you will add a more natural flow to the main part of your presentation, and the main parts of your talk will be more likely to be remembered by your audience.

The simplest way of doing this is to look through the many topics that you captured in your presentation mind map to see if there is a logical way of grouping all of the content into three parts. Some of the topics should seem to fit naturally. For example, if you have an introductory topic it will more likely be in the first group of three as you'll want to speak about this in the earlier part of the presentation. Other topics can be a little more complicated to fit into the rule of three. Often, you'll have to create a topic that encapsulates the topics into a logical group.

To highlight how this works, we can turn to the example mind map that we have been working on for our GPS presentation. Figure 3.8 shows the mind map with nine different topic areas, together with the opening story we recently added.

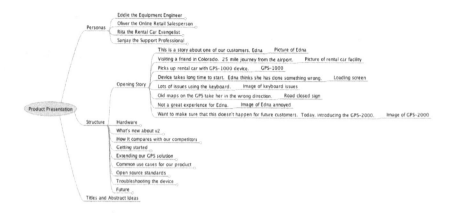

Figure 3.8 - The current mind map with the opening story and nine different topic areas.

For the purpose of fitting the diagram into the book, I've collapsed the details for each of the main nodes. As you can see, however, we have nine areas:

1. Hardware,

2. What's new about v2,

3. How it compares with our competitors,

4. Getting started,

5. Extending our GPS solution,

6. Common use cases for our product,

7. Open source standards,

8. Troubleshooting the device, and

9. Future.

All are really strong topics that will hopefully make for a great presentation.

Let's now start putting these into groups. It's pretty clear that the first group should be about an introduction to the new device. This new group should likely include: What's new about v2, Getting started, Common use cases for our product, and possibly Hardware.

Reading through the list, there are also several topics that seem to be more on the advanced side. Extending our GPS solution, Open source standards, Troubleshooting the device, and Future could well fit in here.

If my math is correct, this leaves one remaining: How it compares with our competitors. There are no rules about the number of topics that can be in a group, as long as we end up with only three groups, so we'll place this in it's own group called Competition. The area of competition could also be large, so this makes sense.

Figure 3.9 shows the mind map after the nodes have been rearranged into the three groups.

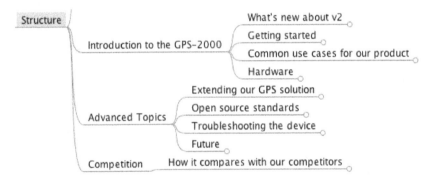

Figure 3.9 - The topics rearranged into three logical groups.

Things are starting to come together, but there's definitely more to do. Firstly, it is probably more logical to talk about the area of competition before talking about advanced topics, so we should switch the second and third group around. In addition, the ordering of the second level topics probably needs some adjusting. In the introduction group, we'll probably want to lead off with the topic of common use cases, and finish this part with showing the audience how they can get started with the device. This will probably be a more natural flow. In the advanced section, we should probably talk about troubleshooting the device before talking about how others can extend the GPS.

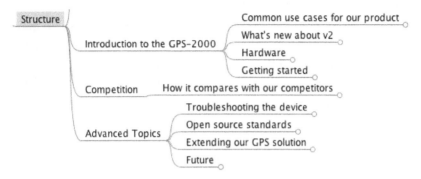

Figure 3.10 - A more logical rearranging of the topics in the mind map.

As you might be able to see from Figure 3.10, we now have a much more natural flow. We have three top level groupings, which seem to work well, together with a second level of ordered topics. There is, however, one last step. The rule of three applies to the top level grouping, but it also applies to the second level. We need to change the topics on the second level so that they are also in logical groups of three.

Fortunately, this is relatively easy to do. For the introduction group, it seems logical to take the section about hardware and move it into the previous section, What's new about v2. The hardware is new, so this makes sense.

For the competition group, as we only have one element, we'll have to do something different. Here, we will actually promote the three competitors that we are going to be talking about to the second level.

Finally, for the advanced topics, the subject of open source standards is related to extending the GPS solution, so we can move the open source node to a child of this.

Figure 3.11 - The first and second level nodes now in groups of three.

After a little more rearranging, and as seen in Figure 3.11, we now have three top level nodes, with each node having three second level nodes. Reading through from top to bottom, you should also be able to see that we have a structure beginning to form. The presentation is going to begin with an introductory section that will cover the common use cases, what's new about the product, and how to get started. The second section will focus on competition, outlining three of our top competitors. The third and final section will focus on advanced topics, namely troubleshooting the device, extending the GPS solution, and what the future holds.

Although the topics in your own presentation will be very different, hopefully you can see how this logical grouping of three helps to form a structure. As you move topics into these logical groups, some decisions will have to be made about which areas get combined with others, or which areas don't make sense to include in the presentation. It's these types of decisions that make using a mind map so powerful. The decisions that you are making at this stage are relatively cheap to make. Playing with the structure by copying and pasting a node on a mind map costs you only a few seconds. Imagine trying to do this with a near-complete slide deck. The cost would be way higher as the potential impact of moving slides, rearranging animations, or deconstructing parts of slides would be very expensive.

So far, we have applied the rule of three to the first and second levels of the presentation mind map. One question that you may be asking is whether this same rule applies for all the other levels of the mind map? Do you need to do this for every level in order to complete the structure? My recommendation is to try and follow the rule of three where it makes sense. On a detailed mind map, I typically find that I can apply the rule to the third and possibly fourth level before things don't start to make sense. At that point it's fine to have a grouping of less or more than three items.

For the purpose of the example, we will apply the rule of three up until the third level. This will be enough to take us into the slide creation, and hopefully demonstrate the groupings.

Figure 3.12 - Three levels of the example presentation mind map adhering to the rule of three.

As can be shown in Figure 3.12, we have refactored the mind map so that the first three levels are grouped into threes.

When three just doesn't fit

There are times where the bulk of the presentation cannot be distilled down into three goals or sections, or you find yourself really force-fitting content into three areas where another number might work better. This can often apply to deeply technical presentations where there are multiple facets of a product or subject that just can't be categorized into a rule of three. Although it should be viewed as an exception, there are a couple of variations that can be considered: The rule of five and the rule of ten.

As the name suggests, the rule of five breaks down the main portion of the content into five different areas. I've used this on several occasions, and it's been quite effective. Most recently, I've been working on a presentation where the bulk of the main content focused on five use cases, or scenarios, from a fictitious company.[3] While five isn't quite as rememberable as three items, it can still work with the audience.

There are, however, a couple of caveats to this approach. Firstly, the second level beyond the initial five sections is always split into threes. Even though you may have five distinct sections, each of the sections is subject to the original rule of three for the sub levels of the mind map.

Secondly, because you are dealing with five top level sections instead of three, time management becomes much more important. For example, if you have an hour presentation, an 85% main section will account for approximately 50 minutes. Based on this, a main part with five sections equates to about 10 minutes per section. This isn't necessarily so bad, but it's definitely going to require a quicker pace compared to a main part with three sections. I've been caught out on a couple of occasions where I've overrun on a five-part main section, partly because my brain has been conditioned to think about the main part as three sections.

If three or five still doesn't work, the rule of ten might be an option. As you may have guessed by now, the rule of ten involves breaking the main part of the presentation into ten sections. Although it sounds daunting, this can be useful for presenting a topic that naturally falls into a list of ten. For example, "Top Ten Tips for Using NodeJS" or "Ten things you never knew about MongoDB." If the main part of your presentation is 50 minutes in length, each item out of the list of ten gets approximately 5 minutes. Again, time management will be key here, but 5 minutes is certainly enough to get across a single point in such a list.

Presentations that use this rule of ten tend to be most effective when presented in reverse, meaning that you present number ten first, and gradually bring the audience up to number one. Assuming that number one is indeed the most important item in your presentation, this can be an effective way of bringing your audience to the crescendo point in your presentation—something that we'll be covering shortly.

Are there other numbers aside from 3, 5, and 10 that can be used for the main content? For sure. I've experimented, and seen other presenters experiment, with all kinds of different ranges. As you get more comfortable with structuring the main part of your presentation, I would encourage you to try other combinations depending on the topic that you are presenting. I created one presentation a few years ago that covered "100 top tips" about a particular subject. The title definitely drew the crowd, but due to the pace that I had to go through the content, I'm not sure how many the audience actually remembered!

Identifying potential weak spots in your main content

If you've been following along by creating your own presentation mind map, you are likely in the position where you have a well thought-out structure for the main part of your presentation, ordered into some kind of grouping. Before going too far, a good exercise at this point is to review the current structure against your personas. The benefit of this is that it acts as a checkpoint for your structure, validating that the topics you have are still relevant to your expected audience.

The structure of your presentation should ensure some kind of balance across the personas. It's a cruel fact of life, but it will be very unlikely that every speaking point in your presentation will be 100% relevant to everyone in your audience. Typically, audience members will find certain parts of your presentation especially relevant, whereas other parts might be less relevant—although they could still be interesting. This equally applies to the personas. By mapping the relevancy of the presentation to the personas, we can get a sense of any gaps in the structure.

To demonstrate this, we can again use our GPS example presentation mind map, together with the four personas that we created in the previous chapter.

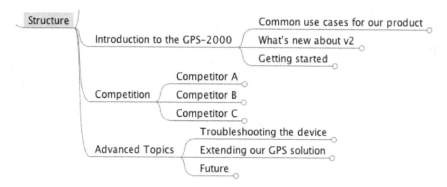

Figure 3.13 - The current presentation mind map shown to 2 levels.

To see how relevant the mind map is for each of the personas, we simply run through the mind map in Figure 3.13 in order and allocate a 1–10 value based on our understanding of each of the personas. In a table, the output might look as follows:

Mind Map Level	Subject	Eddie the Equipment Engineer	Oliver the Online Retail Salesperson	Rita the Rental Car Evangelist	Sanjay the Support Professional
1.1	Common use cases	5	10	8	9
1.2	What's new	6	10	10	8
1.3	Getting started	4	8	10	10
2.1	Competitor A	4	10	10	6
2.2	Competitor B	4	10	10	6
2.3	Competitor C	4	10	10	6
3.1	Trouble-shooting	7	4	4	10
3.2	Extending	10	3	5	9
3.3	Future	10	7	8	9

Table 3.1 - Applying a relevancy score for each area of the structure.

Running through Table 3.1, we can start to see how relevant the content will be for each of our four personas.

The first section (Common use cases, What's new, and Getting started) is likely to be relevant for anyone in the audience that has not yet seen the new GPS device before. Oliver, Rita, and Sanjay have not seen the device before, so they will likely be interested and we give them scores ranging from 8–10. Eddie however has already been using an early prototype of the device, and therefore most of this information will probably be known to him. As this is the case, we'll give him scores of between 4 and 6.

The second section is the deep dive into the competition. We suspect that this will be critical information for both Oliver and Rita, so we are going to score them 10. For Eddie and Sanjay, while they may be interested in the topic, it probably won't be that relevant. For Eddie, the relevancy might be a 4, whereas Sanjay might view this as a 6.

Finally, the third section is about the advanced topics. This is what Eddie has been waiting for. He'll likely be interested in the troubleshooting section, and will definitely connect to the parts about extending the GPS with the SDK, and the future roadmap. For Sanjay, this will also be an important section as many of the topics here will directly affect his ability to support customers that will be calling in with queries. This also scores highly for him. For Oliver and Rita, however, this will likely be less interesting. While they may be interested in some of the futures topics for sales conversations, there's little chance of them requiring the ability to troubleshoot or extend the device after it's been sold!

As I hope this demonstrates, applying a score across each of the personas is a simple but effective way of measuring the relevancy of each area of the mind map. One way to extend this table, which can also be useful, is to look at the averages for each subject area, and each persona. This can be shown in Table 3.2.

Mind Map Level	Subject	Eddie the Equipment Engineer	Oliver the Online Retail Sales-person	Rita the Rental Car Evangelist	Sanjay the Support Professional	Avg
1.1	Common use cases	5	10	8	9	8
1.2	What's new	6	8	10	9	8
1.3	Getting started	4	10	10	10	8.5
2.1	Competitor A	4	10	10	6	7.5
2.2	Competitor B	4	10	10	6	7.5
2.3	Competitor C	4	10	10	6	7.5
3.1	Trouble-shooting	7	4	4	10	6.25
3.2	Extending	10	3	5	9	6.75
3.3	Future	10	7	8	9	8.5
Average		6	8	8.3	8.1	

Table 3.2 - Our updated relevancy table, with averages for each subject area and persona.

As shown, the averages show a value for each topic area and each persona. What we are looking for with these values are numbers that dip too low, as this might be an indication that a subject will be less relevant to the majority or the audience, or a persona that might not get enough out of the entire presentation.

In our example, there are two red flags. The first is the troubleshooting section (3.1), which scores an average of 6.25. Based on our understanding of the personas, content here may only resonate with Sanjay where as the others may get little value. If this is truly going to be the case, and we feel strongly about it, it might cause us to think about how we could restructure the presentation or that topic more effectively.

The second red flag is the total score for Eddie's persona. While all of the other personas seem to be above 8, Eddie's overall relevancy score comes in at a 6. While this may not adversely affect the presentation, it might be enough to cause us to revisit Eddie's persona and decide whether we need to adjust the structure to better accommodate his expectations.

Other than those values, everything else appears to be looking good. Another key indicator are the values for the beginning and end of the table, as we want the start and finish of the content to be relevant for as much of the audience as possible. If we were seeing low figures here, it might indicate that we need to adjust the opening and ending of the content to appeal to a broader audience.

Again, the scores are only as accurate as our persona definitions and gut feel of relevancy for those personas, so don't take them as scientific measurements or guarantees of success for the presentation. What they can help with however is identifying the potential weak spots in your structure while you still have the time and flexibility to change things around.

Transitioning between topics

We are now to the point where the structure is taking shape. As shown in Figure 3.14, we have three high level topics, together with multiple groups underneath.

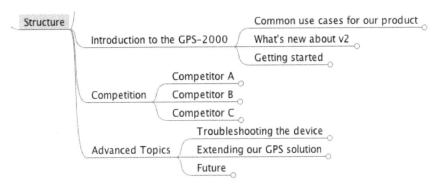

Figure 3.14 - The current presentation mind map for our example.

Before we move on to looking at some concluding topics, it's important to spend some time on transitions. As a presenter it is your job to help navigate the audience through your structure. This navigation should be smooth as possible, ideally so that the audience feels that they are being naturally led through the content rather than seeing the seams of your presentation. This is where transitions come in.

If we look back at Figure 3.14, we can start to look at some of the transitions we will need to deal with. Let's take the "Introduction" node as an example. Under here, there are three topics: "Common use cases," "What's new," and "Getting started." While they all form part of the introduction, we still need to think about the transition between all three. At the end of the "Common use cases" section, we need to make sure that the transition is smooth into the section about "What's new." At the end of the "What's new" section, we need a good transition into "Getting started."

To investigate the first transition point, let's expand the mind map slightly.

Figure 3.15 - Expanded mind map for the "Common use cases" and "What's new" sections.

As shown in Figure 3.15, the "Common use cases" section has three subtopics: "General driver navigation," "Finding local points of interest," and "Staying up to date with traffic information." Assuming that these represent the order of the presentation, we need to find a way of transitioning from "Staying up to date with traffic information" to the section on "What's new about v2." Instead of ending the section abruptly, we need to think about how we can connect these sections.

Typically there are three types of transition: the related topic transition, the question transition, and the summary transition.

- **Related topic transition.** The related topic transition is a transition that links the two areas through a common subject or speaking point. In our example, if one of the new features had included traffic information we might have used a related topic to introduce it. At the end of the traffic section, the transition might have gone something like, "The subject of traffic information is also one of the new features that we've been working on" or "Speaking of traffic information, let me show you what we've included in this new release." The use of a related topic is a very natural way of transitioning between sections using a topic that the audience has just heard about.

- **Question transition.** The question transition is where we link two areas by posing a question to the audience. In this case, we attempt to wrap up the subject, and pose a question to the audience that will transition to the next topic area. In our example, the speaker might turn to the audience and ask, "You might be thinking, 'what are we doing to support traffic information in v2 of our product?'" and then move on to the new section. The question transition can also work well to group all of the topics together before transitioning. For example, "What are we doing to make all of these use cases better in v2 of our product?"

- **Summary transition.** Finally, the summary transition is where the topic or topics are summarized before moving on to the new section. Here, the speaker pauses to reflect on what has just been said before moving on. In our example, this could look like this: "To summarize, the common use cases are: General driver navigation, Finding local points of interest, and Staying up to date with traffic information.

Now let's move on and investigate what's new in v2 of our product."

Which transition to use where will come down to your presentation style, together with the topics that you are presenting. If the topics are closely related, the related topic transition can often work well. If the topics are somewhat related, but taking the audience in a different direction, you might want to think about the question transition. If the topics are completely unrelated, or you feel it's necessary to echo something that the audience has just heard, the summary transition is often best. Moreover, I find that the related topic transition and the question transition work best at the 2nd level of the mind map, whereas the summary transition is the one transition that works best when transitioning to the 1st level of the mind map.

Once you have decided on the transition that is going to work best, you should also add it to your mind map. I choose to add the transition nodes using italics to keep them separate from the actual content. Figure 3.16 shows this in action for our example.

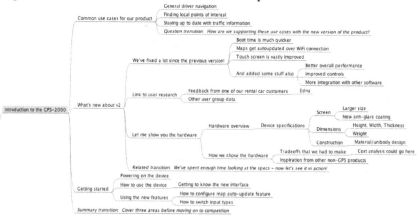

Figure 3.16 - Three transition points added to our example mind map.

As you can see, we've added three transition points in our example. The first transition moves the audience from the subject of "Common use cases" to the "What's new" section. Here, we are going to pose a hypothetical question to the audience, "How are we supporting these use cases with the new version of the product?" This question will be used to indicate to the audience that we are moving on to a new topic.

Moving from the "What's new" section to "Getting started" will work best with a related transition. At the end of the "What's new" section, we will have just finished speaking about the hardware for the new GPS device. In the beginning of the "Getting started" section, we will be talking about powering on the device, so a related transition will fit nicely here. At the end of the "What's new" section, we can address the audience and say something like, "We've spent enough time looking at the specifications—now let's see it in action!"

Finally, we have the transition from the introduction section to the next section on competition. Here, we are going to leave the introduction topic completely, so this transition could benefit from a summary of everything the audience heard in the three introductory topics before moving on to the area of competition.

Crescendos

By this point you've likely developed a solid structure for your presentation. In our example, we've gone through the rule of three, rearranged many of our topics, matched the structure against our personas, and worked out transition points. The final piece of developing structure involves introducing crescendo points into your presentation.

For those who haven't come across the term, a crescendo is known as a gradual increase in volume to a particular point in a piece of music. For those with a musical interest, Bolero by Ravel is an excellent example of a piece leading up to a crescendo. Many other musical pieces have multiple crescendos throughout, and almost all of these have a final crescendo towards the end.

This same effect found in music can have a powerful effect within your presentation. Crescendo points during your presentation can keep the audience interested in your content for longer, and a final crescendo can have them talking about your presentation for a long time afterward.

71

Unlike music, however, using a crescendo in our presentation doesn't mean raising the volume of our voice. Instead, a crescendo in a presentation is a particular topic, subject, or announcement that is going to have the most impact with the audience. During his time with Apple, the late Steve Jobs was famous for having a crescendo point at the end of his keynote presentations. He would save one of the most significant and exciting announcements of the presentation until the end, and just as the audience was thinking that the presentation was close to being over, he would reveal this under the guise of having "one more thing" to talk about. This crescendo point became such a common highlight of his talks that many audiences grew accustomed to waiting for his "one more thing" phrase, knowing that he would likely be saving the best for last.

While it's likely that you won't have the luxury of saving important product announcements to a "one more thing" section in your own presentation, you can still take advantage of these crescendos in your talk.

To show how this can be done, let's review our current mind map for the introductory section of our fictitious presentation, as shown in Figure 3.17.

Figure 3.17 - Current view of our example mind map.

As you may recall previously, we inserted different types of transition points in our example. We had one transition point for each 1st and 2nd level transition. In general, crescendos work best just before these transitions. For those visually inspired, imagine this as series of waves throughout the presentation that peak at the crescendo point, before the audience is transitioned to the next topic. If you've ever heard of the phrase "leave the audience on a high note" this will sound familiar.

Using this representation of waves, we can apply the same logic to our introductory section. Within our introductory section we have three topics: "Common use cases," "What's new," and "Getting started." The order of these actually follows a natural crescendo. "Common use cases" will set the scene of the audience, "What's new" will introduce some new information, and we hope that "Getting started" will start to whet the appetite of our audience about our new product. We can also validate this with the previous work that we did matching the relevancy of the content to the personas. If you look back at Table 3.2, you'll see that the section on "Getting started" appears to be a natural crescendo point by being most relevant to the personas.

Let's go deeper in the mind map to see what the crescendos look like at the next level down. Under "Common use cases," we have three topics: "General driver navigation," "Finding local points of interest," and "Staying up to date with traffic information." The relevancy table doesn't help us at this level as all of these topics are probably equally relevant to each persona, but we can get a gut feel of where the crescendo point should be. In our example, it so happens that while "Staying up to date with traffic information" is interesting, it's probably not going to cause such a positive reaction as "Finding local points of interest." Let's say that this is a key topic that the audience will likely resonate with. If this is the case, we should consider rearranging the topics so that the "Finding local points of interest" becomes the crescendo point of this section.

A result of this will be a branch, as shown in Figure 3.18.

73

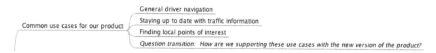

Figure 3.18 - Rearranging the topics to find a natural crescendo point before the transition.

As you can see, "Finding local points of interest" now becomes our crescendo point, which means that we'll be leaving the audience on this high point before transitioning to the next topic. You'll also notice that the transition supports this move. Our transition is going to be a question about the use cases, which works equally well regardless of the order of the use cases that we talk about. If the transition point had been related to the previous topic, we would have had to change this to support the new order.

As you can imagine, we can take this same concept and apply it to each of the sections that we have in our presentation. As with transition points, for your own presentation you'll probably only need to do this on the 1st and 2nd levels of your mind map. Creating crescendos beyond this will likely take too much work, and will be so subtle that the audience will likely not pick up on them.

We do have to think about one more crescendo point, and that's the finale. This is the last speaking point before we move on to the conclusion. In our example mind map shown in Figure 3.19, this is represented by the "Future" topic in our "Advanced topics" branch.

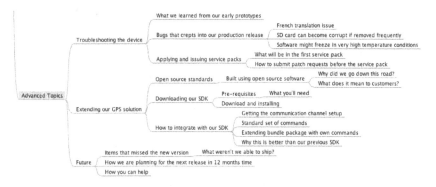

Figure 3.19 - Building a crescendo for the the final topic in the presentation.

By this point in the presentation, we will have covered a lot of information for the audience, and we now need this section to stand out. It needs to be memorable for the audience to ensure that the presentation concludes on the high point that it deserves.

Although there are many ways of constructing a final crescendo, the most effective ones tend to be the ones that "give" the audience something. This could be some new information, it could be something physical, or something intangible. To figure out what might work here, we can ask ourselves a few questions:

- Can we show something to the audience that they have never seen before?

- Can we involve the audience in something that they would otherwise not have the chance to participate in?

- Can we give something to the audience - or can we setup the opportunity for the audience to receive something tangible?

You may have seen many examples of these types of questions in the final crescendo of other presentations. A Jobs-like "one more thing" act is a good demonstration of the first question to announce a new product. The second question could be answered by showing a sneak peak of the next version or a follow-up product. The third question is often answered in large conferences where the speaker will cover a product and then announce that "Everyone in the audience will be getting one of these on the way out of the room!"—often to rapturous applause.

In our example, as we don't have a new product to announce at this stage and it's probably too early to show the next version of the product, we might want to consider the third option of giving something to the audience. Obviously, we likely will not have a budget to give away new GPS units for everyone in the audience, but we might be able to do something related. As we were just talking about the SDK and how it could be used to enable people to create apps for the GPS in the previous point, this might make a good connection. We could "give away" the SDK to everyone in the audience (as there is no cost of doing this) and then potentially offer some free GPS units to the first people who develop new software based on the SDK, as shown in Figure 3.20.

Figure 3.20 - Adding the finale crescendo point to the example presentation.

What you choose to do in your presentation will of course be very different, but hopefully you can see how the final crescendo point should empower you to "give" something to the audience. It might be new information, it might be something physical, or it might be something intangible, but the key point is that the audience leaves the presentation having received something—in addition to the great content of the rest of your presentation, of course!

Speaking of crescendos, that wraps up this section on the topic, and indeed the bulk of defining the main content for your presentation. We are now going to move on and look at how we finish the presentation through something called the related conclusion.

Related conclusion

In the 10/85/5 model that we've been covering during this chapter, the final 5% is given to the conclusion. When you do the math, the conclusion is therefore one of the shortest sections of the presentation. If your presentation is estimated to be an hour in length, then 5% will result in about 3 minutes.

There are many speakers who prefer longer conclusions, and I've often heard a common saying that a presentation should have a "strong beginning, strong ending, and who cares what is in the middle." To this, I respectfully disagree. Your presentation should be strong all the way through, and the conclusion should function as the name implies—to conclude your presentation, and not to fool the audience in forgetting a poorly delivered middle part.

A good conclusion should have three parts to it. It should summarize what the audience has heard during the presentation, it should instruct the audience to do something after the presentation, and it should end by tying back to the opening story. The goal of the conclusion is to "round out" the presentation, putting a proverbial bow on the slide deck and handing it off to the audience before you walk off stage.

Although it's only 5% of the presentation, it is however still important to have a well thought-out structure for the conclusion. While a poorly executed conclusion won't necessarily ruin the presentation for the audience, it still needs to resonate with everyone in the room. Remember that the audience will have just come off the high of your final crescendo. While there will always be a come down from this, we don't want an uncomfortable and awkward bump as we wrap things up.

Let's now look in detail at the three parts of the conclusion to see how this can work for your presentations.

Summarize what the audience has heard

The first goal of the conclusion should be to summarize what the audience has heard. Due to the time allocated to the conclusion, this will be very short, so the intent here is to summarize briefly as opposed to re-covering all of the points of the presentation. To this end, I recommend covering the 3 or 5 main topics that you covered in your presentation and presenting them back to the audience. If you have followed the structure of the main content as outlined in this chapter, you can simply pick your top level mind map nodes.

To show an example of this, let's refer back to our fictitious presentation for the GPS product.

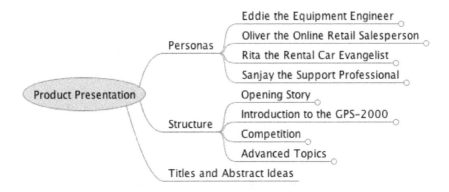

Figure 3.21 - Top level nodes for the GPS Product Presentation.

As you may recall from earlier on in this chapter, and as summarized in Figure 3.21, we created three top level nodes: "Introduction to the GPS-2000," "Competition," and "Advanced Topics." These three work perfectly for the conclusion as we can wrap up the presentation, and then echo to the audience what they've just heard.

You should be able to imagine presenting this to your audience using a message of "What did you just hear?" with the three items listed. This message would talk through each of three bullet points in turn, spending no more than a minute for the slide for a 60-minute presentation.

When you have decided on the topics for your conclusion, you should add a "Conclusion" node to the mind map, as all of this is going to be used to create our slide deck in the next chapter. For our ongoing example, we end up with a map, as shown in Figure 3.22.

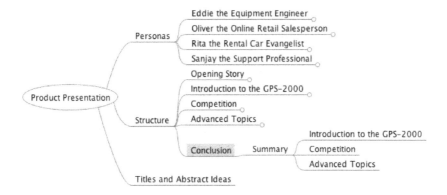

Figure 3.22 - Adding a conclusion node and summary to our presentation mind map.

Instructing the audience to do something

By the time you reach the conclusion part of your presentation, both you and your audience will have invested a lot of time. The audience especially will have likely sat through a significant amount of content to get to this point. After all of this investment from the audience, it would be a shame if the conversation and train of thought came to a stop when your presentation ended. Often you'll be presenting on a topic or subject that lives well beyond the 60-minute duration of your talk.

Recognizing this, an important function of the conclusion is to instruct the audience what to do next. Upon leaving the room very shortly, what should the audience do as a result of investing their time and listening to you? How will they be able to take the content they've heard to the next level? Is there anything that you need them to do?

For your presentation, this section of the conclusion should outline either 3 or 5 actions that you would like the audience to take, or you feel the audience would benefit from. It could of course be a mix of both.

Examples of actions that the audience could do after the presentation include: going to a follow-up session, visiting a website, downloading some software, filling out a survey, and hold meetings or presentations of their own to further share your message with their own audiences. You may want to revisit the structure that you've created in the mind map to search for examples. For instance, if you are giving the audience something as part of the final conclusion, you may want to add a call to action to instruct the audience how they can make good on your offer.

In common terminology, the list that you will create is known as a "call to action" list.

Although every presentation will have very different calls to action, we can look at our example to see how this might work. Based on the content that we have developed so far, we may decide that there are five distinct calls to action. These are:

1. Download the SDK,

2. Visit the product website,

3. Report feedback on the company's survey site,

4. Test out the device when they are shipped to the local offices, and

5. Keep up to date on the competition.

With such a list of items, it's also very important to qualify how the audience can perform the call to action. Each call to action should have an explicit next step that takes the audience in this direction. As examples, this could be the address of a website, an email address, the date and time of the next meeting, etc. The key point is that there is no excuse for the audience thinking, "I want to do that, but I don't know how."

How could this work for our list? Items 1, 2, and 3 are relatively easy as we can supply the URL for the audience. Item 4 is a little trickier as it involves shipping items to a physical office. For this, we might want to point people to a document with the estimated shipping dates and a prompt to add them to the calendar. Item 5 is the one that needs some work. Although it's a very valid call to action, we need to make it actionable for the audience. To do this, we might want to include a link to a competitive report, or set of documents, that the audience can start reading right away. This will make the call to action something that the audience can actually start when they leave the room.

As many of the above actions include URLs in your presentation, we do need to think about how we are going to present these to the audience. Remember that many in the audience will likely be writing down these actions as part of the notes they will be taking. One of the common mistakes I've seen from a number of presentations is including URL addresses that are so horribly long that they cannot be remembered or written down in the time allocated for the slide. Presenters will copy and paste URLs from the browser straight into their PowerPoint slide. Here's a nice example:

> http://mycompany/Pages/Documents?feed.aspx?
> index=91628393&name=Annual%20Product
> %20Report.docx&download=true

The result is a URL that works when it is clicked on, but one that no one in the audience has a hope of jotting down. The result is either forcing the audience to download your slides after the talk, or I've even seen cases where people in the audience will quickly grab their cellphones in order to take a picture of the slide so that they can type it in at their leisure later on.

Please don't do this to your audience! If you have long URLs similar to these, use a URL shortening such as https://bitly.com or http://goo.gl to produce something that can be written down quickly and also potentially remembered by the audience.

The final thing that we need to do to the list is to place the items in the desired order. Although the order is not as strict as other pieces of information we've already discussed, there are a couple of rules that you should follow.

Firstly, the list should be chronologically listed if it applies. For example, if the audience member has to visit a website in order to download the SDK we should think about swapping the order of the first two calls to action items. Secondly, the list should always end with the most important call to action. As a presenter, it's a good idea when presenting this list to add emphasis on the final—and more important—point. Although it's subtle, you are saying to the audience, "If you only do one of the things here, please do this one."

For our example, we might determine that reporting feedback is the most important ask of the audience, so we should move this to the last spot. Reordering this list appropriately and then inserting this into our mind map results in Figure 3.23.

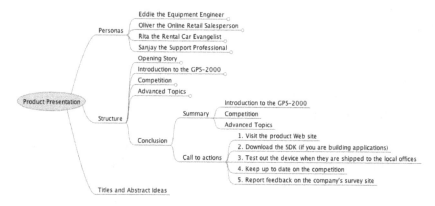

Figure 3.23 - Reordering the calls to action within the presentation mind map.

Final comment

The conclusion now includes a summary of the presentation and a list of actions for the audience. The final piece to the conclusion is to include a final comment which should, if possible, tie back to your opening story.

This final comment can be a great way of concluding a presentation as not only does it remind the audience of how you started, but it also is a chance to introduce a final piece of emotion to close out the talk. The conclusion so far has been very operational. You've summarized the presentation using a list of topics, and then asked the audience to do one or more things. All of this tends to be very instructional and as a result it's difficult to infuse any emotion. Rather than leaving the audience on this tone, the final comment allows you to close out on a softer note that can connect you back to the audience.

Although there are many ways of doing this, a strong final comment will relate back to the opening story, and paint a picture for the future, with (ideally) the audience playing a part. To construct this, you should look at your opening story and find a way of relating the conclusion to this, while leading the audience on this journey and thanking them for their involvement. To put this into perspective, let's create one for our GPS product presentation and add it to our mind map, as shown in Figure 3.24.

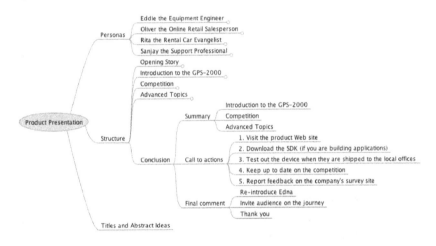

Figure 3.24 - Adding the final comment to the conclusion.

As you may recall, our opening story was about Edna, positioning her as a customer who was frustrated with the current model of GPS device she was using, and setting the scene for the rest of the presentation. For our final comment imagine the presentation switching to an image of Edna with a script that could go something like this:

Hopefully you remember Edna, who we introduced at the beginning of the talk. If you recall, Edna was frustrated with her experience using our current product, the GPS-1000. I hope you'll agree that everything we are introducing with the GPS-2000 means that future customers will have a far superior experience that puts us well ahead of the competition.

What we've done here is tied the conclusion back to Edna and shown how the new product will mean that this won't happen again. We still need to include the audience on the journey and thank them for their involvement, however. To do this, we might add something as follows:

Of course, this product won't succeed in the market without the help of everyone in this room. Whether you are in sales, support, or engineering, I hope you'll join me and my team on this journey to make this the most successful product we've ever launched. Thank you!

And it's a wrap!

Choosing a title and abstract for your presentation

The final part of this chapter on structure involves choosing a title, and if required, an abstract. Choosing an accurate title for presentations is often one of the overlooked details of presentation design.

A poorly chosen title has the potential of setting expectations incorrectly with the audience—or worse, attracting the wrong type and size of audience to your presentation. You could have the most amazing presentation content ever, but if the audience is the wrong people with the wrong expectations, it will always be poorly received.

Many speakers overlook the title in favor of the session code, abstract, or other material promoting the talk. From experience, I can say that the majority of attendees use the presentation title as the primary criteria for deciding whether or not to attend a session. In a small study that I did several conferences ago, I was amazed to find that not only is the abstract never read, but often it's not even available! Many large conferences now offer "quick conference guides" or mobile apps that list only the sessions by title, which further adds to the problem. In addition, many attendees often find themselves not planning ahead and having to quickly pick a session to attend. The majority, if not all of these, will be basing their decision on the session title alone.

What type of presentation am I creating?

In creating a title and abstract, it's important to know what type of presentation you are creating. Using either your own presentation mind map or the example we have been building throughout the book, we can start to classify the presentation type in order to derive an effective title. You may be thinking that you already know what type of presentation you are creating, but there are some subtle differences that are important to cover.

In general, there are three types of presentation: Informational, Educational, and Visionary. All of these presentation types have a lot of things in common, but they all serve a slightly different purpose. It's also possible to have a mix of these types in a single presentation. For example, a presentation might start off as educational, and end with a more visionary slant. Let's go through each of these in turn to look at how they differ:

- **Informational.** Informational presentations are talks that provide information to the audience. As a speaker, your goal is to make the audience more informed, and ensure that they leave with more knowledge, or a different perspective, than when they first came through the door. After hearing an informational presentation, the audience will typically walk away knowing something new that they had not known before entering the room. An informational presentation could be one that announces a new product, shares some new details, or introduces a topic that is new to the audience.

- **Educational.** Educational presentations are similar to informational sessions, except the primary goal of the talk is to educate the audience on a topic. As a speaker, you are imparting your knowledge and, in essence, training the audience to do something new, or to do something better, as a result. With an educational presentation, the audience will leave with new skills that they can apply to a subject that they were often already knowledgeable about. An educational presentation could be one that shows the audience how to use specific features of a product, provides instructional learning, or dives deep into a subject that the audience is familiar with.

You may be asking what the difference is between informational and educational. Aren't they really the same? While the audience is leaving with more knowledge in both scenarios, the key difference is understanding what the audience can do with the knowledge that they have just been given. A good question to ask is, "What will the audience be able to do differently on the Monday after the conference?" If they will learn something that they can immediately apply the following week, the presentation is more likely to be educational in nature. If they learn something new, but they can't really do anything practical with it, this normally indicates a more informational presentation.

• **Visionary.** The third and final category is a visionary presentation. With a visionary presentation, the goal of the talk is to inspire the audience. As a speaker, you are presenting a vision, typically one that you hold, and hoping that your audience comes away enlightened as a result. The audience will leave the presentation passionate about the topic, even if they are not immediately able to act upon this information. A visionary presentation could be one that shows the audience a glimpse of a future product, a revolutionary way of doing something, or focuses on broad topics that have far-reaching impact beyond the audience in the room.

How do you know what type of presentation you are creating? An effective exercise is to run through the presentation mind map to get a sense of whether the content is informational, educational, or visionary. You can ask questions such as:

• Am I informing the audience?

• Am I educating the audience?

• Am I being visionary?

We can apply this approach to the example presentation mind map that we've been building upon in this chapter. Based on the opening story, and the three sections covering the new product, competition, and advanced topics, we can make an educated guess that this will be an informational presentation. The majority of the content is informing the audience about the new GPS product that is being released. While there are sections that cover educational aspects (such as the support section) and visionary aspects (such as the future section), we can safely say that this presentation falls into the informational category. If the presentation had been designed to take the audience through an in-depth scope of the workings of the SDK or the device, it may have leaned more towards an educational talk. If this presentation had been focused on showing the future for an upcoming release next year, it would have certainly been classified as visionary.

What does this have to do with the title?

Based on which category your presentation falls within, there are rules and boundaries for what the title should be. By creating an effective title you should be implicitly telling the audience whether this will be an informational, educational, or visionary session before they step into the room. To put this into perspective, let's look at some examples.

For informational sessions, your title should guide the audience to what they will hear without being too specific. Your presentation might be announcing something new, or introducing a new product, in which case you should use these words. Where it makes sense, including some reference to the audience who will benefit from this talk can also be effective. Here are some examples:

> Introducing Microsoft PowerPoint for Speakers
>
> Announcing a New Software Platform for Realtors
>
> A First Look at Your New Benefits Website

Given that we decided that our GPS example was also an informational talk, we can include a title here, as well: "Introducing the New GPS-2000 Product Range."

As you can see in the above examples, the titles do a good job of guiding the audience into what they will be hearing without being too specific. You'll also notice that the length of the title is around six to eight words. While this isn't a strict rule, this tends to work best for informational talks. A title that is too long (such as "A First Look at Your New Benefits Package, HR Website, and Company Perks") could be misinterpreted as an educational talk, as well as being a little overwhelming.

Let's now look at presentations that fall within the educational category. Because the content will be targeted more towards educating the audience, the title also needs to be much more precise. As with the informational presentation, we are guiding the audience, but this time we need to narrow down the focus to ensure that we have the right people in the room. To do this, instead of mentioning the intended audience in the title, we should instead focus on the intended outcome of the talk. Here are some examples:

> Leveraging Microsoft PowerPoint to Create User Interface Prototypes
>
> Using the New Realtor Software Platform to List Your First House

Navigating the New HR Website to Set Up Your Benefits Package

As you can see from the above, educational titles are much more precise and the outcome to the audience is clearly demonstrated. As a result of this, the titles also tend to be slightly longer.

Another option for educational titles is to call out the number of sections in the main content. If you recall from earlier in this chapter, the main content is likely divided up into three sections, but it could also be five or ten. Using this as part of the title can also be effective.

The Art, History, and Science Behind Improving Your UI Design

Decrypting SSL in Five Easy Steps

Top Ten Tips for Setting Up Your Development Environment

Finally, let's look at titles for visionary presentations. Out of the three, this is the one that is least bound by rules. In general, a visionary title should be somewhat generic and forward looking. Unlike the informational and educational titles, it should also be open-ended for the audience to interpret. A good test to see whether this truly is a visionary title is to see whether the title works with an exclamation mark to the end, even if you choose not to use one.

Next Generation Presentation Software: Myth or Magic?

Real Estate Software in 2030

Cloud IDEs Evolved

As you can see from the above, visionary titles are forward looking, and open to some interpretation by the audience. Where things get interesting however is when the title of a presentation is mismatched to the content within. This is something that we can look at now.

Mismatched titles

Although it might seem obvious, things can go wrong with

mismatched titles, especially when a title from one category is applied to another. A common example I've seen is speakers who choose an educational title, but where the presentation is mostly informational and visionary. The audience comes into the session expecting to be educated, and often leaves disappointed, leaving feedback such as "This presentation was full of fluff" or "I did not learn that much" on the evaluation forms.

On several occasions, I've also seen the reverse, where a visionary title has been used for an information or educational session. In some ways this is actually worse, especially if the title really is appealing, as this has a side effect of attracting a larger audience. Suddenly you are dealing with a large discontented audience, which is never fun.

Such a case takes me back to a conference a few years ago. My team was responsible for one of the tracks of a developer event, for which we were selecting speakers and sessions. Out of our sessions, we had selected a session called "How to Teach Your Grandmother to Build Rockets" and we were under the impression that this would be a very visionary session speaking about the future of making software simpler to build. After a set of missed rehearsals, however, we found out too late that this was much more of an informational session, with the majority of the content covering the speaker's own experience and opinions on a particular software topic. Unfortunately, it was too late to change the title as the conference agenda had already gone to print, and the title was locked. On the day of the presentation, we sat helplessly as over five hundred attendees packed the large room, and witnessed a great number of these people get up and leave around halfway through once they realized that it wasn't going to be the visionary masterpiece that they had hoped for. Needless to say we heard about it many times in the resulting evaluation forms. For not only the speaker in question, but for me as an organizer of the track, this was a great lesson in the importance of selecting a title that matches the type of presentation that will be delivered.

Subtitles

In many cases, along with the title, it will be possible to include a subtitle for the presentation. Subtitles can be used to give more detail on a presentation over and above what the title is trying to convey. Subtitles can be used for any type of presentation, although tend to work best with informational and visionary sessions, especially when the title is very short.

Let's take one of our previous visionary examples:

Cloud IDEs Evolved

If we wanted to augment this title with additional information to add clarity for the audience we might choose to append a subtitle similar to this one:

How IDEs Will Change Over the Next Decade, and What You Should Be Doing About It

In this case, the use of a subtitle is effective as it still keeps the goal of a visionary talk, while adding more details to the potentially inquiring audience member.

If you do choose to use a subtitle for your presentation, I would advise doing so with caution. While they can be effective with short, informational or visionary titles, they can quickly lead to long sentences that are difficult to digest for potential attendees. My recommendation would be to try the subtitle out with a few people to see whether it's really necessary. If you find that you are just using it to play safe, you can probably drop it.

Presentation levels

Many conferences, especially technical ones, will also ask for a presentation level when you submit your title and abstract. Normally this will be based on a 100, 200, 300, or 400 scale, with 100 being introductory and 400 being advanced. If you haven't come across this before, this scale is modeled after the US college system. As with the title, you can use the presentation type and your mind map to determine which level should be attributed to your talk. For large conferences, it's important to get the level accurate, as this can greatly affect the expectation of the audience. As a rule of thumb, you can use the presentation type as a guide:

- **Informational.** Most informational presentations will likely be 200 level or 300 level depending on the topic, and any familiarity or prerequisites required from the audience. Level 100 is usually too low for an informational presentation, unless the session is part of a keynote or mandatory session, in which case, the bar of entry will likely be lower. Level 400 informational presentations are rare as presentations of this type tend to focus on introducing and announcing new topics, and it's difficult to get to 400 level within the allocated time.

- **Educational.** Most educational sessions will range between 200 and 400, again depending on the topic. For an educational session, level 200 can be seen as beginner, level 300 is intermediate, and level 400 is advanced. The detail of the topic, together with the expectations and prerequisites of the audience, is likely to dictate this level. Level 100 educational sessions are rare as most of the content presented will likely be informational in nature.

- **Visionary.** Visionary sessions will likely be level 100 or 200. The broad nature of the visionary topic means that the level of detail will likely never reach anything higher. If you are finding that your visionary session is leaning towards a level 300 or 400 session, it might be that the content of the session could be more informational or educational in nature.

While this rating scale is useful for conferences and organizers who ask for this information, I would recommend against using the scale in situations where it might not be recognized. For example, I've seen presentations with titles such as:

HTML5 101

Advanced Arduino Programming—A Level 400 Session

While these might make sense to the speaker, it assumes that the audience knows the 100–400 rating scale. As the rating scale is based on the US educational system, it assumes that everyone in the audience will be familiar with it which might not be the case, especially those traveling from overseas. Immigrating from overseas myself, I was a little confused when I first came across the use of "101" in a session title, having been through an educational system in another country that did not use this concept!

Session codes

Often related to the presentation level is the concept of a session code. If you are presenting at a large conference or event, your session will often be given a session code. Different conferences have codes in many different formats, but the most common is a combination of the track, presentation level, and a unique identifier.

As an example, let's imagine that you are presenting at a large developer conference. You have been awarded a session in the "Cloud" track, and you are planning a 200 level talk. Given these variables, your session code might be CLD230. CLD indicates that your session is in the cloud track. The "200" part of the 230 indicates that this is a level 200 talk. The "30" part of the 230 is to create a unique code to identify your session from others in the same track.

While the session code indicates the track and level for the presentation, I've found time and time again one important fact: Attendees very rarely look at the session code! As a presenter you may be mistaken for thinking that a session with a code CLD230 would intuitively indicate a level 200 session in the cloud track for the potential audience. On many occasions, however, I've found that this is not the case. I've seen audience feedback complaining that the session contained too much information about a certain topic—where that certain topic in question was indeed the overall subject of the track! I've also heard audience members complain that this was not a level 400 session as they expected, when the session code explicitly stated that it would be a level 200.

The moral of this? While the session code might indicate the track and level to you and the conference organizers, don't assume that the audience will either read the session code or even understand it. Ultimately, the title and abstract are much more important than any code given to you by the conference organizers, and will determine the type of people you attract to your session.

Writing a good abstract

If you are presenting to any large group, and most certainly when presenting at a conference, you are going to need to submit an abstract for your talk. Although abstracts can vary greatly, they are typically two or three paragraphs of text that inform your potential audience about what the talk is about, and hopefully what they will get out of it, should they attend.

As a speaker, the goal of the abstract should be to draw the right audience to your presentation. The abstract should concisely frame the presentation and what's on offer to the audience. Ideally, the abstract should also be inviting, acting as a teaser to encourage participants to come to your session.

An effective abstract has three components to it. Firstly, it must set the scene or problem statement for the potential audience. This should frame the topic for the audience. Secondly, it should introduce the content that reflects the main sections of the presentation. Questions are a good way of doing this, and we'll look at this shortly. Finally, it should end with a teaser to attract the audience. In one to two paragraphs, this should be a concise way of attracting the right people to the presentation.

To put this in some perspective, let's take a look at an example. Building on from the other session titles that we've been using in this chapter, let's imagine that we are putting together an abstract for a presentation on code refactoring tools and techniques. The abstract might look like something as follows:

> In a recently conducted study, it was estimated that developers using code refactoring tools are on average up to 20% more productive than their peers. As a result, the number of plug-ins and utilities offering refactoring capabilities has almost doubled in size over the past five years.
>
> With this growth and interest, you'd be right to ask how you can capitalize on this upward swing. What types of refactoring will add most value to your project? What are the fundamental features to look out for? How should you go about selecting between commercial and open source tools?
>
> In this session, we'll building answering these questions and more. We'll take a 360-degree look at refactoring techniques, including the best practices and pitfalls from recent projects. You'll leave the session with a complete understanding of the space, ready to incorporate refactoring tools and techniques to your project!

Although this is a completely fictitious example, you can hopefully see how much has been covered in these three small paragraphs. Firstly, the abstract references the recent study and another statistic from the industry. Not only does this set the scene for the potential attendee, but it also adds a level of credibility by citing sources outside the presentation's content. Secondly, the abstract asks four potential questions on the trend, types of refactoring, fundamental features, and selecting the right tool. Three of these questions will map to the main sections of the presentation. Finally, the abstract uses three sentences as the teaser. The first and second promise coverage of the main questions, and the third is future looking, promising a positive outcome for anyone who attends.

Using a similar approach, let's see how this would work for our equally fictitious GPS product example that we've been building within this chapter.

> Our previous line of GPS devices have been very successful in the market over the past five years, but customers' expectations have never been higher. Customers looking for a GPS today are asking for new features and pushing the boundaries of how navigation works within the vehicle. To take our company forward, we are embarking on a new journey to meet these needs, and will be releasing the GPS-2000 model to customers.
>
> With such a major new release, you'd be right to ask how this device improves the in-vehicle experience for customers. What new features does it have over the previous models? How does it stack up against our competitors? How can the new device be extended to new platforms and hardware?
>
> In this session, we'll be answering these questions, and much more. We'll be demonstrating the product for the first time on stage, as well as showing you a glimpse into the future of what we believe this product is capable of. You'll walk away not only with a full understanding of this amazing product, but also with the opportunity to be involved in making this new GPS device a success with our customers!

As you can tell, although it's a completely different set of questions and objectives, using the sample template for the GPS example is very effective in setting the scene, covering the content of the presentation, and planting a teaser for potential attendees. Using this template, you should now be in a position to put together a similar abstract for your own presentation.

When should you select and submit your title and abstract?

You may have noticed that we left the subject of title creation to the very end of the chapter on structure. This was done on purpose as the job of classifying the type of presentation is far easier once you have a structure to work against. Although this might feel contrary to the way that you've done things in the past, I really do recommend that you do not come up with a title of your presentation until you have the majority of your structure defined. With a complete structure in a mind map, not only will it be easier to come up with the title, but the end result will likely be more accurate.

There are, of course, times that this can be difficult. Often, to even get accepted into a conference, the first step is to submit a title, abstract, and bio. If you are planning to speak about a new topic, there's a good chance that you won't even have a mind map to reference at this point. In this situation, my recommendation would be to submit a placeholder title and abstract getting as close as you can to what you believe the structure will be. If you are then accepted, the first thing you should do is to find out when the last possible date is to change the details of your session (this will often be when any agendas or materials go to the printers) and submit a revised title and abstract as close to this date as you possibly can. The result will be a more accurate title and abstract that reflects the true content of your presentation.

Time for your first rehearsal!

This might sound a little strange, but it's time for your first rehearsal! I can hear what you are thinking. You haven't created any slides yet, so how can you possibly rehearse anything? We will, of course, be doing a rehearsal using the completed presentation mind map. Rehearsing the mind map with one or more people that you trust will give you the confidence that your content is sound, and will give you early warning for anything that needs changing. As previously mentioned, the cost in time and effort of moving things around on the mind map is relatively cheap. Moving things around when you are close to completing a presentation can be a lot more time consuming. Therefore, any major feedback that comes out from your first rehearsal will be easier to address at this stage.

Who should you rehearse to? The rehearsal can be to anyone, of course, but if possible, I would recommend finding people that match most closely with your personas. If you can find a group of people that match all of your personas, and get them in the same place at once, this can be very effective.

The rehearsal can be done over the phone, via an online meeting, or in person, with the latter two being more preferable. You won't be showing slides, but having the ability to share and walk through your mind map is important. If phone is your only option, be sure to send a copy of your mind map ahead of time. Given that there is likely a lot of content in the mind map at this stage, and the person you are doing the rehearsal to may not have the mind map software you are using, I would recommend sending the map as a multi-page PDF.

The rehearsal will involve walking the person (or people that you've assembled) through your mind map. You will introduce the opening story, cover the main content of your presentation in some detail, and cover the conclusion. At this point, you are not actually presenting the content, but instead walking them through what you will be presenting. As you do this, you'll be saying things, such as "At this point in the presentation, I'm going to talk about X" and "This is where we move on to topic Y." Also, try to get into the habit of expanding on the subject without the use of the mind map. For example, if one of the nodes on your mind map reads "Feature X," offer some detail to your reviews about what Feature X is, and why it's important to mention. Having nodes in the mind map trigger conversation will help your review, and will also be invaluable as triggers for when you start putting together your actual presentation.

This review session should also be an opportunity to test the selected title and abstract with the audience. This is the best way of seeing how other people interpret the title, and to get a gut check of what content they believe will be presented and whether it matches the mind map that you are walking them through. If you have a couple of titles that you feel could go either way, this is also an excellent opportunity to get a feel for which one resonates the best with a potential audience.

Allow your audience of reviewers to offer feedback at any time, and don't be afraid of updating the mind map in real time to reflect their suggestions. This will make them feel like their input is more valuable and they will likely offer more suggestions as a result. You can also pause and prompt for feedback at various points. "Does this section make sense to you?" or "Do you think this will work for the audience?" are great questions to gather feedback, especially if your reviewers are on the quiet side.

Finally, in terms of time for the rehearsal, don't try and come up with an estimated time for the presentation as there are still many unknown factors as this stage. Instead, ensure that there is enough time to cover the mind map in some detail with your reviewers and get feedback without worrying about how short or long your presentation will be.

Can you actually present from the mind map?

For a conference in mid-2005, I actually ended up ditching Microsoft PowerPoint altogether and presenting directly from the mind map to an audience of around fifty or so attendees. At the time, I was curious to see whether this approach would work, and I was running desperately behind on time, so it was also an excuse not to put a slide deck together!

Although I wouldn't recommend this unless you are very familiar with presenting mind maps and want to try something completely different, the feedback from the audience was actually very positive. As well as breaking up the monotony of the slide decks that the audience had been subjected to all week, the mind map allowed for a more conversational approach.

One major drawback of this approach, and probably one of the reasons that I've not tried this since, is that there is little to no re-use for the mind map. There was nothing to distribute after the talk aside from a large PDF version of the mind map, which the attendees couldn't do that much with.

Where are we?

This brings us to the end of Chapter 3 where we have covered a lot of content about structure, creating a presentation mind map, introduced the

10/85/5 rule, chosen a title and abstract, and performed a first rehearsal.

After incorporating the feedback from your first rehearsal, and likely editing more of the mind map as you continue to build out your structure, there will come a point where you need to call it done. The mind map is going to form the basis of your actual slide deck, which itself is going to take some time to put together.

A good of rule of thumb of knowing when you are done is to see what changes you are making to the mind map. If you find yourself comfortable with presenting the mind map and mostly fine-tuning the map as opposed to adding or editing major chunks of content, it's probably a sign that you are getting ready to move on!

When you are ready, in the next chapter we are going to make the transition from the mind map to putting together the first parts of your presentation, known as the slide canvas!

---

1. Please note that the "GPS-1000" and "GPS-2000" models are used throughout the book for illustration purposes, and are not meant to represent any devices using similar or same names.

2. TED (Technology Education and Design) is a conference series that was started in 1984, and releases amazing presentations under a Creative Commons license. You can watch many of the videos from previous conferences at http://www.ted.com

3. For reference, this presentation can be found here: http://www.slideshare.net/simonguest/enterprise-social-networking-myth-or-magic-15147041

CHAPTER 4: Your Slide Canvas–The Pencil Sketch

* * *

I want to start this chapter by making a claim that may be new to some: People cannot read and listen at the same time. This is one of these truths that takes a while to fully sink in, but once it does, it immediately reveals how ineffective many presentations are.

Imagine if you put a piece of written content in front of someone and ask them to read it. There are many articles[1] that have shown that while they are reading and absorbing it, the person has the ability to hear, but finds it very difficult to listen. A lot of this stems to our human, primal instincts. In simplistic terms, we have two channels—one for audible and one for visual cognition. While both channels are technically open at the same time, priority is always given to one of the channels. For example, if halfway through reading the text you suddenly shout, "Hey! Watch out for the falling rock!" then chances are good that the person reading will stop and pay attention quickly. Despite a lot of focus on the visual channel, the audible channel is open to these types of primal threats. If, however, you "equalize" the channels and talk in a normal voice, reading some other text to this person at the same time that they are reading the text from the paper, there's a very good chance that they will not be able to recall one or the other in complete detail. These two channels are like a Y-shaped valve that can absorb information via either visual or audible inputs, but can't effectively handle both at the same time.

As presenters we often ignore these two channels and instead put up a slide's worth of bullet points or other text on the screen for the audience to read, and while they are reading this, we provide our own narration over the top. What we are doing is presenting people a piece of text to read using their visual channel, and then asking them to listen to us at the same time using their audible channel. Just like the Y-shaped valve, people will only tune into one at a time, and as a result will likely miss most or all of one of the inputs.

This is actually fun to experiment with. Don't look at it yet, but Figure 4.1 shows a slide full of bullet points, something that you might find in a regular presentation about mobile devices. Before you read it, turn on the TV and tune into one of the news channels. When you are ready, read all of the bullet points on the slide and simultaneously try to listen to the news report on TV. After you've finished reading the slide, reflect on the information you absorbed and how you tried to process information from either channel. Were you able to get to the end of the slide of text before your attention was diverted to the TV? Are you able to recall anything from the news stories? Were you frequently switching between both materials, but don't feel that you have a complete picture of either one? Chances are, your brain did not multitask between the two, but instead focused on one of these input channels at a time and temporarily shut down the other as it switched between the two. If you were able to read the majority of the text, you might have "heard" the news, but were you actually "listening" to the news?

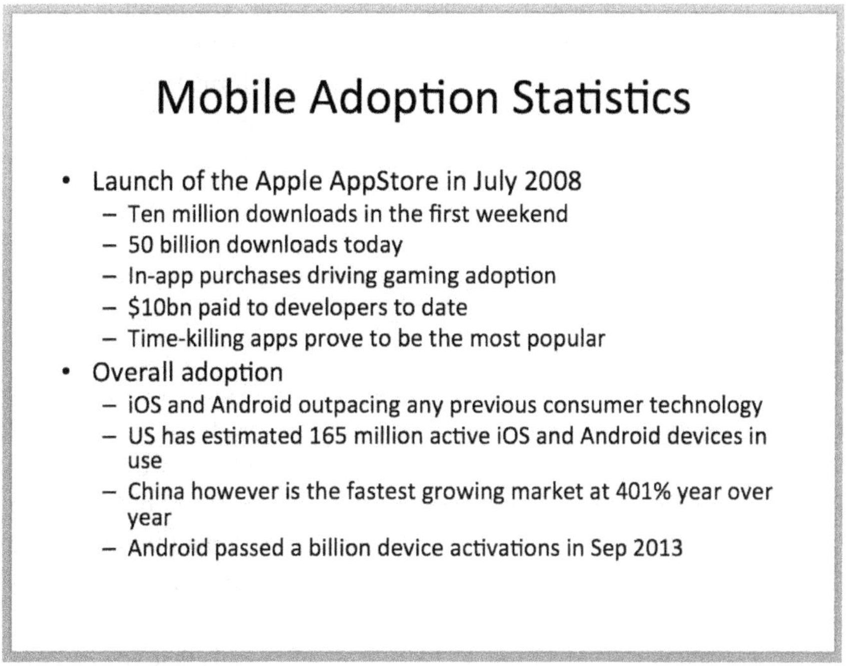

Mobile Adoption Statistics

- Launch of the Apple AppStore in July 2008
  - Ten million downloads in the first weekend
  - 50 billion downloads today
  - In-app purchases driving gaming adoption
  - $10bn paid to developers to date
  - Time-killing apps prove to be the most popular
- Overall adoption
  - iOS and Android outpacing any previous consumer technology
  - US has estimated 165 million active iOS and Android devices in use
  - China however is the fastest growing market at 401% year over year
  - Android passed a billion device activations in Sep 2013

Figure 4.1 - A slide full of bullet points on mobile adoption.

As presenters we run into this mistake time and time again. We put up slides full of text, similar to Figure 4.1, expecting the audience to read it, while at the same time giving our own narration over the top. What happens with most audiences is that they switch to their visual channel, reading the text once you advance to the next slide. It's new information, and they are keen to read it. While they are spending the 15–20 seconds to read your bullet points, their audible channel is hearing that you are speaking, but they are not listening to your words. Once they have finished the slide, these inputs will switch. Their audible channel will begin to listen to you more attentively and their visual channel will stop reading the slide in detail. The problem being, at this stage, it's often too late. As each slide gets displayed, the audience is effectively missing the first 20 seconds or so of your narration, and it can take more time for

103

them to actually then tune into what you are saying. The result is a lot of switching between the channels. Multiply this by 50 slides in a deck, and it quickly results in missing vital pieces of information, the brain becoming tired of having to constantly switch channels, and ultimately the attendee becoming disconnected and likely bored with your presentation.

How do we address this? Unless you want to do a silent presentation, there's not much we can do about the audible channel. As presenters we need to speak! Instead we need to effectively modify the visual channel, which is something that we'll be focusing on starting in this chapter.

The first step on the path to modifying the visual channel is to change the perspective of what goes into a slide deck. Instead of thinking about your presentation as a set of slides, bullet points, and text, I'd like you to instead start thinking about it as a beautiful piece of art on a canvas. While there will be text in your presentation, the important things in your slide deck are the important things that you will find in a good piece of art.

In this chapter we are going to be covering the tools that you can use, building up the layers of your canvas, and overall composition until your work of art is ready to be shown to the world!

Layers

I've had the opportunity to study techniques that many presenters use to put together slide decks. One common trait, especially among less experienced presenters, is the tendency to create the presentation in a serial fashion.

For example, a presenter might create a new slide deck starting from the title slide, then create an agenda, move on and create the first content slide, and so forth. Each slide is "polished" at the point of creation, adding diagrams, images, videos, builds, animations, and any other assets that might be needed.

While this doesn't sound too bad at first, try to imagine an artist creating a painting of a vase of flowers using the same technique. The idea that the artist would sketch, draw, paint, and finish each part of the picture individually seems implausible. Imagine the artist starting the picture by fully completing a table leg, before moving on to a flower petal, before finally moving on to a window. While the result might look close to what the artist intended, the composition of the picture as a whole would likely suffer as a result. It would likely look like a patchwork of parts rather than a true painting.

To overcome this, many, if not all, artists instead use layers. The artist will likely start by first creating a light pencil sketch of the whole scene, outlining major objects, perspectives, and the broad detail of the painting. Secondly, the artist will start building some of these broad elements into actual objects. She will start painting the background and major components, adding depth and texture to the painting. Finally, the artist will concentrate on the finer details. This might include the shadow falling from the flower vase or the patterns on the curtains in the background.

Each layer builds upon the previous, enabling the artist to truly create the painting as a cohesive picture as opposed to assembling multiple parts together. The artist also uses each layer to reflect on the state of the picture at any one time. For example, after completing the pencil sketch, she might take a minute to stand back from the canvas and really judge whether the perspective is correct. Is the vase proportional to the rest of the objects in the picture? Is the window in the right place? Does the angle of the floor look skewed? Any changes can be dealt with early and quickly before the artist has invested time in applying any paint.

Applying layers to presentations

Similar to how an artist uses layers to create their canvas, we can and should use the same concept when creating a presentation.

The first layer is analogous to the pencil sketch. This is where we define the main sections and boundaries of the presentation, the rough outline for any text, and any foundational templates that we'll be using. The presentation doesn't look much like a presentation at this point, but it will have all of the foundational and structural elements required.

The second layer represents the paint. Creation of the presentation focuses on the fonts, colors, backgrounds, images, and videos. This adds a level of depth to the presentation, bringing sections and areas of the presentation to life.

Finally, the third layer can be thought of as the detail. The finishing touches are added to the presentation, including diagrams, screenshots, clippings, builds, and animations. Ultimately, this is the polish for the presentation, adding the pieces that are going to result in something that looks great in front of the audience.

Just as the artist reflects on their painting at each layer, as presenters we can do something similar. For example, at the end of the first layer, we can start to get a sense for the timing of each of the sections. Is the first section too long? Does the middle bit of the final section belong there? Is there something that's off with the ending? As with the painting, edits are much easier to correct at this stage as opposed to realizing this once the slide deck is complete.

Choosing a tool for your canvas: Microsoft PowerPoint...

Of course, every good artist has a set of tools that they use to create a great painting. As presenters, and taking the analogy forward, we need to make sure we have the same.

Since its release in 1990, Microsoft PowerPoint has earned a reputation of being the de facto standard for creating presentations. This standard has resulted in multiple books, training courses, videos, and other materials on how to use the popular software product.

When many presenters are looking to increase their presentation skills or change the way they present, they often first start by looking at the tool. Many will question whether using a different tool might give them access to different features and functions, while at the same time differentiating them from other presenters.

While this book doesn't aim to do a feature by feature breakdown of Microsoft PowerPoint compared to other alternatives, in case you are also going through the same thought process, I did want to take an unbiased summary of how Microsoft PowerPoint stacks up compared to others.

Compared to Apple Keynote

At the 2003 MacWorld conference, Steve Jobs unveiled Apple's newest creation, a new piece of software for creating presentations called Keynote. Keynote had been Job's personal tool for creating presentations for prior MacWorld and other events, and over the past few years Keynote has evolved through multiple releases, with v5.3 being available at the time of this writing.

After having used both Microsoft PowerPoint and Apple Keynote extensively over the years, and frequently interchanging between the two, I want to share some of the differences between the competing products:

- **What type of machine do you have?** A key question to ask as Apple Keynote only runs on a Mac, whereas Microsoft PowerPoint is available for both. If you only have a PC, then unless you are prepared to switch machines, or have access to a Mac, it's going to be difficult for you to run Keynote.

- **Compatibility and re-use.** With many more years in the market, Microsoft PowerPoint has enjoyed much more adoption than Apple Keynote, and as a result, if you are planning on sharing your presentation with others, the PPT (or PPTX) file format used by Microsoft PowerPoint is likely to be more widely accepted than the KEY file format used by Keynote.

- **There are ways around this, of course.** Keynote does support an "Export to PowerPoint" feature, which aside from fonts and tables, appears to do a reasonable job at exporting. You can also save your Keynote file to a PDF (Adobe's Portable Document Format) file. Although recipients will not be able to edit the PDF document, the presentation will preserve the fidelity of the original presentation.

- **Graphs, media, and animations.** Although both tools support creation of charts, inserting media, and the ability to animate numerous elements, from my experience Apple Keynote is superior in all three of these areas. Some of the charting effects in Apple Keynote add a level of quality beyond Microsoft PowerPoint, and certain animation effects (such as Magic Move, which we'll cover at the end of Chapter 6) offer transitions that are beyond the default set found in the Microsoft product.

Compared to online presentation tools

In addition to Apple Keynote and others, over the past few years we've also seen a number of online alternatives to Microsoft PowerPoint. These have included SlideRocket (www.sliderocket.com), Zoho Show (zoho.com), and more recently, a tool called Prezi (www.prezi.com). While the concept of creating slides still holds true, many of these tools focus on animations and transitions between the slides as a differentiator. The result is "decks" that zoom in, zoom out, and offer transitions in multiple ways to introduce different areas of content in your presentation. I recently sat through one presentation that mimicked the stops on a virtual train line, introducing a new slide of content at each "station."

While I would definitely encourage you to check out Prezi and other similar tools, I would also recommend that you think about potential re-use. While the link to online content will be easy to share through links, there are many occasions where the actual deck might be requested and expected by others.

It's really not about the tool!

While using a different presentation tool might give you a new feature or a novel way of presenting an idea, there's a good chance that it won't dramatically affect your presentation skills. I've seen many people switch to a different tool in the hope that it will make their presentations stand out and become slick and different, when in reality all they face is frustration with having to learn something new or finding missing features halfway through creating their presentation.

My advice would be to stick with the tool that you have most experience with and are most comfortable using. By doing so, you can focus on improving the creation and delivery of your content rather than relying on a new tool or set of features that you haven't used before.

For the purpose of this book, we'll be showing the slide creation using Microsoft PowerPoint, and I'll point out how to do certain things in Apple Keynote where appropriate. With this in mind, however, remember that nothing shown (especially in this chapter) will keep you from using any other tool of your choice.

First layer: Your pencil sketch

Now that we've covered the concept of the canvas, and have taken a brief look at tools, we can start looking at the elements that go into the first layer of the presentation.

This first layer focuses on five elements. Firstly, we will import the existing mind map into our presentation tool. Once the import is complete, we'll mark some of the sectional boundaries that will form the broad picture of the presentation. After this, we will review and edit the text of each slide to make sure that it makes sense. Following the text review, we'll investigate the use of templates to help correctly shape the slides, and finally we'll review how different elements are going to be revealed.

This might sound like a lot of work, and there's definitely much to do, but by the end we'll have an actual working presentation that we can rehearse from.

Importing the mind map

The first stage is to import the mind map presentation into a new slide deck. To start, using the tool of your choice, create a new slide deck (see Figure 4.2). Pick the default white template. That's all we need for now.

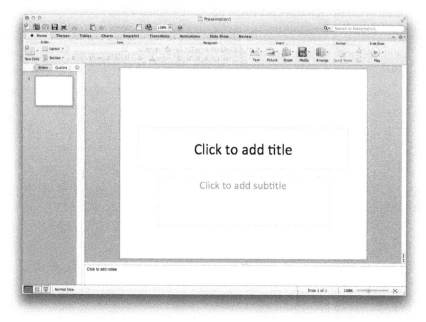

Figure 4.2 - A new presentation in Microsoft PowerPoint.

Once this is created, open your mind map. What we now need to do is take the whole of the structure node that we created earlier and move it to the presentation. This is not a trivial exercise, and will take some time to do. Some mind map software applications support automatic export to Microsoft PowerPoint, but your mileage may vary, and if this is your first time through this exercise I would recommend doing this piece manually.

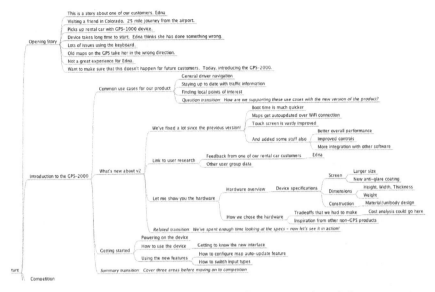

Figure 4.3 - Expanded structure of our presentation mind map.

Figure 4.3 shows the expanded structure of the example presentation mind map that we created in the previous chapter. To convert this to individual slides, we start at the top, which in this case is the opening story, and create a single slide for each node, traversing the mind map as we go. For example, our first slide will contain a single line of text called "Opening Story." Our second slide will contain a single line of text with "This is a story about one of our customers, Edna." Our third slide will have a line that reads "Visiting a friend in Colorado. 25 mile journey from the airport". And so forth.

Within Microsoft PowerPoint, simply create a new slide with the default template (which should be title and text block), and enter the text for each node in the title. For the first three nodes in our example mind map, this will produce something similar to Figure 4.4.

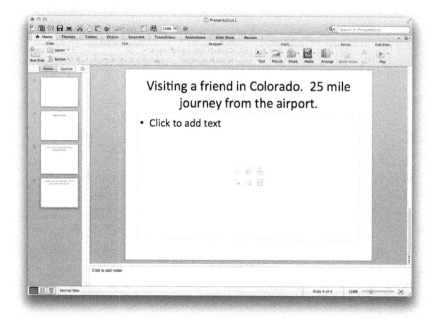

Figure 4.4 - A new slide with text imported from one of the nodes on the mind map.

Now, continue this process until your entire mind map is converted to slides. Make sure that every node in the mind map has a slide, including the transitions, as shown in Figure 4.5. Don't worry if some of your titles are long and go onto multiple lines. We will be trimming these down after we have all of the map converted. Also, if you come across a node that represents a potential demo, video, or other image, just use placeholder text to represent this.

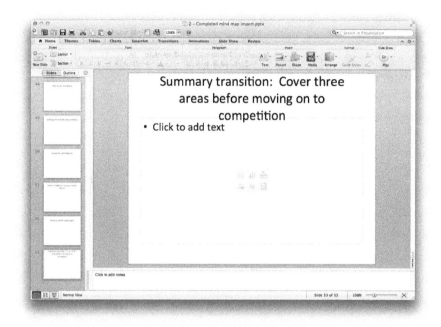

Figure 4.5 - The opening story and introduction section in slide format.

Once you've completed the conversion of your mind map into slides, congratulations! You are now in a position where all of your mind map has been converted into some kind of slide format. Of course, there is still a lot of work to do, but give yourself a pat on the back for reaching this stage!

What you'll also likely have noticed is that you have a presentation that contains a lot of slides. Maybe 100? Possibly 200 or 300? For the purposes of this book, I only converted the opening story and introductory node for our example, and I'm already at 53 slides. For the time being, don't worry about the number of slides. We'll be making a lot of adjustments and touching on this very concern at the end of this section.

113

Creating section boundaries

At this point in the process we have all of the nodes in the mind map represented as slides in the deck. What we now need to do is to break the presentation into sectional boundaries. This is a fairly easy exercise to do and involves running through the deck, and creating boundaries for each major section.

For example, Slide 2 in our example presentation (shown in Figure 4.6) introduces our opening story. This is clearly the start of a new or different talking point in our deck, as we will now be talking about a completely new topic.

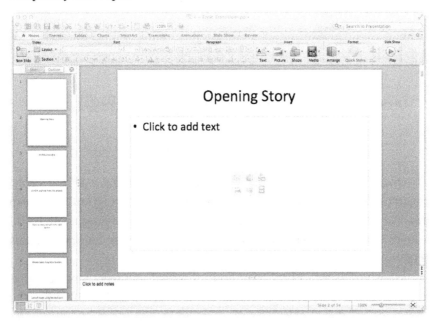

Figure 4.6 - Slide 2 is the introduction of a new section.

All we need to do is to mark this as a new section. To do this in Microsoft PowerPoint, simply right-click on the slide and select Add Section and give the section a name. If you are using Apple Keynote, you can use the Tab button in the Slide column to get a similar effect. I'm going to name this section "Opening Story," which will insert an appropriate section break, as shown in Figure 4.7.

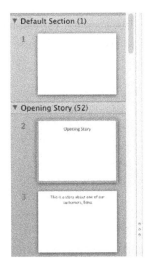

Figure 4.7 - A new section break for the opening story section.

The next section break in our example presentation will come at Slide 11 where we transition from the opening story about Edna into introducing the new GPS product. We can now go through and add section breaks throughout the deck. The transition slides will be a great help here, and feel free to peek back at the presentation mind map if you need help determining where the major break points should be.

The end result (as shown in Figure 4.8) for our example introduction presentation is six section boundaries:

1. A Default Section (this is the title slide—we'll get to this in Chapter 6),

2. The Opening Story,

3. Introduction,

4. Common Use Cases,

5. What's New?, and

6. Getting Started.

Obviously, if you do this exercise for your entire mind map, you'll end up with many more than six—typically one representing each 1st and 2nd level node of the map.

Figure 4.8 - The six sections in our example presentation.

In the mind map, recall how the "Introduction" node is the parent node for the next three. As a result, notice how the introduction section is only one slide. Although it might seem strange to have only one slide in a section, this is actually fine, and will work out well as a placeholder for introducing the rest of the content.

Now that we have the sections of the presentation in place, let's take a closer look at some of the text.

Converting text to visual cues

With the import of the presentation mind map complete, it's now time to look at some of the text that we've just imported. The goal of the text on the slide should be to act as a visual cue to us as a presenter, not as a long sentence or paragraph that you will read to the audience. Therefore, anything that you can do to reduce the amount of text on the slide, and ultimately convert it to a visual cue, will promote this point.

As an example, let's take a look at Slide 3 in our example deck.

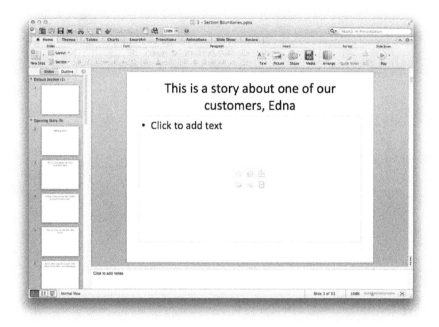

Figure 4.9 - Slide 3 in the example presentation deck.

As shown in Figure 4.9, the current text reads, "This is a story about one of our customers, Edna." Although it represents what we will be presenting, it's a little long to read—and it's probably going to repeat what we actually say—so we can and should convert it to a visual cue by reducing the amount of text. We might shorten it to: "This is a story about Edna" or even better, just "Introducing Edna" (similar to Figure 4.10).

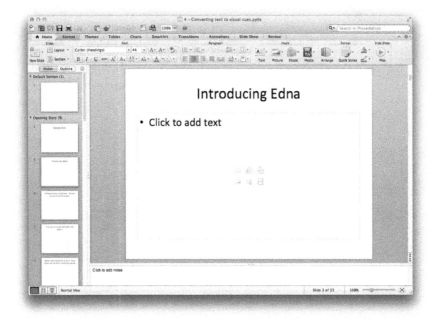

Figure 4.10 - Reducing the amount of text on Slide 3.

Again, the goal is to have the text as a visual cue for what you will be speaking about. As a presenter, when I look at the screen and see "Introducing Edna," this will be my cue for explaining that Edna was a customer that we met as part of our research group, and then lead into the rest of the story. You shouldn't reduce the text so much that you forget the meaning of the visual cue, but the rule should be that less text is better. As we covered at the start of this chapter, remember that your audience will read the text on the slide first before starting to listen to you, so the less text the better.

You might come across slides that have long sentences that might need to be broken up into multiple slides. Slide 10 in our example presentation is a good example of this.

118

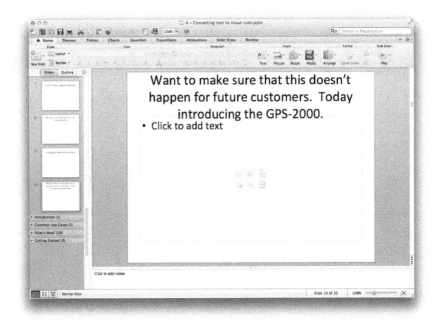

Figure 4.11 - Slide 10 with a long sentence that needs splitting.

As we can see in Figure 4.11, we have two topics as part of the same sentence. The first topic is related to making sure that the problem doesn't happen for future customers. The second topic introduces our new product. As it would be a little difficult to reduce these into a single visual cue, we'll just split these into two separate slides for now, with each sentence being given a new slide. However, after we have the topic split into two, we'll still reduce the text. The first slide will now read, "Avoiding this for future customers," and the second will be "Introducing the GPS-2000" (as shown in Figure 4.12).

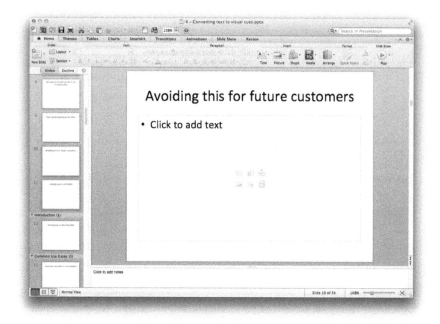

Figure 4.12 - Splitting the sentence and reducing to two visual cues.

If you are following along with your own presentation, go ahead and complete your run-through of the deck, reducing the text to visual cues where it makes sense. The one exception is the transition slides. Don't worry about modifying the text on these slides as we'll come to these later.

Creating lists

Lists are very common in many presentations. A software product presentation might show a list of features, a sales presentation might show a list of top regions, and a financial presentation might show a list of top performing funds.

At this stage of presentation creation, one of the important things we need to do is identify these types of lists. By doing so, we can further add structure to the slide deck as well as combine multiple slides into single slides.

As you step through your deck, you are probably going to find multiple slides that represent lists. The key at this stage is to determine whether the list of items should exist as separate slides or whether it makes sense to combine them into a single slide. There are actually three types of list that we need to be on the lookout for.

To demonstrate these three types, here are a couple of examples from our fictitious presentation:

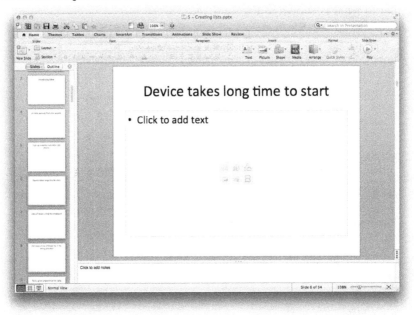

Figure 4.13 - Example of a list in the example presentation.

Slides 6–8, as shown in Figure 4.13, contain a list of three items. These slides represent the list of issues that Edna has been having with the GPS, namely "Device takes long time to start," "Lots of issues with the keyboard," and "Old maps on the GPS take her in the wrong direction." We could keep these items on separate slides, but there aren't many talking points for each one. There's a good chance that when we read this list we won't add anything in addition to what is displayed on the screen. As a result, if these were separate slides, we'd probably be skipping through them quickly and the audience would get several slides thrown at them in the space of only a few seconds.

As this is the case, we are going to combine these three slides into a list. To do this, we will simply copy and paste the titles of each of these slides into the text of the previous slide. After we've copied the text, we can also delete the old slide. The result is something that should look similar to what is shown in Figure 4.14.

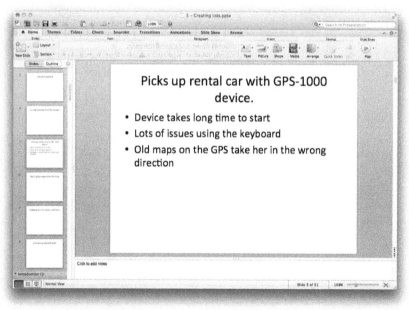

Figure 4.14 - The three slides combined into a list on Slide 5.

The result is that we now have a list of related items under the main heading of picking up the rental car. Now, as you are looking at the slide in Figure 4.14 you might be thinking that this is looking like a regular slide with bullet points, and you would be somewhat correct. Coming back to what we learned at the start of this chapter, we definitely do not want to present this entire list to the audience in one go. Many years ago, I learned a rule from a good friend of mine, and excellent presenter, David Chappell. No matter how small the content, David never puts anything on the screen that he is not directly talking about.

To apply this rule here, we are going to add a build to the list. Although we are going to cover animations in much more detail later on in the chapter, adding a simple build now will get us into the habit of exposing this list in the correct way, and will be useful in our next rehearsal.

To do this in Microsoft PowerPoint, click on the list to select it, click on the Animations tab, and click the Appear animation. This will apply a very basic build to the list, as shown in Figure 4.15.

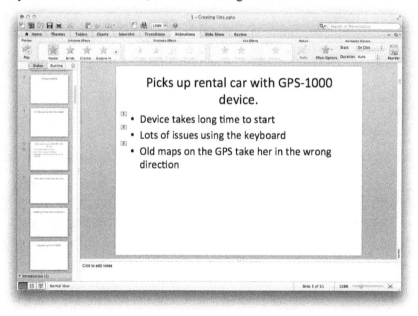

Figure 4.15 - A very simple build applied to the new list of items.

To test that the build is working correctly, you can play a slideshow from this point (by selecting Play from Current Slide on the Slideshow menu). If everything is set correctly, you should see the title slide, and then one line appear when you hit the space bar or mouse button. Don't worry about this being a basic build as this is exactly all we need at this stage.

Before we move on, let's investigate the second type of list. This is a list that is currently represented as single slides, but where it makes sense to keep them as single slides. Slides 30 through 38 in our example presentation (shown in Figure 4.16) demonstrate this well.

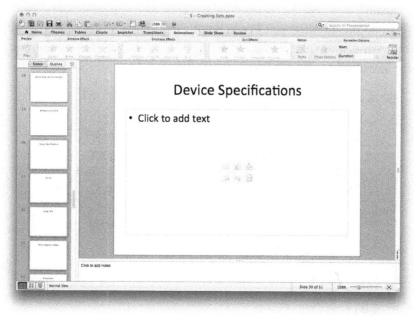

Figure 4.16 - Slides 30 through 38 showing another list.

This particular set of slides is a list of device specifications and covers the screen, size, antiglare coating, dimensions, weight, and construction of the unit. While we could potentially collapse all of these slides into a single list, we will probably want to spend some time on each of these items. The audience might want to know why we picked that type of antiglare coating or have different visuals for each of the

124

specifications that we are talking to. As this is the case, we will probably decide to leave this list as separate slides.

Finally, let's investigate the third type of list. This is a list representing upcoming sections in the presentation. If you remember from our presentation mind map we had an introduction section that referred to common use cases, what's new, and getting started sections. When we imported this into slides, we ended up with a single slide for the top level introduction node.

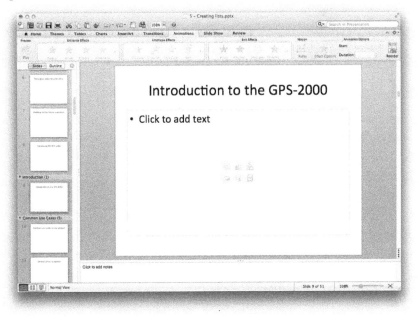

Figure 4.17 - The introduction slide representing the top level node in the mind map.

As shown in Figure 4.17, we have a single slide that will be used to lead into the next three sections. As a result, we should build a list within this slide to show which three sections are upcoming.

To do this, we follow the same approach as we did with the first list. Add a new line for each section in the text field, and add a basic appear animation. The result is something similar to Figure 4.18.

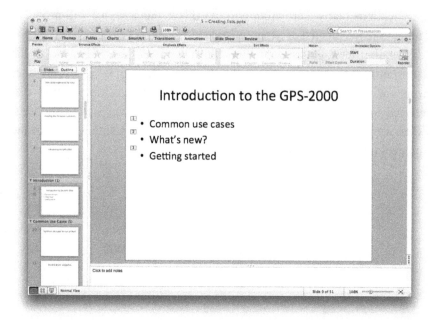

Figure 4.18 - Introduction slide with the upcoming three sections.

That's pretty much all there is for creating lists. Again, if you are following along with your own presentation, I would encourage you to go through all of the potential lists in your slide deck at this stage.

Inserting content placeholders

By this stage, your presentation should be taking shape. You've converted your presentation mind map into a slide deck, created the section boundaries, converted text to visual cues, and created lists. Before we apply templates and go into our next rehearsal, it is important to spend time walking through the deck and thinking about the content that each slide will represent. To do this, we'll walk through the deck and add placeholders to best represent the content that might work. We'll use a selection of slides in our example deck to demonstrate this refinement.

As you go through your deck, one of the first questions to ask is

126

whether the slide should exist. The process of converting the presentation mind map and adding section boundaries often leaves some slides that are placeholders. This is especially true of the first slide at the start of each section.

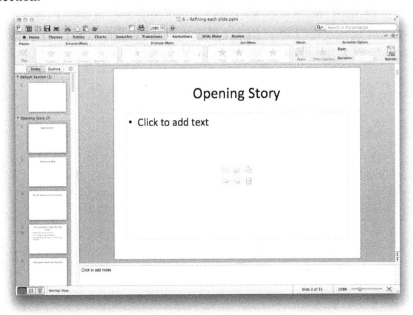

Figure 4.19 - The Opening Story slide is not needed.

A good example of this in our example presentation is the first slide after the "Opening Story" section, as shown in Figure 4.19. This first slide isn't really adding much value, as we are not likely announcing to the audience that this is our opening story. It makes much more sense just to go straight to Slide 3 and talk about Edna. As this is the case, we can go ahead and delete Slide 2.

As we move through the deck, for each slide that does have a clear purpose, we should ask the question: What should be shown on this slide to support the visual cue? What will the audience connect with best? It might be an image or a screenshot. It might be a diagram. It could even be a demo.

Using the example presentation, let's take a look at a couple of examples. Our new Slide 2 is where we will introduce Edna. What could we use to support the topic? A picture of Edna could work, if we have access to it. If we don't, we could potentially use an image of some customer files with "Edna" drawn on one of them. Either way, let's add a placeholder to this slide to represent this thought.

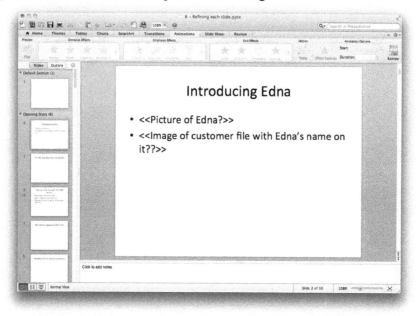

Figure 4.20 - Adding thoughts on the images used to support the visual cue for Slide 2.

As shown in Figure 4.20, we add a placeholder directly into the text of the slide. Notice how I use the angle brackets to denote the placeholder. This is purely a personal preference, and you can choose to use something different if you'd like. The important thing is to be able to recognize that these are placeholders (and not text that you'll want to share with the audience) that you'll have to come back and change later on. You can potentially use the notes section of Microsoft PowerPoint to achieve the same effect, but having the text in the actual slide will work much better for your early rehearsals.

Let's move on to the next slide, which is about Edna's goal of getting to her friend's house from the airport. The current visual cue is "25 mile journey from the airport." Here we might also want to use an image. Maybe a long road or some kind of directional sign, as shown in Figure 4.21. We'll spend some time shortly looking at where we can acquire these images from, but for now we are just inserting a placeholder to capture these ideas onto the slide.

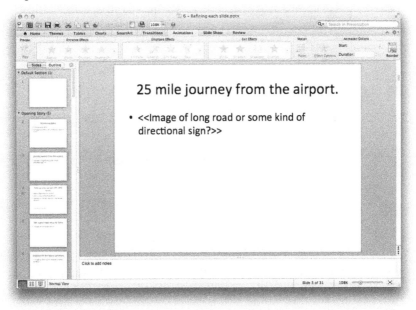

Figure 4.21 - Additional thoughts added to Slide 3.

Placeholders don't have to be images, either. As you apply this process for your own presentation, you'll often find that some slides warrant a diagram. Maybe it's a flowchart or schematic of something that you would like to show. One of our slides in our example deck will speak about the specifications of the device, so a diagram of the device outline with height, width, and length might work well here. The placeholder for this is shown in Figure 4.22.

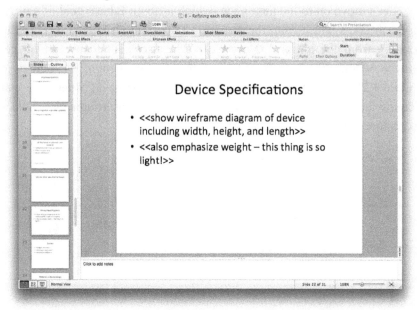

Figure 4.22 - Diagram placeholder for the specifications slide.

Finally, placeholders should also be used for demos. In our example presentation, we have several slides in the "Getting started" section about how to use the device and looking at the new features. Assuming we have access to the actual device on stage, we might want to do a demo here. To support this, I will collapse all of these slides into a single slide with a placeholder for a demo, as shown in Figure 4.23.

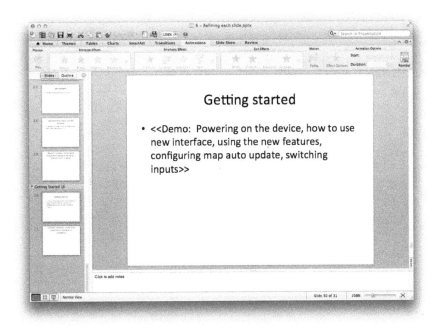

Figure 4.23 - Collapsing multiple slides into a single demo slide.

We'll be spending a lot of time in Chapter 8 talking about demos, so there's no need to worry about the details of what the demo will look like until then. The important thing is that we have a placeholder in the deck to represent that some kind of demo will likely be happening at this point.

The final part of this section is to finalize the transition slides. As you might recall from the presentation mind map, the transitions offer a more natural way of switching between topics within the presentation, and as we discussed in Chapter 3, there are three types of transitions: the related topic transition, the question transition, and the summary transition. Fortunately, we have one of each of these types of transitions in our example deck. Let's go through and refine these slides.

The first transition, as shown in Figure 4.24, is a question transition, and takes us from the "Common use cases" section to the "What's new" section.

131

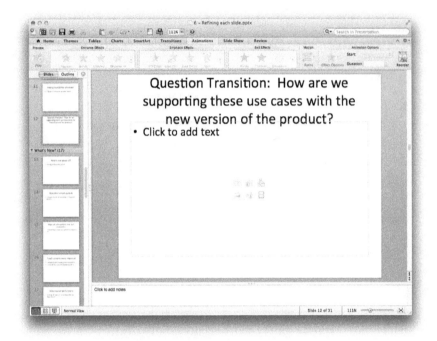

Figure 4.24 - A question-based transition in the example presentation.

As shown on the slide, we'll be posing the question to the audience of how we support the use cases with the new version of the product. This is, of course, a rhetorical question. We are not actually going to ask the audience, but instead use the question to get the audience prepared for the next section.

As the question speaks for itself, there's very little that we need to do on this slide. For these types of transitions, we can simply remove the "Question Transition" wording (as we won't be showing this to the audience) and leave the question intact, as shown in Figure 4.25.

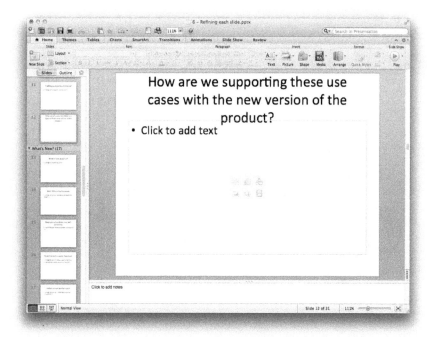

Figure 4.25 - The updated question transition slide.

The next transition is a related transition found at the end of the "What's new" section, designed to lead into the "Getting started" section, as shown in Figure 4.26.

133

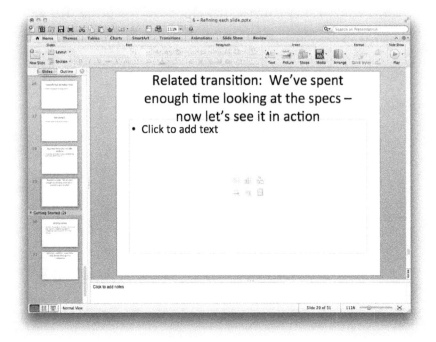

Figure 4.26 - The related transition in our example presentation.

This is very similar to the question-based transition in that it's a single sentence that we pose to the audience in order to prepare them for the next section. As with the question-based transition, we'll remove the prepending text and also shorten the visual cue a little, similar to the slide shown in Figure 4.27.

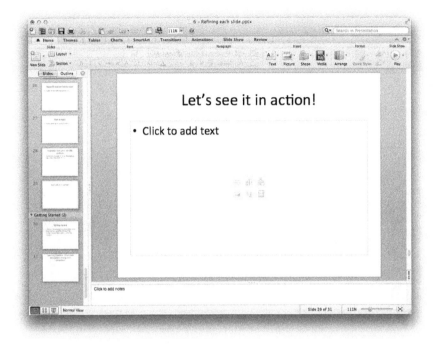

Figure 4.27 - The modified related transition slide.

The final transition is the summary transition. This is a major transition as it wraps up the entire introduction section before we move on to the competition section. The current slide, created from our mind map is shown in Figure 4.28.

135

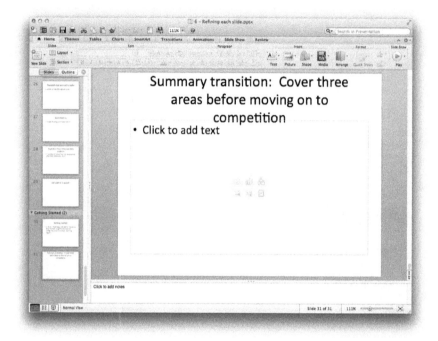

Figure 4.28 - The summary transition in our example presentation.

Unlike the question-based or related transition, the summary transition isn't going to be one sentence that we show to the audience. Instead, we need to summarize the three areas that we covered. To do this, we can create a list that represents those three areas.

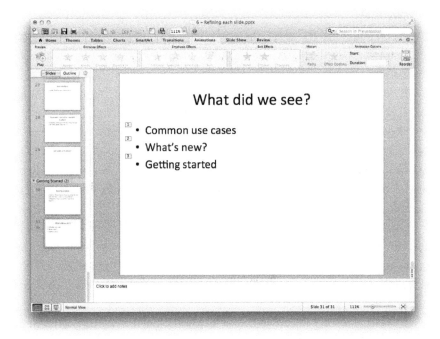

Figure 4.29 - Summarizing the three areas in the example presentation.

As shown in Figure 4.29, we have created a list that represents the three sections that we have just covered. In addition, we have animated the list using the same technique as described in the last section. Finally, we updated the title to be a better visual cue to wrap up the section.

You may notice that this slide is very similar to the introduction slide, which itself is a very similar list. This is by design and helps frame this section as part of the presentation.

This covers the section on content placeholders, and if you are following along with your own presentation, go ahead and insert content placeholders throughout your own deck before moving on.

137

Templates

When someone mentions the term "PowerPoint Template," I suspect you immediately think of the template used by your organization or specific to a conference. This is not what we are going to be talking about in this section, and in my opinion these templates should be avoided at all costs (we'll be covering what to do with these at the end of Chapter 6)!

Slide templates are one of the most underused and also misused features of Microsoft PowerPoint and other similar tools. We tend to associate the template as something that applies a single theme throughout the deck, whereas in this section we'll be exploring how to use them in a more powerful way.

Using a template at this stage of creating the slide deck allows us to start developing a style specific to each section. Doing so will make our rehearsal easier, and it will also lay the groundwork for many of the upcoming topics where we incorporate background images and alternate fonts.

To start, let's go ahead and create a template for the opening story section. To do this in Microsoft PowerPoint, select Slide Master from the View/Master menu. Doing so will open the slide master view, as shown in Figure 4.30.

Figure 4.30 - The slide master view in Microsoft PowerPoint.

The default slide master view has a template with 11 different layouts. We aren't going to use any of these layouts in our presentation, so to be efficient we can go ahead and delete them. To do this, select the layout and hit the Delete key. You'll find that you will be able to delete all of them except the first two as they are in use by the current document. (We can come back and tidy these up later). When you are finished, your master template should look similar to the one shown in Figure 4.31.

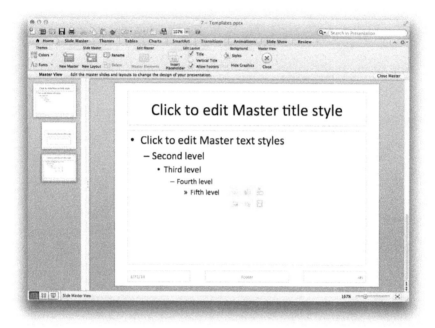

Figure 4.31 - Master template with extra layouts removed.

From here, go ahead and copy/paste the layout. This should create a new layout as a copy. Once the layout is created, right click and rename it "Opening Story." After the rename is complete, right-click again on the layout and select Format Background. This will display the properties window. Select a color from the color picker (I've chosen black), and apply it to the template. If you've selected a dark color, you should also change the font color to white or something light. The result of this should look similar to Figure 4.32.

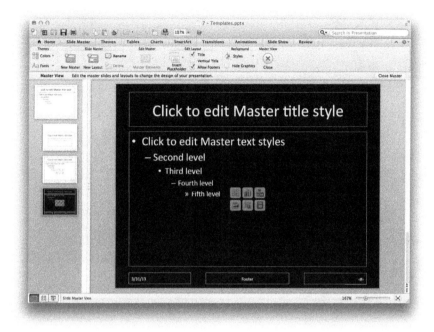

Figure 4.32 - A new layout in the master with a defined background color.

As shown in Figure 4.32, we now have a new layout in the slide master with a background color set. Assuming yours looks similar, go ahead and close the slide master to return to the deck.

Now, select the entire opening story section. You can do this by either selecting each slide individually or you can just click on the section header to select all of the slides in that section. Once selected, pick the "Opening Story" layout from the Layout drop-down bar in the Home ribbon.

The result, as shown in Figure 4.33, will show the new layout from the master applied to all of the slides in the opening story section.

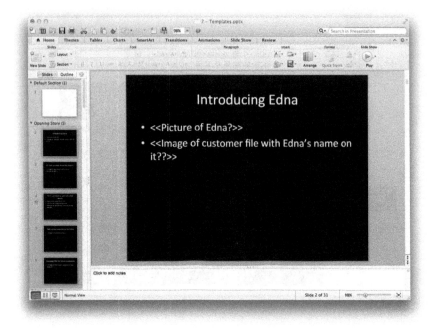

Figure 4.33 - The new master layout applied to the opening story section.

That's all we need to do for now. Although it doesn't look like much, having a template associated with each section will become incredibly valuable as we start adding background images and titles. Why the background color? This will help us distinguish sections of the deck as we continue to develop it, making it much easier to edit and also helping greatly with rehearsals.

Go ahead and repeat this process for all of the sections in your slide deck. When you are doing this, however, select a different background color for each section. You can either select a totally random color, or alternate between colors. The goal is to be able to quickly determine when you change sections when you are viewing the presentation in full screen mode. For the purposes of illustration in this book, given that you might be reading this on a grayscale eReader device, I'll be creating layouts that alternate between black and white.

When you are finished, you should have a slide deck divided into sections, with each section having its own layout in the master template. For the purposes of illustration, Figure 4.34 shows the example presentation shown in slide sorter view. Notice how each section has a different background color from the proceeding and following sections. Also, don't worry about the template for the title slide at this stage as we'll complete this at a later point.

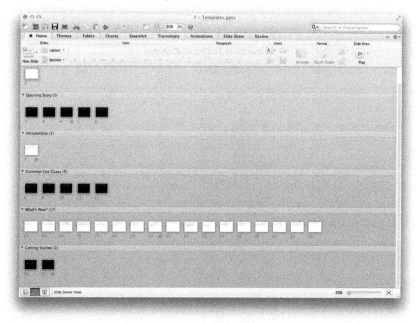

Figure 4.34 - Slide sorter view of the example presentation.

When you reach a similar point, congratulations! Even though it has been a lot of work to get to this point, the "sketch" of your presentation is really starting to take shape. Now it's time for your next rehearsal.

Are you sure this isn't too many slides?

As we come towards the end of this chapter, you might be concerned about the number of slides in your presentation. Maybe you are past 100?

Close to 200 even? Even in our example, which only focuses on a third of the total mind map, we've reached over 30!

Please trust me on this one: Don't worry about the number of slides in your presentation—as it really does not matter! The arbitrary number of slides in your deck holds no bearing to the quality of the presentation or how it will be received by the audience. I have seen phenomenal presentations with only a handful of slides and equally great talks with over 200. A good friend of mine and ex-colleague at Microsoft, Miha Kralj, has a lot of experience in delivering talks using a Japanese technique called Pecha Kucha.[2] This technique mandates the speaker changes the slide every 20 seconds. Miha has done several longer versions of these presentations, each one with an average of 180 slides per hour.

The number of slides in a presentation is analogous to the number of scenes in a movie. What's a good number of scenes in a movie? Who cares? Will a shorter or longer amount of scenes hold any bearing over how good or bad the movie is? Probably not.

Why then do people get so held up over the number of slides? Because in their head they are equating the number of slides to the length of time that the presentation will take. As many of us have grown up with traditional slide decks each with 7 bullet points per slide, we've equally become accustomed to having a certain number of slides taking a certain amount of time. On many occasions, I've seen people open a slide deck, look at the 40 or so slides, and claim, "This looks like about an hour's worth of content."

This slide-to-time ratio is also very common among conference organizers. Over the years, I have submitted numerous slide decks for conferences only to have the organizers contact me directly to actually make sure that this presentation fits within the hour. Just like scenes in a movie, the number of slides in your presentation means very little. It will likely not affect the quality of the presentation or how well the story is received by the audience. What does matter is running time. Just like a movie has a running time associated with it, you should know what the running time is for your presentation. Instead of thinking of your presentation as a "presentation with 80 slides," you should think of your presentation as a "presentation that takes 55 minutes." This concept will also serve you well when showing your presentation to others, including conference organizers. I've learned that when people gasp at the number of slides in my deck, if I simply respond with "Yes, it might seem like a lot, but the presentation only runs for 55 minutes," I can quickly get past any sticking point.

Of course, the question you are probably thinking now is "How long will my presentation take?" This will start to become clearer in our next rehearsal!

Your second rehearsal

Believe it or not, it's time for your second rehearsal. (I am assuming, of course, that your first rehearsal was when you went through your presentation mind map at the end of Chapter 3.)

While the first rehearsal focused on the validity of the information in the mind map, the goal of this second rehearsal is to get a sense of timing. At the end of this exercise, the goal is to answer the question of how long your presentation will take in front of a live audience.

Fortunately, for this rehearsal, you don't need to rehearse to anyone. All you will likely need is a quiet room, a stopwatch, your presentation, ideally a presentation remote and/or mouse, and enough time.

This rehearsal is easy. Start your stopwatch, put the presentation in full screen mode and simply present the complete deck to yourself. This is where the concept of the quiet room comes in useful! I actually like standing up and presenting this in a loud voice to become accustomed to the actual presentation environment. If you have access to a presentation remote, this will be even more effective.

Even though the slides only contain text at this stage, the goal of this rehearsal is to present the entire deck using the pace that you plan to use in front of a live audience. If you come to a piece of the presentation that is not complete (e.g., a demo or a video that you'll be showing), estimate

145

how long you think this might take and add it to the total time. Don't worry about the format of the presentation or even if you forget what part of the presentation comes next—simply run through the entire deck, speaking about each slide and talking point in turn. Remember that the slides are prompts for your talking points. Don't simply read aloud the text on each slide and click next. Treat the text as a visual cue, and speak about the topic—just as if someone had said, "Please tell me about this topic."

After running through the presentation you should have a sense of the running time for your deck. At this stage, we are not after a perfect number as we'll continue to add images and other assets, so don't worry about calculating the time to the exact minute. Do, however, look out for any major deviances in running time. If you were thinking that this might be an hour presentation, but it took closer to two on your first rehearsal, there might be a problem. I would recommend looking at each section and potentially hiding certain slides and pieces of content that you might deem superfluous and then re-run through the deck. Remember to hide the slides, as opposed to deleting them, as this will make it much easier to re-include them at a future point in time, if needed.

If you ran through the presentation in 15 minutes instead of 45, you may want to question whether you have sufficient content or whether you were going too quickly through the slides. Did you really tell the right stories and expand on each of the visual cues, or were you just reading the text?

What type of presentation remote?

A presentation remote is one of the most valuable tools for a presenter. It allows you to advance the slides remotely, which means that you are no longer tethered to pressing the space bar or mouse button, which means that you can advance the slides without necessarily taking your eye off the audience and have additional freedom to move around the stage or floor.

I have seen and/or used almost every presentation remote available, and the best one I've found is the Logitech Professional Presenter R800, as shown in Figure 4.35. Not only does it support advancing the slide, but it also has a visible countdown timer that will vibrate as you reach a certain amount of time remaining. The subtle vibration won't be seen by the audience, but can be a gentle reminder to either slow down or speed up during your presentation. Moreover, the R800 also works flawlessly with both PCs and Macs, both PowerPoint and Keynote, with no additional drivers or software required. It's a little pricier than others, partially due to having the LCD display, but in my mind it's worth the extra cost of have a professional tool on hand.

Figure 4.35 - The Logitech Professional Presenter R800 Remote.

Rehearsal of the example presentation

To help you get a sense of the flow of the rehearsal, I wanted to share a run through of a few of the slides of the example presentation, together

147

with the talking points that I would use for each of the slides. My hope is that this gives you a sense of how long you should be spending on each slide, and what types of talking points work.

Introducing Edna

- <<Picture of Edna?>>
- <<Image of customer file with Edna's name on it??>>

I wanted to share a story about Edna. Edna is one of the many customers that we've been working with since last year. (click)

25 mile journey from the airport.

- <<Image of long road or some kind of directional sign?>>

When we met Edna, she had just landed in Colorado. She was visiting a friend, who lived about 25 miles from the airport. Because of the journey, she hired a rental car from the airport. (click)

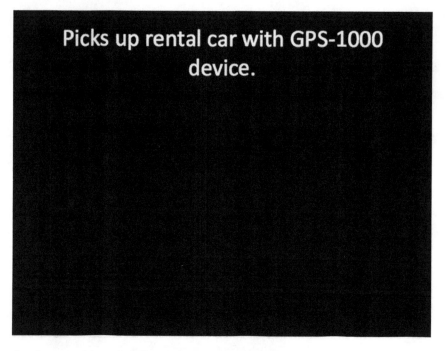

At the rental car facility, Edna picked up her car which was equipped with our current model, the GPS-1000. Although she was initially pleased with the GPS, her experience didn't start well. (click)

Picks up rental car with GPS-1000 device.

- Device takes long time to start

Firstly, the device took a long time to start. Edna waited for up to 5 minutes before the GPS loaded all of the maps from memory and was able to get a good satellite lock. (click)

Picks up rental car with GPS-1000 device.

- Device takes long time to start
- Lots of issues using the keyboard

When the device did finally acquire a signal, Edna had issues using the keyboard. Every time she tried to enter the city in the address, the onscreen keyboard seemed to freeze. (click)

Picks up rental car with GPS-1000 device.

- Device takes long time to start
- Lots of issues using the keyboard
- Old maps on the GPS take her in the wrong direction

And to make matters worse, once she did get going, she discovered that the unit was loaded with an old set of maps. Because her friend lives in a new development, the GPS was unable to locate her house accurately. (click)

As you can imagine, Edna didn't have a great experience with our GPS device. She did get to her destination eventually, but using the product wasn't as smooth as it should have been. (click)

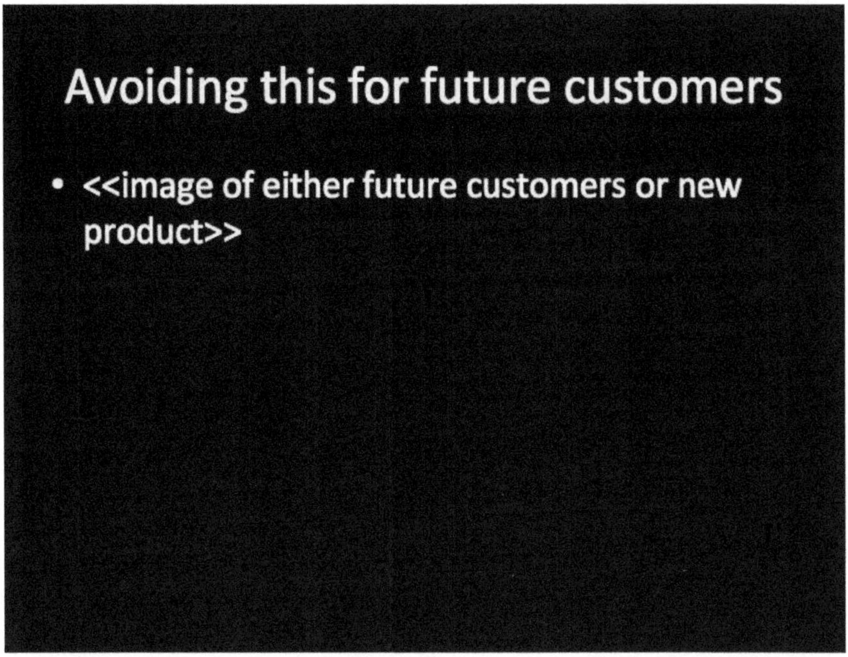

Avoiding this for future customers

- <<image of either future customers or new product>>

Being part of the product team, we are keen that this experience doesn't happen for Edna again. In fact, we've learned a lot since then, and today I'm very proud to announce our next product—the GPS-2000. (click)

Introduction to the GPS-2000

The GPS-2000 is an amazing device, and I can't wait to tell you about it. (click)

Introduction to the GPS-2000

- Common use cases

First, I'd like to share some of the common customer use cases that we've used to make sure that we have the right set of features for our customers. (click)

Introduction to the GPS-2000

- Common use cases
- What's new?

I want to then expand on this, and show you the new features in the device, and how it compares to the previous models. (click)

Introduction to the GPS-2000

- Common use cases
- What's new?
- Getting started

Finally, I want to cover the out-of-the-box experience. What's it like to get started with one of these amazing new GPS units?

If everyone is ready, let's get started.(click)

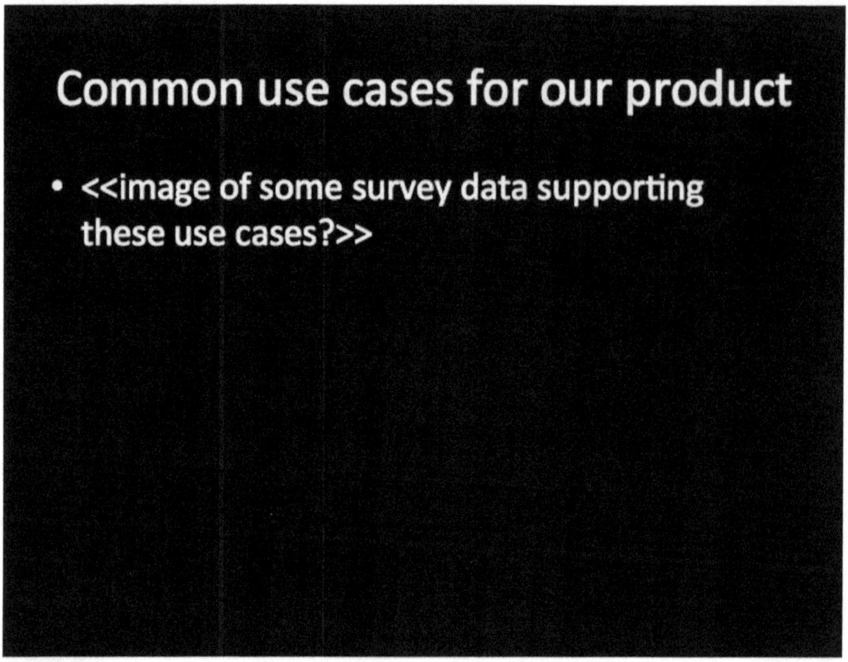

Common use cases for our product

- <<image of some survey data supporting these use cases?>>

Let's cover some of the data that we received as part of the global customer survey last year...

I could continue, but hopefully you get a good sense of the rhythm and pace of our example slide deck. Again, I've just covered a small piece of the introduction in our example presentation, but from this you should get a feeling of the timing and narrative required between slides, builds, and sections.

At this stage, I would encourage you to run through your own rehearsal, primarily to get an idea of the timing of your presentation, but also to help edit content also. At any point in the presentation, don't hesitate to break out of full screen and modify the slides or text as you feel it helps the flow.

Finally, don't worry about how you start or end the presentation during this rehearsal. We'll be covering these in much more detail during

Chapter 7.

Where are we?

We have covered a lot of new information in this chapter, taking your presentation mind map into an actual presentation, creating section boundaries, visual cues, lists, content placeholders, and templates. In addition, we had our second rehearsal. Ultimately, the goal of this second rehearsal (and subsequent rehearsals over the next few chapters) is to build your muscle memory for your presentation. I guarantee that the first time you run through the slides everything will seem very awkward and you might even be questioning this whole presentation technique! You might not know what section comes next, or may even forget what the text on the slide is supposed to be prompting you to say. If this happens, please don't worry! I guarantee that after running through a few more times, the structure will start to stick in your mind.

Similar to how a golfer learns how to swing by developing the right muscle memory, you'll learn the structure and flow of your presentation in the same way. This will pay off in dividends in front of your audience, as this muscle memory will help you naturally know what comes next, placing you in a more relaxed state overall, and also translating to a much more polished presentation for the audience.

In our next chapter, we are going to continue developing the slide canvas, looking at some of the composition elements in your decks that will start to bring your presentation to life!

---

1. A great summary of reading, listening, and comprehending can be found on Matt Zimmerman's blog, here: http://mdzlog.alcor.net/2010/07/12/read-listen-or-comprehend-choose-two/
2. http://en.wikipedia.org/wiki/PechaKucha

CHAPTER 5: Your Slide Canvas—Composition

* * *

In the previous chapter, we spent a lot of time converting the mind map to an actual presentation and refactoring a lot of the structural elements. As mentioned, this was analogous to creating a pencil sketch for a piece of art. To take this analogy forward, we are now going to fill in some of the major parts of the painting, which for our presentation will include designing and importing backgrounds, images, fonts, colors, and many other visual elements that will make your presentation start to stand out.

Backgrounds

We will start this second layer of our canvas by looking at slide backgrounds. When we talk about slide backgrounds, we are referring to full screen images that take the whole slide, with visual cues and other content layered on top.

There are two ways to use background images in your slides. The first is to have a unique image for each slide. As you move to the next slide, a different image is shown to represent the concept being discussed. Using unique images for each slide can create a very powerful, visual set of slides, and I've found it works well for the opening story and conclusion of a presentation.

The second way to use background images is to have a single image that persists through a section of a presentation. Using this technique, the background image remains constant until you move to the next section. This helps maintain consistency for topics that might take a number of slides to explain.

Let's start by taking a look at the first technique, using unique images for each slide. To demonstrate this in action, we'll use the first slides of the opening story in our example presentation, as shown in Figure 5.1.

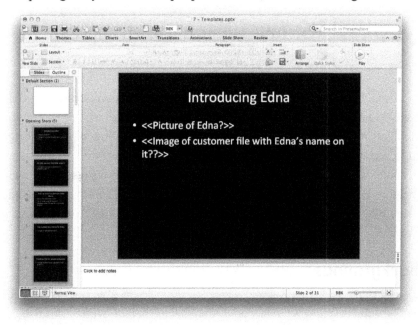

Figure 5.1 - The first slide in our opening story.

As shown in Figure 5.1, this is the slide where we introduce Edna. You'll recall that during the last chapter we added some placeholders for what this slide might show, namely a picture of Edna or an image of a customer file with Edna's name on it. We'll talk about image acquisition shortly, but for now let's imagine that we have a suitable image of Edna (or at least someone that we'll be portraying as Edna!) for the presentation.

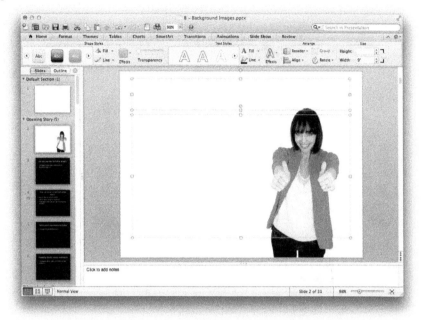

Figure 5.2 - An image used to represent Edna for our presentation.

As Figure 5.2 shows, we've inserted a full screen image of Edna, and set the arrangement of the image so that it is behind the text. Unfortunately, now we can't see the text, so we'll change the color to black so that it will work with the background.

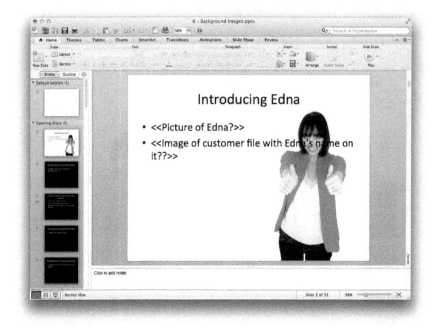

Figure 5.3 - Reseting the color of the text to work with the image.

As shown in Figure 5.3, we clearly need to tidy this slide up. Firstly, now that we have the image, we can delete the placeholder text (as this was only for our reference). Secondly, the "Introducing Edna" text should be made into a better visual cue. To do this, we will set the background of the text box to black, expand it to be the full width of the slide, set the opacity to 75%, change the font color back to white, and left justify the text. The result can be seen in Figure 5.4.

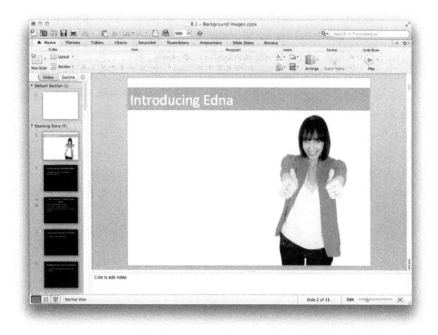

Figure 5.4 - Tidying up the text on the slide.

We are going to do some additional work with fonts in the next section, but as you can see from Figure 5.4, even with a few small adjustments to the text box we are transforming the slide from a "traditional PowerPoint slide" into something that looks a little more visually appealing.

Slide ratios

As you start applying background images and these styles to your own slides, one of the important things to consider is the size of your slides, specifically the ratio. Up until now we've been working with the default for Microsoft PowerPoint, which is a 4:3 ratio (4 inches wide for every 3 inches high). While this works well for the traditional "slide with 7 bullet points" approach, wider ratios tend to be much more effective for decks that are heavy in images and visuals. This principle is akin to what the TV industry has experienced over the past couple of decades, with many sets moving from 4:3 to 16:9 and other widescreen ratios.

The one caveat to "widescreen" slides however is the projector. While the latest slide projectors are moving towards 16:9 ratios, many current projectors are still 4:3. Using a 16:9 ratio slide deck on a 4:3 projector will still work, but it will be subject to a "letterbox effect" with a black bar at the top and bottom of your display.

Although this is a trade off, I now default to using 16:9 for all of my slide presentations. I find that the additional slide real estate works very well for images and backgrounds, and even though many projectors are still 4:3, the sacrifice of the letterbox effect is worth it.

You can find the aspect ratios in Microsoft PowerPoint, under Page Setup from the File menu, as shown in Figure 5.5.

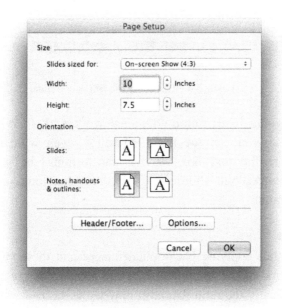

Figure 5.5 - The aspect ratio drop-down in the Page Setup window.

Moving forward with the example presentation in this book, I'm going to apply a 16:9 ratio. If you do choose a different aspect ratio for your own deck, I would recommend that you make this choice early on. Converting to a different aspect ratio will unfortunately stretch any images that you have already placed in the deck. While are there are tricks[1] for making this easier, it's likely that you will have to go back through your deck and resize all of your images to work with the new ratio.

More background techniques

Using the same technique that we applied to the "Introducing Edna" slide, we can now work on Slide 3, which is where we talk about Edna's journey to her friend's house. Figure 5.6 shows the slide in its current state.

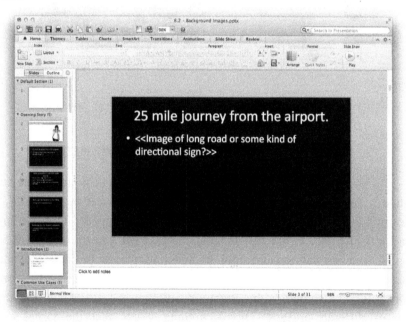

Figure 5.6 - The "journey from the airport" slide.

Let's now apply a background image, and modify the title text box, in the same way as we did with the previous slide. The end result can be shown in Figure 5.7.

Figure 5.7 - Slide 3 updated with a background image and new title.

As shown in Figure 5.7, we've used exactly the same technique for Slide 3. As I'm sure you'll notice, the one difference is that the title is towards the bottom of the slide, right justified as opposed to at the top and left justified. I find that moving the title (or what should now be called, our primary visual cue) to different places in the slide and changing the justification of the text can help add further variety between slides. It can also help with correctly positioning the visual cue over the top of different images. There's nothing worse that the visual cue covering someone's face!

In your own presentation, you should feel free with experimenting placing the title in various positions for greater effect. The only position I would recommend avoiding is the very bottom edge of the slide. The text in Figure 5.7 is positioned as far down as I would go. Aside from visual composition, the primary reason for this is that a lot of presentation rooms have people sitting in rows behind many other people. Any text right at the bottom of the slide can often be obscured by the head of the person or people in front them. If you place your primary visual cue right at the bottom of the slide, you'll likely have a lot of shuffling in the audience as people try to adjust their viewing angle to read your text.

Let's move on and look at Slide 4, as it introduces a requirement for lists. Figure 5.8 shows the current slide.

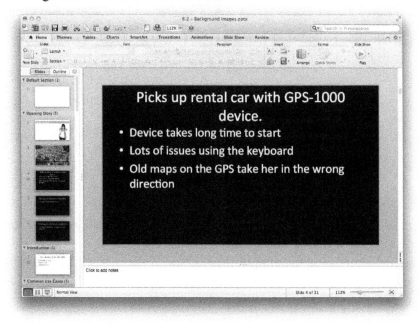

Figure 5.8 - Current version of Slide 4.

As you might recall, this is the slide depicting the part of the story where Edna will pick up the rental car and then face frustrations with using the existing GPS device. Using the same technique from the previous two slides, we can go ahead and apply a background and tidy up

171

the visual cue. The result is shown in Figure 5.9.

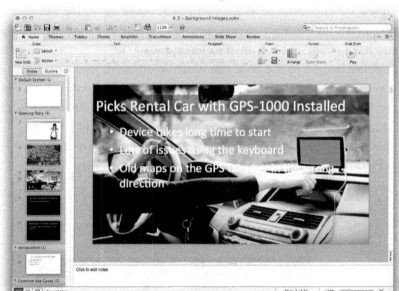

Figure 5.9 - Applying a background image and visual cue to Slide 4.

While the overall slide looks good, unlike the other slides we have text on this slide that needs to be kept. (If you recall, this is a list of items that we'll be speaking through.) As you can see, this list of three items doesn't really stand apart from the background image and is generally difficult to read. No matter what font color we select, it's never really going to do well against that background.

There are several ways that we could format the list to make it stand out more. For example, we could add an opaque background to each of the line items, or create a larger opaque shape as a background. While this might work visually, there is another technique that can have a good visual effect, but also add an effect to the way that we speak through the talking points.

To do this, we duplicate the slide and remove the list of items in the first slide. The result is two slides (now Slides 4 and 5), with the list of items appearing on Slide 5, as shown in Figure 5.10.

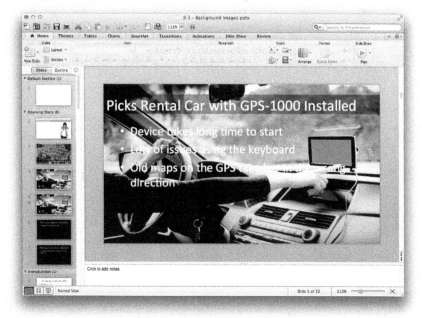

Figure 5.10 - Duplicated slides for Slides 4 and 5.

Next, we obscure the image on Slide 5. To do this, we right-click on the background in Slide 5 and select the Format Picture option. Under the Artistic Filters menu option, we will select the Blur filter with a radius of 25, as shown in Figure 5.11.

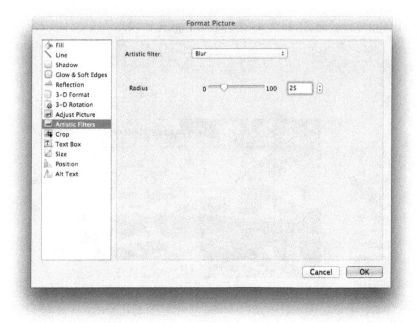

Figure 5.11 - Applying a Blur filter to the background in Slide 5.

After this is done, we now select the Adjust Picture menu option. Here, we are going reduce the contrast from 0% to −30%, as shown in Figure 5.12.

Figure 5.12 - Reducing the contrast of the background image by 30%.

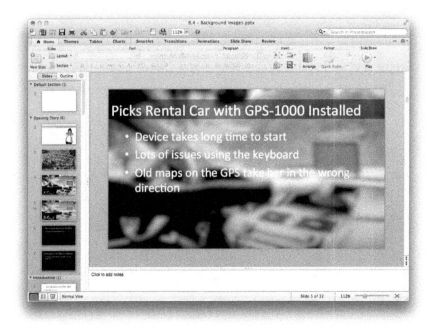

Figure 5.13 - The background image with a Blur filter and reduced contrast.

As shown in Figure 5.13, the effect of applying a filter and reducing the contrast of the background image results in the three items being more clearly displayed. There is also another positive side effect in that it forces the focus of the audience to the list of three items that will be displayed sequentially (remember that we applied an animation so that each list item comes in after we click on the next button).

To demonstrate this, let's look at how this might work when presented in full screen mode, together with the rehearsal text from the previous chapter:

176

At the rental car facility, Edna picked up her car, which was equipped with our current model, the GPS-1000. Although she was initially pleased with GPS, her experience didn't start well. (click)

Firstly, the device took a long time to start. Edna waited for up to 5 minutes before the GPS loaded all of the maps from memory and was able to get a good satellite lock. (click)

When the device did finally acquire a signal, Edna has issues using the keyboard. Every time she tried to enter the city in the address, the on-screen keyboard seemed to freeze. (click)

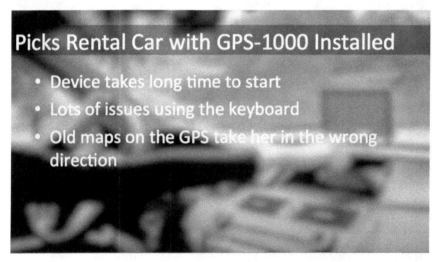

And to make matters worse, once she did get going, she discovered that the unit was loaded with an old set of maps. Because her friend lives in a new development, the GPS was unable to locate her house accurately. (click)

As I hope you can tell from this example, this technique helps apply focus on the troubles that Edna is having with the device as we talk through the speaking points on the slide, yet keeps everything in context with the scenario of her picking up the rental car.

Let's show how we can now wrap up the opening story using a similar technique.

Figure 5.14 - Slide 6 showing a poor experience for Edna.

As shown in Figure 5.14, we've edited Slide 6 and inserted an image of Edna, suitably frustrated by her experience. Notice also how we've changed the text of the visual cue (the title prior used to read "Not a great experience for Edna"). This has been done on purpose, as often you'll find that the text should be modified slightly to match the expression or emotion of the selected image. This is also a great time to review the visual cue to make sure it makes sense, together with correctly changing the case and any other grammatical errors.

For the next slide that speaks about how we can avoid this for future customers, we have used a similar artistic effect and image colorization, as shown in Figure 5.15.

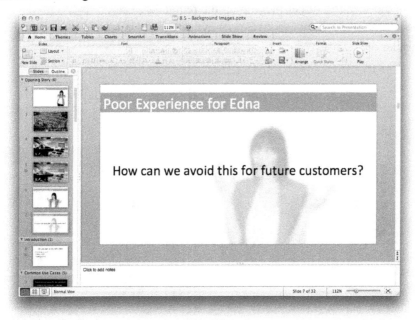

Figure 5.15 - Blur effect and image colorization used on Slide 7.

Because we still want to make out the shape of Edna's profile, we've used a blur radius of 10 to apply the necessary effect without completely distorting the image. Instead of reducing the contrast, we've applied a "black and white" filter to make the black text overlay work correctly.

As you can see, this effect allows us to use the same slide format with the text that we had on Slide 7. Instead of a new image of "future customers" we are able to reuse the image of frustrated Edna, which also has the advantage of carrying through the story to this last slide of the opening story.

Acquiring and selecting images

So far in this chapter, we've inserted a handful of images into our presentation to start building out the backgrounds for our presentation. At this point you might be wondering where to get these images? Acquiring images is easy—the Internet is a wonderful resource and it's trivial to find all kinds of images related to a topic. Acquiring the right image can take time, however, and this is something that I wanted to cover here.

Free vs. Commercial images

One of the first decisions to make is whether you should search for "free" images or whether you are prepared to pay for images. Both have their pros and cons. Firstly, "free" images can be discovered very quickly. Using the image search capabilities of Google and other search engines will return hundreds, if not thousands of results. I purposefully put "free" in quotes because even though you might find a suitable image via a search engine, it doesn't necessarily mean that you should use it. Many images are protected under copyright or trademark, and while this may not seem to be a big deal for a small internal meeting, there's no guarantee that images or slides from the presentation might not be used inadvertently for other presentations. I was caught out by this once after realizing that one of my presentations was being placed on a post-conference DVD and sold to attendees who couldn't make it! Although there were no repercussions at the time, it could be argued that taking images from a site and inadvertently selling them (albeit in a slide deck) isn't great business sense.

There are, however, many ways to get free images while adhering to the copyright claims of the origin photographers. The first, and arguably most popular, is Flickr (http://www.flickr.com). One of the nice features of searching Flickr is the ability to search only for images that have been submitted using a Creative Commons[2] license, and to even specify images that may be used commercially and/or modified, as shown in Figure 5.16.

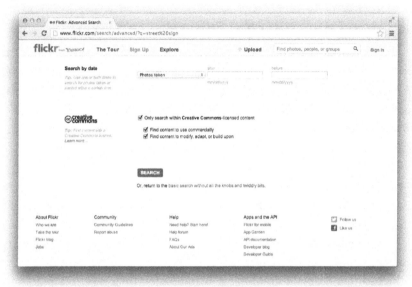

Figure 5.16 - The Creative Commons search option in Flickr.

If you are on the hunt for additional free images, you may also want to check out stock.xchng (http://scx.hu), another very popular site for image search and download. Although the site has recently become more affiliated with commercial entities, there is still a good collection of free images with clear licensing terms.

Finally, it's also worth revisiting the clipart provided by Microsoft's Office Online (http://office.microsoft.com). When many people hear Office clipart it conjures up images of the cartoon duck smashing a computer with a sledgehammer (if you are too young to know what this means, please look it up!), but Office Online today, however, features not only a set of clipart, but also a good collection of photographic images. The library is fairly small, and you often have to try different search keywords if you are not finding what you are looking for, but the images tend to be good quality and useful, especially for slide backgrounds.

On the commercial side, there are many sites that offer low-cost, royalty-free images. One of the most popular, and the one that I've used for many of the images in this book, is iStockPhoto (http://www.istockphoto.com). While you will be looking at paying around $10–$20 per image from iStockPhoto, the quality of images tend to be very good and the selection is vast. iStockPhoto and other similar sites also have extended license options for images, for adding further legal protection if this is something that you are interested in.

Regardless of the image or site that you choose, however, I always recommend placing the URL of the image as a footnote in the bottom corner of your slide, or at the very least in the notes section. By doing so, you are giving credit for where the image has been sourced from, and additionally it's always useful to have a reference of where certain images were obtained, especially for others that might be reusing your deck.

How to search for images

Searching for images sounds simple enough, but can actually take a lot of patience. Often you'll have an image in mind that you are particularly looking for, and despite all the best searching you can't find anything that comes close. Here are a few tips for overcoming this:

- **You need to think like a thesaurus.** If you are searching on a keyword and nothing suitable is appearing in the results, you need to think about what other keywords you can try instead. In our previous example presentation, for the slide where Edna is visiting a friend, I used the keyword "road" to look at various images. This didn't really turn up anything that I thought looked suitable, so I tried others. "Highway," "freeway," and "interstate" were all other examples. Eventually I decided to search using "house" and "real estate" to try and select an image that would relate to Edna's friend's house instead of the actual journey. The one image that I settled on came from this last search.[3]

- **I would recommend thinking about the audience connection with the images that you select.** Try to find images that are elegant and convey their meaning immediately to the audience. The audience should be able to create an immediate connection between the image shown and the point that you are trying to make. Under no circumstances do you want the audience to look at the image and start pondering about how that photograph or picture relates to the point that you are trying to make. Look for simple images that instantly convey a message rather than complicated, busy images that might have the audience puzzled.

- **Searching for images of people can be very difficult and time consuming.** You want to make sure that the image of the person conveys the story that you are trying to tell. You can of course use some artistic license here (even in our example presentation we are talking about Edna, when we all know it's not really Edna!), but at the same time, the person that you select must still be believable by the audience. Moreover, finding multiple emotions for the same person can be challenging. I was fortunate in the example presentation to find several images that conveyed different emotions so that I could pick out both happy and frustrated to tell the story using the same person. You'll definitely need to spend some time here. If you are thinking about using the same person to convey a set of emotions through the entire deck, there are several sites that will offer a grid of emotions, an example of which is shown in Figure 5.17.

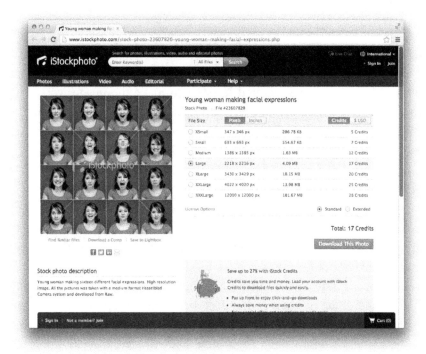

Figure 5.17 - A grid of different emotion-related images offered through iStockPhoto.[4]

The images such as the one shown in Figure 5.17 can make for a character that lasts through the entire deck with various emotions. For a conference in 2009, I put together such a presentation[5] that talked about the subject of cloud computing through the eyes of an IT manager named "Jim." All of the images and visuals for Jim used this exact same approach.

Finally, if you still can't find an image that matches what you are looking for, you can always consider creating your own. Having been interested in photography for many years, I have used many of my own images in many presentations that I've delivered. Not only does this get past the subject of copyright ownership, but it also makes for an interesting conversation when attendees ask "Where did you get those great images from?"

Editing images

Of course, when you find an image, there's a good chance that some level of editing will be required in order to make the image work with your slide. This might include stretching and cropping, repositioning the image, and applying an alpha mask. I wanted to cover these techniques to help ensure that all images you find can work with your deck.

Stretching and cropping images

Rarely will an image fit your background perfectly. There will always have to be some stretching or cropping required. When it comes to stretching an image to fit, there are two important rules. Firstly, always ensure that the image you select is of sufficient resolution such that it works when it is displayed full screen. There is nothing worse than seeing a pixelated, blurred image that has been blown up to full screen. Secondly, all stretching should be done proportionally. This means that the height and width of the image should be adjusted in relation to each other. Holding down the Control/Command key in Microsoft PowerPoint will ensure that the image is proportionally stretched. For Apple Keynote, you'll need to edit the image properties in the inspector to ensure that the constraints for locking the width and height are set.

Even if you stretch the image proportionally you'll likely find that it will not fit exactly on the background of the slide. With this being the case, you'll want to stretch the image (proportionally) until it's larger than the slide, then crop the image so that it fits.

There will of course be times where proportionally stretching the image won't be possible. For example, if the image is square, no amount of stretching is going to make it look good when stretched fully. You may have noticed this in our previous example with the initial image of Edna.

Figure 5.18 - Initial image of Edna.

As shown in Figure 5.18, our initial image of Edna was 848 pixels tall and 566 pixels wide. As you can see in Figure 5.19, no matter how we try and stretch this, it looks terrible as a full-size background image, and certainly isn't very flattering for Edna.

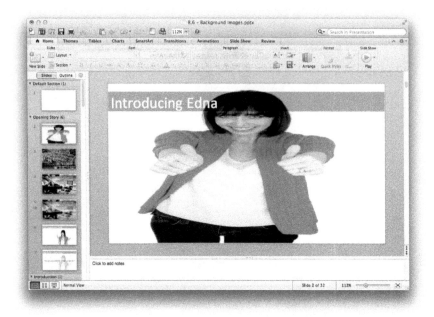

Figure 5.19 - Attempting to stretch the image to make it completely fill the background.

Likewise, just placing the image in the middle of the slide doesn't really work either, as shown in Figure 5.20. Although the image is displayed proportionally, it looks lost in the middle of the slide and is in stark contrast to the background.

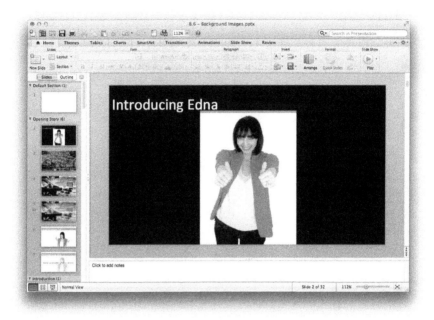

Figure 5.20 - Placing the image in the middle of the slide.

We are fortunate in that the image for Edna has a plain, white background. This makes it easy to create a background that is larger than the original image. To do this, we create a solid rectangle, filled with a white background, and with no line (sometimes called a stroke). When we make this rectangle the size of the slide and arrange it behind everything else, the image of Edna works much better.

189

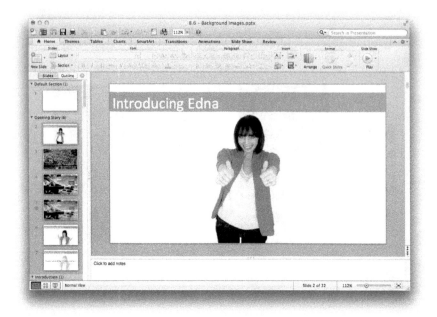

Figure 5.21 - Creating a new, white background for the image.

This effect can be seen in Figure 5.21. The slide will definitely work like this, although we can improve it further by applying the "rule of thirds."

Applying the "rule of thirds"

The "rule of thirds" is a common design principle widely used in many industries. I remember first learning about this rule in a photography class just after college, and from that point on it changed the way I thought about composing photos. The rule involves taking an image or photograph and dividing it into thirds, both on the horizontal and vertical planes. The result will be a square or rectangular frame in the middle of the image. For effective composition, the rule states that objects should then be placed along this inner frame.

Let's see how this works with our previous slide. Firstly, we will need to enable a feature in Microsoft PowerPoint called Static Guides. To do this, select the option from the Guides submenu under the View menu. The result will be two lines, one vertically and one horizontally. Next, position the guides so that one is about a third of the way from the left, and the second is about a third of the way from the bottom. This is shown in Figure 5.22.

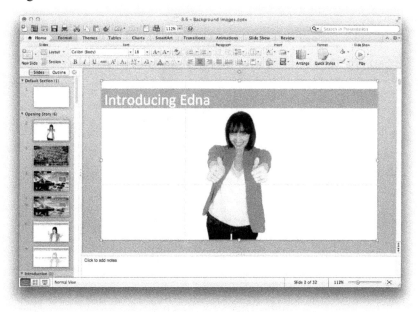

Figure 5.22 - Initial snap guides.

Next, hold down the Option key (CTRL key if you are using Windows) and drag one of the guides in order to duplicate it. Move this duplicated guide to the other side of the slide, and repeat the process with the other guide line.

Figure 5.23 - Duplicating the guide lines.

The result should be something similar to Figure 5.23, where the two intersecting vertical and horizontal lines should be splitting the slide into thirds. If you are having problems with positioning exactly, you can use the rulers or number guides (that are shown when you are dragging the guides) to calculate the exact dimensions. Also, if you find that you accidentally created more than four guidelines, you can remove one by simply dragging it outside the borders of the slide.

With this guide in place we can now move the image of Edna such that it intersects one of these guidelines, as shown in Figure 5.24.

Figure 5.24 - Positioning the image of Edna to align with the guidelines.

The end result (once we turn off the guidelines) is an image of Edna that aligns to the center box as created by the "rule of thirds" (as shown in Figure 5.25).

193

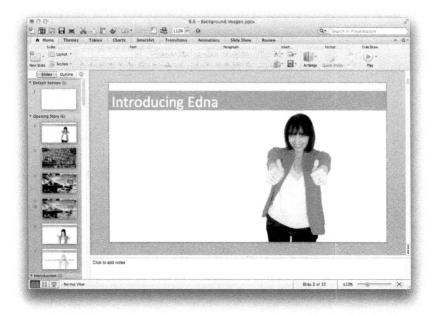

Figure 5.25 - The final layout with a white background using the rule of thirds.

While conforming to this rule of thirds will not be possible for every image, it can be very effective for positioning objects and images on slides, especially when there is a lot of available whitespace to play with.

What if my image doesn't have a solid background?

The previous picture of Edna was easy to manipulate as it had a plain white background, but chances are you won't have that luxury with every photo. Often, we'll need to extract the foreground from a particular image. The process of doing this is known as applying an "alpha mask." The alpha channel is the transparency channel on an image. By creating a mask over certain parts of the image using this alpha channel, we can give the effect of removing the background from a particular image.

While this feature has been part of image manipulation software for many years, this can be done more easily today using the built-in features

194

of either Microsoft PowerPoint or Apple Keynote.

In Microsoft Powerpoint, the Format Picture ribbon contains an item called Remove Background. This feature enables you to select an area around a foreground object and then finely touchup the picture by adding and removing pieces of the image. This is shown in Figure 5.26, with an image of my two boys who are standing in front of a background.

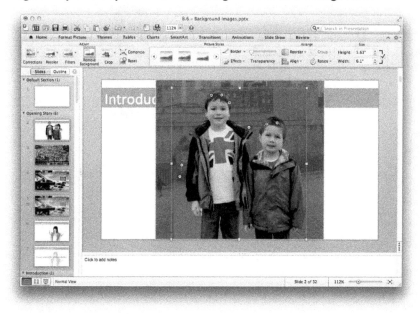

Figure 5.26 - Removing the background using the feature in Microsoft PowerPoint.

As you can see in the image, the feature can be used to turn on/off pieces of the background, denoted in the magenta-like color. When this is applied, the background elements are removed, and the resulting image looks similar to the one shown in Figure 5.27.

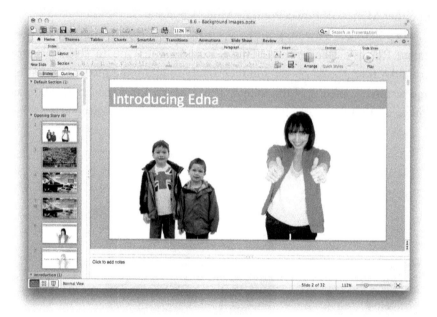

Figure 5.27 - The resulting image with applied alpha mask.

Apple's Keynote has similar functionality called Instant Alpha, which can be found via the Format menu. Both of these methods are not pixel perfect and will likely not produce the same results as a person or object photographed against a solid background, or more professional photo manipulation software, but in many cases will provide a usable version of the extracted foreground image.

Applying background templates to sections

As you've seen so far, we've been composing the deck using a different image for each slide. While this works well for our opening story, we probably don't want to do this for the rest of the slide deck. Not only is sourcing a separate image for each slide an incredible amount of work, but it can actually be very tiring for our attendees. Having to keep up with separate images every few seconds is stimulating, but keeping

196

that going for an hour-long presentation or more can be exhausting.

To overcome this, each section after the opening story will still use different backgrounds and images, but the image and theme will persist for the duration of the section. The result will still be a very visual set of slides, but one that allows the attendee to focus a little more on the content within each section rather than a consistently changing set of images.

To illustrate this, we can take a look at how this style could be applied to one of the sections in our example deck.

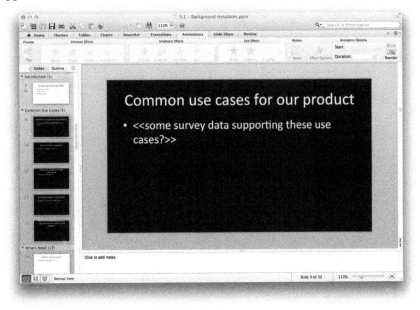

Figure 5.28 - The common use cases section.

As shown in Figure 5.28, the common use cases section in our example deck currently has five slides that relate to the same subject. As you may recall from Chapter 4, we also applied a template with a black background to make the section identifiable.

As this section is going to talk about common use cases of how devices are used in the vehicle, I've selected an image[6] to represent this. Instead of simply pasting the image on to each individual slide, however, as we need this to apply to each slide in the section, we are going to adjust the template.

To do this, we go into the slide master section in Microsoft PowerPoint (or the equivalent in Apple Keynote) and locate the template for the common use cases section that we created in Chapter 4, as shown in Figure 5.29.

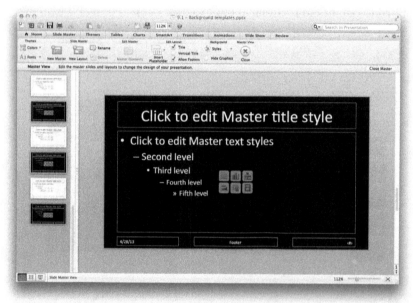

Figure 5.29 - Slide master for the common use cases section.

Using our newly acquired image, we stretch and crop this image, and set it as the background for this slide. There are two ways to do this. We can either copy/paste the image directly on the template slide and arrange it behind all of the layout text, or the background can be set automatically through the Format Background option, found by right-clicking on the slide. While both will work, I would always recommend the first option.

Preserving the image as an image on the slide allows you to manipulate properties of the image, which will come in useful shortly.

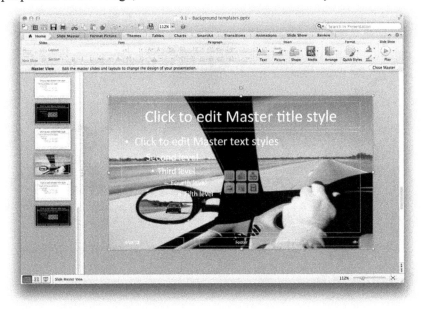

Figure 5.30 - Background image on the slide template.

With a background image set on the slide template, as shown in Figure 5.30, we can now see what this looks like for the actual slides.

Figure 5.31 - The template applied to the section.

Figure 5.31 shows that we now have the slide template applied to each slide in the common use cases section. While we now have a common image and theme throughout the section, there are a couple of problems. Firstly, it might still be a little jarring for the attendee. We no longer have a single image for each slide, which is better, but there is still little that we are doing to ease the attendee into the section. Secondly, there's a good chance that text, images, or other diagrams that we may place later on the slide will clash with the background, especially on images with multiple light and dark points.

To address this, we need to find some way of introducing the background image at the start of the section, and then making it less prominent while the content of the section is being shown. This will be similar to the effect that we used in the opening story earlier on in this chapter, but we are going to see how this can be applied to multiple slides

200

at one time.

To do this, let's go back to our slide master template. Here, we are going to duplicate our master slide for the common use cases section.

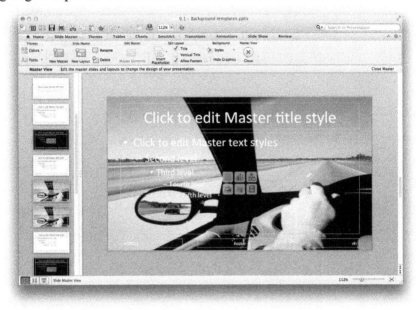

Figure 5.32 - A duplicated master slide for the section.

As seen in Figure 5.32, we've duplicated the master slide for the section. For the new master slide, we've also renamed it to "Common Use Cases—Title" to identify it later on.

Now that we have two master slides, we are going to adjust the image properties to get the effect that we are after. To do this, we select the master slide used by the current slides (hovering over the slide template in Microsoft PowerPoint will reveal which slides are being used by which template). Once we have this selected, we will change the background image by applying a blue accent, increasing the brightness by 20%, decreasing the contrast by 40%, and adding a blur effect. The result is a slide template that now looks similar to the one shown in Figure 5.33.

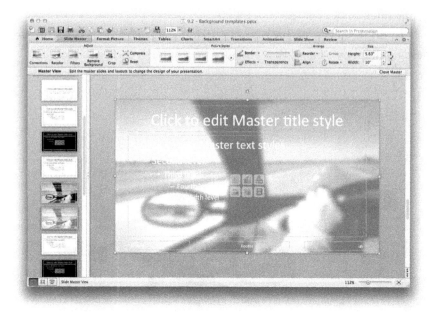

Figure 5.33 - The new slide template with the image adjustments.

With these adjustments in place, we can now return to the slides to see the new template applied to each of the slides in the section, as shown in Figure 5.34. What we now need to do is add an initial slide to the section using the original template.

Figure 5.34 - The new slide template applied to the section.

To add the initial slide, we simply add a new, blank slide at the start of the section. When we add the slide, we select the "Common Use Cases —Title" template. The result is something similar to Figure 5.35.

Figure 5.35 - Inserting the initial slide with the original master template.

The final thing we'll be doing here is fixing the titles. To do this, we'll use a very similar effect to the one that we saw at the start of this chapter. We'll set the background of the title text to black with an opacity of 75%, adjust the height to 0.7 inches, and left justify the text. The difference here, however, is that this will be applied to the sectional template, and will affect all of the slides in the common use cases section, as shown in Figure 5.36.

Figure 5.36 - Applying a title effect to this section.

Although there are a lot of steps to get this right, hopefully you can start to see how this section will work. The first slide we will open the section, where we will be talking about the importance of use cases and the audience will see the original background image in its correct definition. On the next slide, we will start digging into the detail about the survey data and other aspects of the use cases. To support this, the background of the slide will be transformed to the "washed out" look that was used for the second template, and new information will be presented.

Although it's difficult to demonstrate in a book, this concept can be very effective for the sections of content throughout your presentation. The use of the image transformation allows the presenter to introduce a section of material, and then dive into the material while maintaining the context of the section for the attendee. Although different subject areas and topics might be talked about in this section, the attendee implicitly knows that all of the speaking points are related.

Alternatives to background images

So far in this chapter we have looked at using full-size images for backgrounds. While this can be a very effective technique for both individual slides and to represent sections, it's not mandatory and many presenters choose to use plain backgrounds to achieve the same effect.

While you can easily select a solid color for your background, a more accepted and aesthetic approach is the use a a slight gradient to add some depth and to make objects stand out more clearer. This method has been popularized over the past few years by the late Steve Jobs, who used a gradient background that transitions from black at the top to a gray hue at the bottom. This same template can be found in Apple's Keynote product (listed under the Gradient template).

Figure 5.37 - A clip from Steve Jobs' keynote (Jan. 2010) showing the gradient popularized by his presentations.

As shown in Figure 5.37, the use of a gradient background adds depth to the slide and makes objects appear clearer without modification. This particular background effect is very useful for showing smaller images in isolation, such as the iPhone and Mac demonstrated in the image.

Spotlight on texture effect

A slight variation of the gradient effect, and one that is also gaining popularity in many recent presentations, is the use of a spotlight on texture. With this method, a texture is chosen as the primary background element, together with a spotlight effect in the direct center or top center of the image.

Figure 5.38 shows an example of this effect using a honeycomb metal texture.[7]

Figure 5.38 - Spotlight effect on textured metal.

This background technique can be very effective as it plays to the strength of the gradient approach, yet adds a texture and dynamic that can relate to the overall theme of the presentation. For example, a presentation specializing in software that was designed to be "industrial strength" could use a textured metal look to emphasize the heavy, solid elements often found in construction. For other industries, such as a presentation about a retail website, the same technique could be used but instead of a textured metal the presenter could choose a textured fabric instead.

Ensuring consistency for background themes

Regardless of whichever technique you use for your own presentation, the key to success will be consistency. If you plan to use background images for sections, try to keep the image theme consistent for the entire presentation. This will help the audience get accustomed to the flow and style of your presentation. Conversely if you choose a gradient or textured background for some or all of your sections, try to remain consistent here. Constantly flipping between a set of textured slides and a set of slides with image-based backgrounds might look visually impressive, but may not offer a consistent flow for the audience.

Fonts

When moving beyond the standard set of templates provided by Microsoft PowerPoint or Apple Keynote, many presenters find themselves experimenting with images, colors, different gradients, and other effects to try and make their presentations stand out. One area that is commonly overlooked, however, is picking and using different fonts.

The ability for a font to change the tone and story of a presentation is simply amazing and once you try this, I guarantee that you'll be hooked! Moreover, it's not just about picking one of the thirty or so fonts installed on your machine. There are literally millions of fonts available for download. Many of them are free, and if not, many come with commercial licenses available at a very reasonable cost.

Exploring fonts for your presentation

The first stage to realizing what fonts can do for your presentation is simply a case of exploring what is out there. FontSpace (http://www.fontspace.com) is a site that I use often as it has a good search engine, as well as the ability to test out the font before using it in your presentation.

Let's use the example of our presentation for the new GPS product, and let's imagine that we are after a font to represent some of the titles in our presentation. Given that it's related to new technology, I'm going to use "technology" as a keyword to search for appropriate fonts. By customizing the text while searching, I am able to browse through a number of fonts that might be a good fit, as shown in Figure 5.39.

Figure 5.39 - Browsing the fonts on FontSpace using a custom keyword and sample text.

For another example, especially when thinking of calling out important information in the presentation, an "embossed" font can be very effective for the audience. Figure 5.40 shows a font called "Impact Label" available on FontSpace that can work well for these scenarios.

Figure 5.40 - The "Impact Label" font on FontSpace.

As a final example of what you can find, fonts that relate to "handwriting" or "crayon" can be effective, especially for training materials or for presentations that are primarily educational in nature. You have to take care in how much you use these fonts, as using them for every piece of text can result in audience fatigue, but for titles, headings, and other elements they can be visually attractive.

Figure 5.41 - Examples of fonts that simulate handwriting using pens or crayons.

Picking three main fonts for your presentation

As you have likely guessed by now, it's certainly possible to overuse custom fonts. Multiple different fonts used sporadically throughout your presentation can lead to audience confusion as well as distract from the message that you are trying to tell.

To avoid this, and to follow generally accepted design principles, I find it useful to pick and use three main fonts throughout the presentation.

The first font should be used for titles. This should be a clear, bold font typeface that works well for titles and has the ability to echo a primary theme related to the presentation. In many of the technology-related presentations that I've created, I've used a font called "Franchise Bold"[8], which uses small caps (single, upper case) to create a clean, bold, title font, as shown in Figure 5.42.

Figure 5.42 - The Franchise Bold font.

The second font you select should be used for any text in your presentation that is not a title. For this, I would recommend a much lighter font, which complements the title font, but will be easier on the eyes for the audience. Selecting something as bold as the Franchise font works well for titles, but you wouldn't necessarily find it's great for large pieces of text.

Instead, you may want to look at light sans serif font such as Frutiger or Open Sans, as shown in Figure 5.43.

Figure 5.43 - The Open Sans font as a secondary font for main text in the presentation.

Finally, I would recommend selecting a third font for callouts or other areas in the presentation that you'd like to make an impact. This particular font can be very different from the other two, but should still be readable for the audience. (There are a lot of very creative fonts available that look great close up, but are near impossible to read on a projector from a distance, so you may want to experiment here.) For the purpose of our example, I'll use the Impact Label font that we discussed earlier.

The impact of using different fonts

Let's now take a quick look at the impact of selecting and using different fonts in our example presentation. Earlier in the chapter, you may recall the slide that shows some of the issues that Edna was having with her previous GPS.

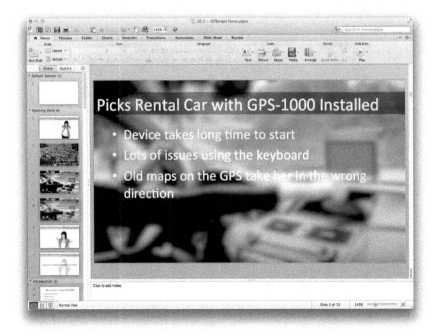

Figure 5.44 - Slide 5 with existing font selection.

As shown in Figure 5.44, we haven't done anything with the fonts so far. They are using the default, which for this particular version of Microsoft PowerPoint is Calibri.

Let's go ahead and change the fonts on this slide to Franchise Bold for the title, and Open Sans for the body text.

Figure 5.45 - Using alternative fonts to change the style of a presentation.

As you can see from Figure 5.45, the simple action of using different fonts, and selecting a bold/light combination for titles and text, drastically alters the feel and theme of the slide. The bold title adds emphasis to the story, and builds on the presentation's technical theme, whereas the lighter text font for the body adds a clean look to the page. We'll come back to the bullet point list when we investigate images further on in this chapter, but hopefully you can start to see how this is feeling more like a customized presentation versus the regular Microsoft PowerPoint look and feel.

We can apply the same effect to another slide as a further example. Figure 5.46 shows the question that takes our presentation from the opening story into the introduction section.

215

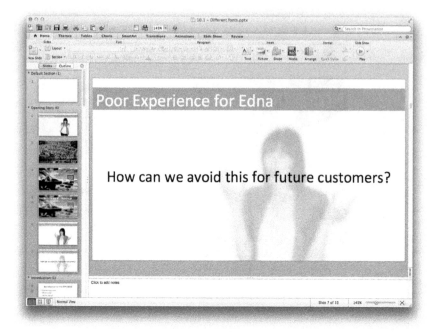

Figure 5.46 - Default fonts as used in the transition slide from the opening story.

Again, with this slide we are still using the default Calibri font set. Let's apply the Franchise Bold font for the title, together with the Impact Label font for the rhetorical question that we will be posing to the audience.

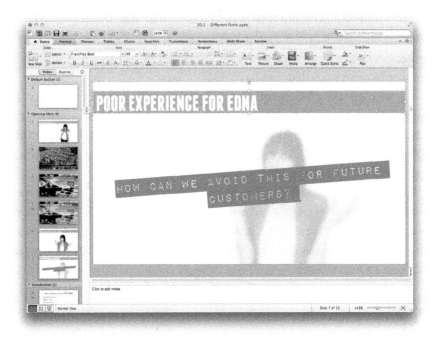

Figure 5.47 - Using new fonts to enhance the transition slide.

As shown in Figure 5.47, applying these new fonts gives us a much more visually interesting transition slide to take the audience to the next section. Moreover, the Impact Label font stands out as something that the audience can really take notice of.

Distributing fonts with your presentation

Hopefully this has been a good example of how selecting and using fonts can go a long way to improving the theme of your presentation to make text elements stand out as part of your story. Using custom fonts, however, is not without its own peril. As well as using too many fonts, or selecting fonts that the audience can't read, understanding how to distribute fonts to your audience as part of your presentation is important. If you plan on sharing your presentation file after your talk, and have

217

used custom fonts, there's a good chance that the fonts that you've selected will not be on the recipient's machine. The end result will be a presentation that opens up correctly, but defaults to fonts that will look nothing like the ones that you have used.

If you are using Microsoft PowerPoint on a PC, there is an option to embed fonts as part of the presentation file. This option[9] has a few restrictions, but in general seems to work well. Unfortunately, this same option does not work if you are using Microsoft PowerPoint on a Mac, and Apple Keynote does not support font embedding, either.

Outside of this option, the most reliable way is to generate and distribute a PDF version of your presentation, which will include any custom fonts that you have used by default. Alternatively, you can distribute the presentation with the links to where others can download the fonts as a last resort.

Colors

Similar to fonts, the use and selection of colors in a presentation is often overlooked, if ever used at all. Despite this, correct use of colors have the ability to transform a presentation, making elements and common themes stand out throughout the deck. In this section, I wanted to highlight some tips and tricks for thinking constructively about infusing color within your presentation.

Selecting a primary color for each section

As you may recall earlier in Chapter 4, we chose a different background color for each section of the presentation in order to more easily identify with the sections throughout the deck. As we go through and use background images for many of the slides, the boundary of the section can become lost. The use of color for the title text, however, can greatly increase the cohesion of slides with different backgrounds that are in the same section.

To demonstrate this, let's take a look at the first few slides in our opening story. As you can see in the slide outline view on the left in

Figure 5.48, we have a selection of different images for the six slides, yet there is no single color element that binds all of these slides together into one section.

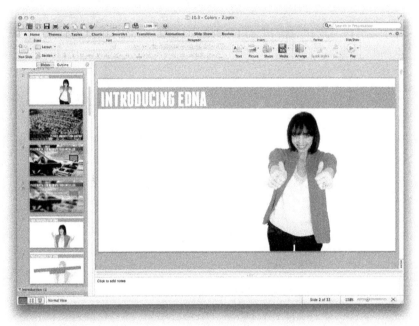

Figure 5.48 - No single color element binds the first few slides together.

To try and address this, we are going to do something very simple and change the background color of the title text to a royal blue (with an RGB value of 0, 0, 144). To prevent washout on some of the lighter slides, we'll also decrease the transparency to 20%.

The result is immediate. As we can see in Figure 5.49, this single color element adds a uniform theme that helps the slides coordinate so that they feel like a single section. This becomes even more obvious as you use different colors to represent different sections later on in the deck.

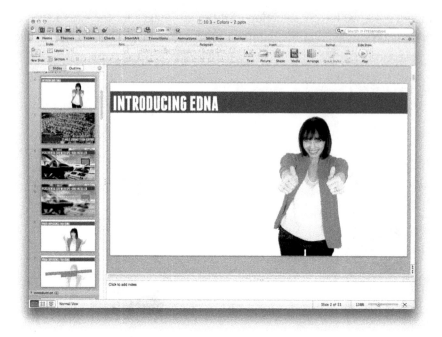

Figure 5.49 - Using a single color to help coordinate all slides in a single section.

Again, a good tip here is to explore different colors to see which ones work well with the images that you have chosen. This is more easily done by changing the color of the title in the master template so that you can make a single change and then see how this affects all of the slides in the relevant section.

When no color is better!

Many presenters overlook the use of color in their presentations. This might mean adding new colors as we saw previously, but in some circumstances it can also mean taking colors away. Removing color from an object or image, converting it into grayscale can add a level of abstraction to the presentation that can be very effective.

To see this in action in our example deck, let's look at Slide 3 of the opening story, as shown in Figure 5.50.

Figure 5.50 - Slide 3 from the opening story.

As you might recall from the previous chapter, this slide depicts Edna's potential journey to her friend's house from the airport. At this point in the story we are not actually taking the journey with her (as she is in the rental car lot picking up her car). Instead, we are glimpsing into Edna's mind about the journey that she will soon be embarking on. As a result, the image that we've selected of the houses is relevant, but it could be more effective if it was made a little more abstract.

To do this, we are going to convert this image to grayscale. This is relatively easy to do within Microsoft PowerPoint (by choosing the grayscale option from the Recolor ribbon) and Apple Keynote (by using the inspector and changing the color depth on the image).

Although a simple change, the effect (as seen in Figure 5.51) is fairly dramatic.

221

Figure 5.51 - Applying a gray scale effect to the background image.

Although this might be difficult to appreciate in the format of this book, converting this image to grayscale adds a level of abstractness that adds to the story. By doing this, the audience subconsciously enters Edna's mind as she is thinking about her upcoming journey before returning to the next slide. In addition, the use of grayscale adds to the fact that this journey could be a little daunting for Edna.

The use of grayscale can also be very dramatic on people and faces, especially close-ups that reveal a high level of detail. If your presentation has to express strong emotion in an abstract way through the use of people's features, converting images to grayscale can have a powerful effect.

Selecting complementary colors

I am unfortunate to be born with red/green color blindness. This has

222

led me into trouble on more than one occasion, including a few embarrassing clothing decisions, so it seems ironic that I should be telling you how to select colors for anything!

Fortunately, even if you are not color blind, there is an excellent tool called a color wheel, that can help you select colors that complement each other throughout your presentation. The color wheel is an organization of color hues around a circle that shows relationships between primary, secondary, and related colors.

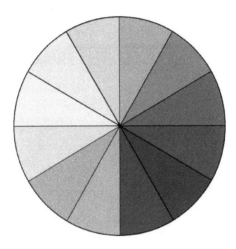

Figure 5.52 - Example of a 12-spoke primary color wheel.[10]

The first versions of the color wheel can be traced back to artists in the early 1700s and they are still used widely today. If you ever selected a color in an application such as Adobe PhotoShop you'll have likely seen the color selector in the form of a color wheel used when selecting a color.

The primary function of a color wheel is to help you select colors that work together in your presentation, and by using simple rules, it's easy to build a color palette. For example, in order to choose a complementary color, simply choose the color on the opposite side of the wheel. Using the previous color wheel, a complementary color to blue would be orange, a complement to green would be red, and so forth. Using a complementary color doesn't necessarily mean that you should mix them together. Even though I'm color blind, I can tell you that red fonts on a green background look awful. Being complementary means than objects of a complementary color will work well together on a single slide.

To illustrate this, let's look at Slide 7 in our opening story.

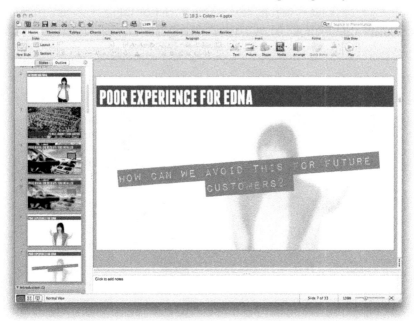

Figure 5.53 - Slide 7 in the opening story.

As shown in Figure 5.53, recall how in the previous section we changed the title color throughout the section to a blue (of RGB value 0, 0, 144). While this worked well on the title, we may want to change the color of the "label" question to be complementary. To do this, I'm going use a color wheel tool from Adobe called Kuler (http://kuler.adobe.com).

224

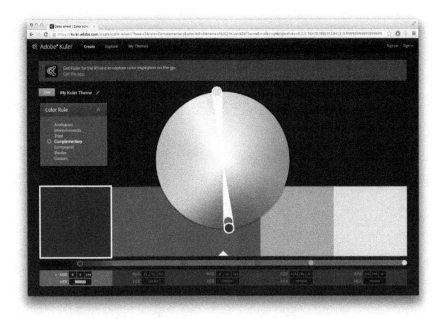

Figure 5.54 - Selecting complementary colors using Adobe Kuler.

As can be seen in Figure 5.54, I have entered the RGB values for the title color, and selected "complementary" from the list of color rules. The result is an orange hue, as we would expect, with RGB values of 178, 146, 0.

225

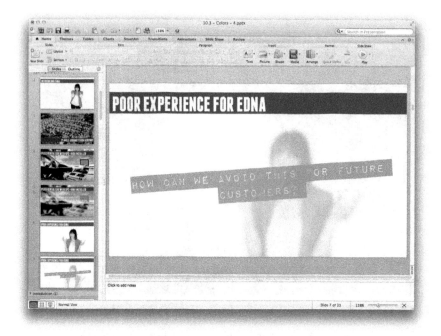

Figure 5.55 - Updating the caption with a complementary color.

The resulting color, as shown in Figure 5.55, looks much more complementary than the previous red label and works well with the blue heading.

Here, we are just scratching the surface of what's possible with color combinations. There are many different color palettes that you can build for your presentation, including monochromatic ranges (palettes on the same axis on the color wheel) and triads (palettes made up of colors at sectional thirds of the color wheel).

All have the ability to add depth and interest to your presentation that can take it to the next level for your audience, and I would encourage you to explore more as you develop your deck.

Standalone images

So far in this chapter we have looked at images for the use of creating effective backgrounds. As you can imagine, there are often times where images need to be used as part of the content material of the presentation.

A well selected, well placed image can help reinforce the text or message as part of a slide, and can also be an effective way of converting bulleted lists of text in to more visually appealing elements.

To illustrate both these techniques, let's take a look at the example deck. We'll start with Slide 12, which is part of the common use cases section in our story. As shown in Figure 5.56, this slide is related to the third use case, which is using the GPS to display traffic information. Although we've updated the fonts and applied a color scheme for the section, this slide still has a placeholder.

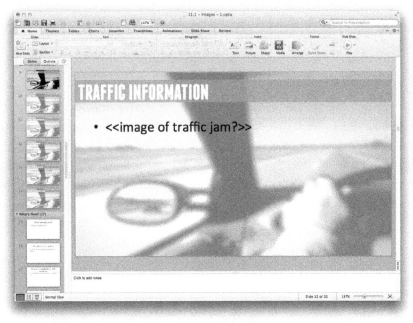

Figure 5.56 - Slide 12 showing a placeholder for an image.

At the start of this chapter, we covered searching for background images. While this focused on looking at different sources where images could be obtained, for this instance we are much more interested in what the image is trying to convey. Generally images within the frame of a slide are used to express one of three functions:

- **Actual representation.** An image that is used to show the audience what something actually looks like. This is useful when showing a new product or item to the audience, and we would definitely use these types of images when introducing the new product later on in the deck.

- **Abstract representation.** An image that is used to show the audience something that relates to the topic being discussed.

- **Humorous representation.** Again, an abstract image, but one that has a humorous connotation. These are often used when recapping or discussing topics that the audience already knows (or are used to bring the rest of the audience up to speed).

As the audience already knows what a traffic jam looks like, and based on our previous work on personas, we are recapping information that the majority of the audience already knows, so we'll use this opportunity to include an image that is somewhat humorous. After a few minutes of searching various photo locations for "traffic jam," I've come up with something that I believe is going to work with the audience.

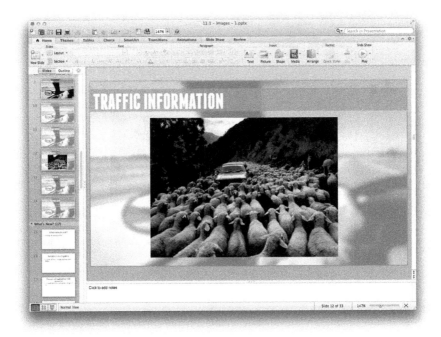

Figure 5.57 - A somewhat humorous picture of a traffic jam.[11]

As we can see in Figure 5.57, what's nice about these types of images is that they help tell the story, yet break up and lighten the presentation for those in the audience who already know the topic. They should definitely be used sparingly and appropriately, as we wouldn't want to try and replicate this on each and every slide, but with the right timing they can be very effective.

Let's now add a couple of effects to help make the image stand out from the rest of the slide. We'll add a white border, apply a paper-like drop shadow, and slightly rotate the image counterclockwise to create a photo-like appearance, as shown in Figure 5.58.

Figure 5.58 - Creating a photo-like effect from our inserted image.

Fortunately, there are several pre-defined effects in Microsoft PowerPoint and Apple Keynote, so you don't need to be a graphic artist in order to create similar looking effects.

We'll touch on the use of humor in Chapter 7, but what's nice about these types of images is that they help add accent to the story. Imagine introducing the slide with the following speaking points:

> "Of course, one of the most useful things we learned about our previous product, the GPS 1000, was the use of traffic information." (Presenter clicks to this slide showing images of sheep)

> "Now, of course, it didn't help in every type of traffic jam, but our research indicated that the majority of customers really valued this

230

feature."

Here, we've told the audience about the importance of the traffic feature in the product, yet at the same time, we've kept the story and presentation interesting for those who already knew that when they walked into the room.

Replacing lists with images

Over the course of the past couple of chapters we've seen several slides and topics that include short lists of items that will be presented in the scope of one slide. Figure 5.59 shows an example of such a list used for Slide 5 of the opening story.

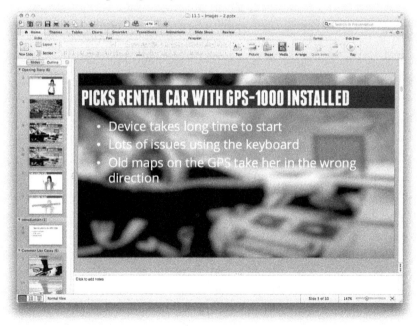

Figure 5.59 - Slide 5 showing a list of three items.

As can be seen in this slide, we have three items that we will be introducing: the fact that the device takes a long time to start, there are lots of issues with the keyboard on the existing GPS model, and the old maps ultimately take Edna in the wrong direction.

In the previous chapter, we created basic appearing animations for these lists for rehearsal purposes. While the animation helps the audience consume this new information piece by piece, the format of the bulleted list could definitely use some improvement. As it happens, using images can help transform this list into something more effective.

When selecting images for items in this list, we still have the option of using actual, abstract, or humorous representations as we discussed previously. Given that we are not going to be showing the actual start time, keyboard, and maps, and based on the fact that this might be new information to many in the room, we are going to select the second option, a simple abstract representation.

To do this, I can acquire or create three icons that represent an hourglass (for the time), a keyboard, and a map. For this example, I'm going to turn to a website called The Noun Project (http://thenounproject.com), which is a project that helps aggregate and catalog many different icons and symbols from designers around the world. Many of the symbols on this site are free, registered under the creative commons license, and others are available at a small charge.

Using the site, I've found three icons that represent the three areas. The icons are available in SVG (Scalable Vector Graphic) format, which means that they can be imported into most graphic design tools such as Adobe Photoshop, Illustrator, or GIMP. After importing them, I inverted the colors (by default the symbols are black, and I want white to present them on a dark background), and created three gradient buttons in Microsoft PowerPoint. The gradient buttons can be created by inserting a rounded corner rectangle (from the Insert Shape option) and then adding a bevel from the Effects drop-down in the Format ribbon. The result of this is shown in Figure 5.60.

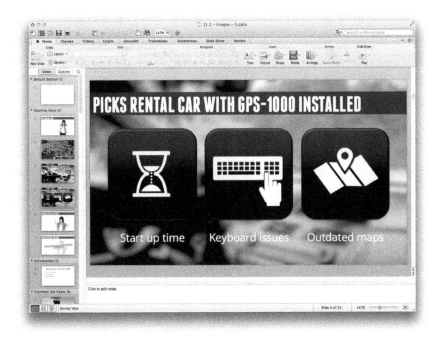

Figure 5.60 - Transforming the bulleted list into three images.

You notice also how the blue in the gradient of the bevel matches the blue of the title heading in order to maintain color consistency on the slide. Finally, I also condensed the text for each of the three items to look more concise with the image. Again, this text is to serve as a prompt for me to explain the issues relating to this slide—as opposed to something that the audience should need to read.

As with the previous bulleted list, the animations are important to preserve for the three images. Each image should be introduced individually with the accompanying text so that the presenter can talk about the topic that the image is referring to before moving on to the next subject.

Although a simple approach, as you can hopefully see in this example, replacing bulleted lists with images—either icons or actual pictures—can be a very powerful way of creating a much more visually impressive presentation. You should definitely be cautious to ensure consistency across items in the list, and certainly don't overdo lists, but in general this can be a very effective way of introducing a number of items in a slide that keeps the audience engaged.

Taking control of your image sizes

As you start adding more and more images to your presentation, it's very easy for the size of the presentation deck to become more and more unwieldy. Before you know it, you'll end up with a slide deck approaching 100 Mb in size that will be impossible to email to others and slow to download.

While keeping an eye on image size is important, it can be difficult. Fortunately, both Microsoft PowerPoint and Apple Keynote have shortcuts for helping manage the size of images in your presentation.

For users of Microsoft PowerPoint, there is a Compress button in the Format Picture ribbon. This option will help you scale down the size of your pictures to a particular resolution. I recommend 150 ppi (pixels per inch) unless you have a need to print high quality versions of the images at a later time. This option will also remove cropped areas of images that you are no longer using.

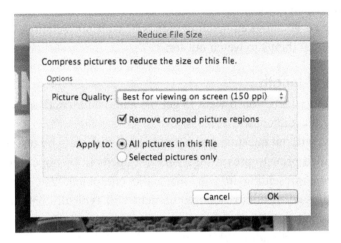

Figure 5.61 - Compressing images in Microsoft PowerPoint.

For users of Apple Keynote, right-click on an image and select the Reduce Image File Size menu option to apply similar changes to a Keynote presentation.

Videos

After spending quite some time talking about images in this chapter, I wanted to wrap things up by talking about the related topic of videos.

Both Microsoft PowerPoint and Apple Keynote support embedding videos that can be played during your presentation. While videos have the ability to add a third-party perspective into your presentation, and can definitely be appealing to some audiences, I would recommend using them with caution.

If you are considering a video as part of your presentation I would encourage you to think about why you are switching to video. If you are showing a new product commercial or trailer, then of course it makes sense. But, if you are simply embedding a random video to make a point to the audience, the risks of using this medium likely outweigh the benefits, and I would recommend seeing whether you could relay the same message as part of your presentation.

If you do go about embedding videos in your presentation, here are a few additional things to watch out for.

Audio and length

With any video, you'll want to get the audio and length of your video perfect for the audience.

Firstly, without question you should make sure that you test the audio of your video prior to presenting. This test needs to be done in the room that you are presenting in with the audio equipment that you will be using. Professional audio/video equipment will typically have a 3.5mm input jack that you can connect to your laptop or other presentation device to support audio. While this sounds simple, you'll want to make sure that your laptop is set to play audio through the headphone jack, and that the volume levels on both your laptop and the audio equipment are appropriate. There's nothing worse than clicking the play button on a video in the middle of your presentation only to have dead silence in the room when you realize there is no audio, so checking this before getting on stage is really important.

Secondly, do make sure that the video you are using is correctly cued up. This means that there's no unnecessary footage before the video starts, and that the video is of appropriate length for your presentation. As a member of the audience, it can be very frustrating to sit through either a really long or miscued video. Make the video concise, and exactly what you need to show to the audience.

Audience immersion dip

One of the problems with playing high quality videos during a presentation is that you risk taking your audience into very immersive media—and shortly afterwards returning them to your presentation with a "bump." This is amplified if your video is exciting, or has a great soundtrack or special effects. For example, if you are showing a trailer for an upcoming game or a new product commercial, the audience is

236

"sucked in" to the video, and when it's over there is often a deafening silence and return to reality as you try to pick up the conversation from where the video ended.

There are ways around this, however. If the video is aimed to inspire and excite people, as soon as the video ends, you can ask a rhetorical question to the audience (e.g.,   "Wow! What did you guys think?" or "Did you like what you saw there?") Assuming that the audience did indeed like the video, and will likely applaud or give other positive feedback, this can be a great way of "easing back" into your presentation flow.

Another consideration can be to place the video at the end of the presentation. Of course, this won't work for every scenario, but a strong video leading out your presentation can definitely leave a memorable impression with the audience. Again, as a presenter, you'll still need to come back and close the presentation. You don't get away with pressing play and walking off stage!

Sharing videos

A final word of caution comes with embedding and sharing videos. Typically, if you embed a video in a Microsoft PowerPoint presentation, you are not embedding or copying the actual video. Instead, you are embedded a link to a video file that lives elsewhere on your machine. This has the ability to catch people out in a couple of ways:

Firstly, if you have embedded a video into a PowerPoint presentation on your machine, when you copy that PowerPoint file to a separate machine, the link to the video will likely not work. On a couple of occasions I've seen presenters copy their slide decks to the "presentation machine" only to discover (halfway through presenting) that all of the embedded videos no longer work! If you have to use a different machine for your presentation, and you are embedding videos, definitely keep this one in mind.

Secondly, as you may have guessed, if you send the PowerPoint file via email after your presentation, all of the embedded links will likely no longer work. There are ways around this, such as placing the videos on the same network share as the original slide deck, but it's well worth noting if you want others to watch the video as part of your shared deck.

Where are we?

This brings us to the end of Chapter 5, where we've covered a lot of ground, focusing on taking your presentation from the pencil sketch stage and adding backgrounds, fonts, colors, and acquiring and using images.

As you run through your presentation using these techniques, your deck should be looking closer to being done, and you're due for another rehearsal. Although we might still be missing some of the finer elements such as diagrams and animations, this is still a great time to re-rehearse your presentation to help let more of the content sink in. This is especially important with some of the restructuring that you may have done, including converting some of the lists to images.

This third rehearsal is also an opportunity to get tighter on the timing of your presentation. If you found that you were significantly shorter or longer when you ran through the presentation at the end of Chapter 4, this is definitely a good time to review the length of some of the sections and ensure that you can work towards a tighter delivery.

In the next chapter, we will continue to further refine the deck by adding the last layer of composition to your presentation—the fine details!

---

1. Scott Hanselman has a great blog post on converting presentations from 4:3 to 16:9, which can be found here: http://www.hanselman.com/blog/HowToConvert
APowerPointPresentationFrom43RatioTo169WithoutDistortedOrStretchedImages.aspx
2. Creative Commons is a nonprofit organization offering a set of easy to use copyright licenses that provide a standardized way of sharing work based on a set of clear conditions. You can find more about the organization at http://creativecommons.org
3. The images that I've used so far in the example presentation can be found here:
Edna Happy
http://www.istockphoto.com/stock-photo-23540446-two-thumbs-up.php?st=237bb75
25 Mile Journey (found using "house" as keyword)
http://office.microsoft.com/en-us/images/results.aspx?qu=house&ex=1#ai:MP900400036|

Car GPS Scene

http://www.istockphoto.com/stock-photo-12938946-getting-direction-on-gps.php?st=96aec79

Edna Frustrated

http://www.istockphoto.com/stock-photo-23540149-frustrated-woman.php?st=237bb75

4. This image can be found here: http://www.istockphoto.com/stock-photo-23607820-young-woman-making-facial-expressions.php

5. You can find the slide deck for this presentation here: http://www.slideshare.net/simonguest/patterns-forc-cloud-computing-2549678

6. The image can be found here: http://office.microsoft.com/en-us/images/results.aspx?qu=dashboards#ai:MP9003998531

7. This image, together with many similar ones, can be found at http://www.99wallpaper.com

8. This font can be viewed and downloaded from: http//www.derekweathersbee.com/franchise/

9. Information on embdedding fonts in the Windows version of Microsoft PowerPoint can be found here:http://support.microsoft.com/kb/826832

10. This color wheel appeared in an article in *Smashing Magazine*, "Color Theory for Designer, Part 3": http://www.smashingmagazine.com/2010/02/08/color-theory-for-designer-part-3-creating-your-own-color-palettes/

11. Image courtesy of: http://s949.photobucket.com/user/seraiwallpapers/media/daily/Tt/Trafficjam.jpg.html

CHAPTER 6: Your Slide Canvas—Fine Details

✱ ✱ ✱

Over the past couple of chapters we have focused on building the presentation by first applying a "pencil sketch" approach to building structure, and then adding composition elements such as backgrounds, images, fonts, and colors. In this third chapter on presentation creation, we'll examine adding the fine details that helps add more polish to the final deck. This will include the creation and use of great diagrams, adding screenshots, clippings and references, and finally introducing builds and animations.

Diagrams

Many presentations have a need for diagrams. Examples include diagrams of networks or systems, a new business process that your company has just implemented, or a product framework that you are sharing with other developers.

If presented poorly, diagrams have the ability to take the presentation and presenter completely off track, and leave the audience quickly confused. I've found in the past that certain presenters include diagrams to show how clever they are, instead of a tool for informing or educating the audience. The presenter will display a massively detailed and complex diagram in a slide, and will then proceed to say something to the effect of, "Of course, you probably can't see the detail of this diagram, but what this is showing is…"

Ugh. If the audience has no chance of even reading the diagram, never mind actually working out what the diagram is trying to represent, why show it? The result is often people in the audience squinting at the slide, trying to make out what is being shown, before trying to pick up the pieces of where the presenter is during the presentation.

To overcome this, regardless of what you are hoping to present, there are a few rules that are worth following to make showing diagrams a benefit not a detriment to your presentation.

Purpose of your diagram?

When considering inserting a diagram into your presentation, one of the first questions to ask is "Why?" Why does it make sense to have a diagram? What are you trying to represent? And more importantly, what will the audience be able to do different as a result of seeing and understanding the diagram in front of them?

Sometimes, answering these questions can be hard. Often a presenter will want to break up many slides of text and an occasional diagram seems to be a great way of inserting something visually different into a deck. Other times, a diagram will be used as a trophy or validation point for the presenter. The presenter will say, "This diagram shows the network that we built to support our worldwide offices." Unless the presentation is training the audience on supporting the worldwide office network, the diagram is likely superfluous, and what they should be saying is, "This diagram shows how clever we think we are. I hope you agree."

A diagram in a presentation should have a purpose for the audience. If you can clearly articulate what the purpose of the diagram is, and how the audience will be able to do something different as a result, then it will go a long way for supporting the use of the diagram in your presentation.

Sometimes diagrams can help structurally define pieces of a presentation. A presenter might show a diagram of a product framework because other sections in the presentation will refer to the pieces being shown.

Diagrams are also useful when showing roadmaps for products or future innovations. The diagram has a clear purpose because it is educating the audience as to what products and features will be coming down the road.

Finally, many diagrams are used to show a business process—the way something has been implemented. The caveat here is that the presentation that follows must build upon the sections or elements referred to in the diagram. Showing a diagram with a "7-step process for setting up your developer environment" without then actually talking in detail about the 7-step process can fall into the trap of trying to appear clever without giving the audience anything of value.

Shapes, lines, and fonts

With a clear purpose for the audience, diagrams also have to look great. Let's first look at one that doesn't!

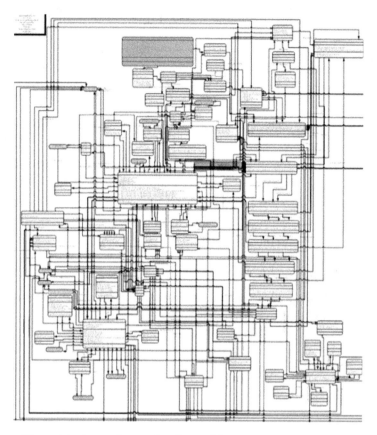

Figure 6.1 - An overly complex diagram[1] for a "customer-friendly" system.

While it's somewhat of an exaggeration, Figure 6.1 shows a style of diagram that I've seen too many times in technical presentations. It's a diagram that has likely been copied and pasted from actual documentation, showing relationships in a database schema in excruciating detail. Not only does this diagram fall into the trap of having no purpose, but the presenter has not even bothered to make the diagram clear for the audience. Unless you are seated in the first row of the audience with a large magnifying glass, you don't stand a chance of being able to read or understand any of this.

A great diagram will have clear shapes, lines, and fonts. While this might sound a little obvious, let's take a look at these elements in some detail:

- **Shapes.** Shapes should be easy to see, bold, and have no ambiguity about what they are depicting. You may choose to use a regular geometric shape in your diagram, or even pick a high resolution icon to show an element, but the goal is to ensure that the audience has no problem reading and understanding what you are trying to show.

- **Lines.** Often overlooked by many, any lines used in diagrams much be of a certain thickness. In both Microsoft PowerPoint and Apple Keynote, the default line thickness (known as weight) is often too thin to see at the back of a large room. If you are including a lot of lines and arrows in your diagram, one of the first things I would recommend would be to increase the weight to a minimum of 3pt thickness.

- **Fonts.** Again, another overlooked point. I've seen many diagrams that have nice looking shapes and structure, but are let down by a font that no one in the audience can read. As a rule of thumb, any font used in a diagram should always be a minimum of 20pt in size. Any smaller, and you risk the audience at the back of the room squinting to make out what pieces of the diagram are trying to represent.

You may be thinking that with bold shapes, thick lines, and large fonts, there will be almost no room for your diagram. This is exactly the point. You want to ensure that everything in your diagram is useful to the audience. If you are finding that you can no longer fit everything on the page, don't try and squeeze the diagram into the page, but instead think about what parts of the diagram you could remove to make things clearer for the audience.

Alignment

You may have the most impressive, clear diagram ever created, but if the shapes and elements don't align with each other, it will always represent an unprofessional and rushed image to your audience.

I've witnessed this a lot of the time. Organizational charts where each team is just a few pixels below their peer teams on the same diagram. Or product framework diagrams where one of the "layers" is just off center by a pinch. You may think that I'm being overly anal and that the audience won't pick up on these, which both might be true, but you would be surprised how many people do pick up on this even at a subconscious level.

Fortunately, both Microsoft PowerPoint and Apple Keynote make it very easy to avoid these kind of alignment issues.

Firstly, both tools have "snap to" guides that can help align objects in a diagram. For Microsoft PowerPoint, under the View/Guides menu, there is an option for snapping to shapes (which will help shapes magnetically align with each other when you drag them), and snapping to grid, which will align shapes based on an invisible grid of 1/12th inch increments. Both these techniques can help avoid shapes being off by a few pixels when you are moving them around on the slide.

Secondly, the Shift key can work wonders in both Microsoft PowerPoint and Apple Keynote. Holding down the Shift key will force lines to stay on a particular trajectory and increase large increments for rotating objects.

Finally, if you need a final sanity check to ensure all of the shapes in your diagram are aligned correctly, you can turn to the Arrange option in the Format ribbon, as shown in Figure 6.2.

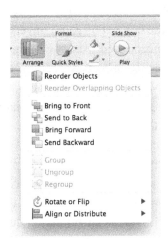

Figure 6.2 - The Arrange option in the Format menu.

Often overlooked, this useful set of options will enable you to not only change the Z-index (foreground and background) of an object, but will also allow you to select a group of objects and align them based on a series of edges. This can be very useful in ensuring alignment to a particular line, or even making sure that a set of elements is exactly centered in your diagram.

Builds

While we've covered the shapes, lines, fonts, and alignment for your diagrams, one thing that remains: How you introduce your diagram to the audience.

The standard way for many presenters is, of course, to hit the "next" button on their clicker to have the diagram immediate appear for the audience. While this introduces the diagram quickly, it runs the risk of taking the audience off track. Putting so much information in front of the audience at one time can easily direct their attention the wrong way. Especially with complex diagrams, the audience will start reviewing the diagram and looking through the parts, while at the same time taking their attention from you. When their attention is restored to your speech, they'll have likely lost the context of your conversation.

Similar to how we introduced lists in Chapter 4, any diagram should be introduced to the audience in parts or sections that map to the speaking points of the presenter. Many diagrams can be broken up logically in this way. For example, if your product framework diagram has five pieces to it, you'll likely want to introduce it in five distinct builds, talking succinctly about each piece in turn.

For now, don't worry about the animation piece of this as we'll be touching on animations and builds later in this chapter. At this point it's sufficient, and often desirable, to break up the build of the diagram across multiple slides. This will work as an animation during your rehearsal, but will have the benefit that you don't have to spend a lot of time getting the animation perfect before including it in your deck.

Putting it all together

So far, this section on diagrams has been largely theoretical. Rather than repeat all of the information with simple examples, let us revisit our GPS example to see how a diagram might look in the context of this presentation.

For the purpose of this example, let's imagine that we've reached a point in the deck where we want to show a simple framework diagram. The purpose of the diagram will be to educate the audience about the main building blocks of the SDK for programming the GPS.

Figure 6.3 - Blank canvas for our diagram.

As shown in Figure 6.3, we are starting from a blank canvas. We've already selected a suitable background, title, and color palette that matches the theme of the presentation. To get a diagram quickly inserted, it would be easy here to simply copy and paste a diagram from some other documentation, but as we can see in Figure 6.4, the result looks fairly terrible.

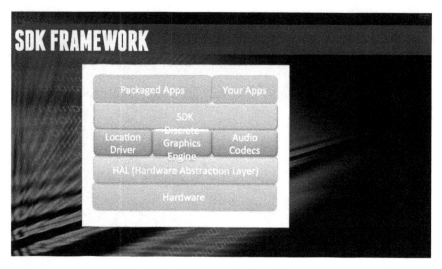

Figure 6.4 - A diagram copy/pasted into the slide.

As you can probably tell, there are a lot of issues here. Not only does the diagram not match any color scheme or fonts we've used previously in the deck, but the diagram is difficult to read, and has multiple alignment issues. Moreover, because the diagram is likely copied as a single image, this precludes the chance of using any animation to build up the diagram layer by layer.

Let's start from scratch by adhering to the principles of correct shapes, lines, and fonts that we've covered thus far in the chapter. Figure 6.5 shows an updated representation of the diagram.

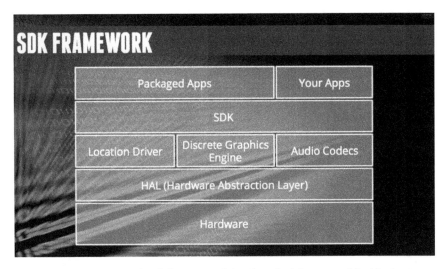

Figure 6.5 - An updated diagram applying the principles covered in this chapter.

As shown, even though the diagram shows the same information, the use of bold lines, readable fonts, and a semi-opaque background greatly improve the diagram. In addition, using a font scheme that we've used previously (Open Sans) in the deck helps make the diagram feel part of the same presentation, rather than something that was copied and pasted as an afterthought. You should also notice that the alignment of the shapes is also accurate. Even though various shapes in the diagram are separated from each other, the spacing around all of the shapes is uniform.

The final piece to the puzzle here is to ensure that the diagram builds correctly. To do this, we can add animation steps for each layer of the framework, working from the bottom up, with each animation being activated when the presenter clicks the mouse. By doing this, we have the opportunity to explain each layer of the framework, without the audience being bombarded by too much information right out of the gate. If we would have displayed the entire diagram and then started explaining the bottom layer of the diagram, there's a good chance that the audience would have skipped ahead by trying to decipher the rest of the framework while we were still talking.

Of course, this is only one example of a diagram style, designed to match many of the visual elements that we've used elsewhere in the deck. In your presentations, you should use the style that you believe best matches the type of message you are trying to deliver while still adhering to the principles that we've covered during this section.

Whiteboard technique

Being in software development, I've always loved whiteboards. During my time at Microsoft, I used to have several of them in my office, and found them to be a great "developer meeting point" for discussing or brainstorming new ideas. One of the unique things about the whiteboard is that the handwritten style makes it very difficult to create complicated diagrams. The results tend to be very clear diagrams that are used to illustrate a point or to convey a solution for the other person in the room.

Taking this forward, I wanted to see if I could replicate and recreate this whiteboard concept for a presentation. What would happen if I created a presentation template for diagrams that emulated a whiteboard?

To start, I created a simple template background using an image from a whiteboard, as shown in Figure 6.6. If you want to do this yourself, multiple images can be found online, or you can even take a picture of your own office whiteboard if you have one. Just make sure you clean it beforehand!

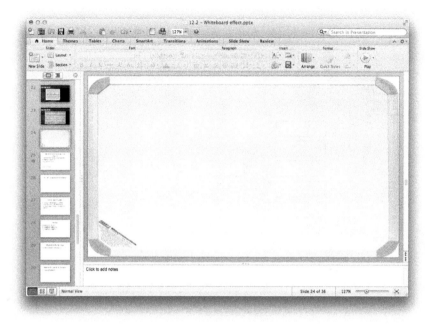

Figure 6.6 - Image of a whiteboard as a template in Microsoft PowerPoint.

Secondly, I wanted to replicate the types of lines and shapes found on a whiteboard. Part of this was ensuring that the thickness of the lines looked appropriate, but more importantly I was able to match the colors of most red, blue, green, and black whiteboard markers to add to the effect. This can be shown in Figure 6.7.

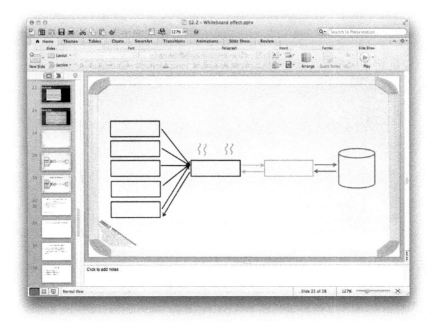

Figure 6.7 - Replicating whiteboard-like lines and colors in the template.

Finally, and arguably the most difficult issue to resolve, was the font. I know I needed a font that looked liked handwriting, but none that I immediately tried had a look and feel of something that had been written on a whiteboard. After much more searching, however, I came across a font called Post Human, which can be found at dafont.com.[2] As shown in Figure 6.8, I hope you'll agree that it has a blend of handwriting, comic, and calligraphic details that make it look perfect for what you might see written on a whiteboard.

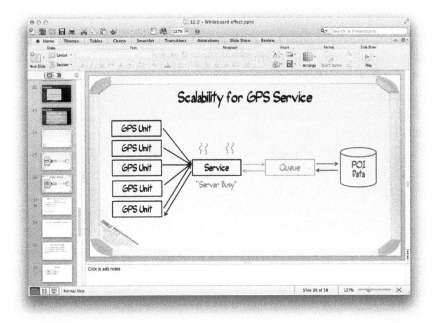

Figure 6.8 - Applying the "Post Human" font to the whiteboard template.

As I hope you'll agree, the result looks quite effective, and I was able to use this style for multiple presentations.[3] What was more interesting than the template, however, was the rethinking I had to go through for diagrams that were displayed in this format. As I was creating diagrams using this template I found myself thinking, "How would I draw this on the whiteboard?" as opposed to "How should I create this in PowerPoint?" Together with introducing the diagrams through animations, I believe the result is much clearer diagrams, especially ones that the audience can quickly understand and relate to.

While the whiteboard template might or might not work for your particular presentation or domain, I hope it demonstrates some of the different thinking that can be applied to diagrams used within presentations.

Screenshots

Screenshots can be an important part of a presentation, especially in place of a demo. We'll cover the use of demos in Chapter 8 in some detail, but in the interim I wanted to share some tips and recommendations for using screenshots in your presentation.

As with many topics that we have covered in this book, of course we have to ask the question of the purpose of using the screenshot. Why is the screenshot being used instead of something else? What will the audience take away having seen the screenshot? What's your goal (as a presenter) of showing the screenshot?

Screenshots can be very useful to show new products, sites, features, enhancements, or other artifacts to the audience, but they have to be done with a purpose in mind. If you are using a screenshot, you want to ensure that there is a clear purpose and takeaway for the audience rather than just including something to fill up some whitespace on a slide.

Assuming that you are confident with the purpose of screenshots, let's now look at some of the tips and recommendations for using them in your presentation.

Full screen or clipped?

One of the first decisions is whether the screenshot you are showing should be full screen (taking up the entire real estate of your slide) or a cropped image embedded within your slide. Using Google to perform a simple search, Figures 6.9 and 6.10 show examples of both.

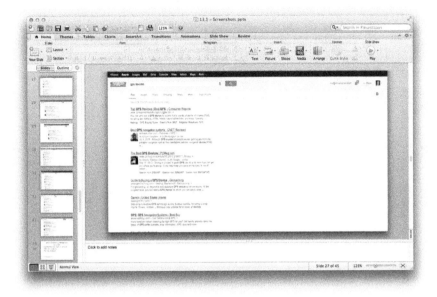

Figure 6.9 - A screenshot that occupies the entire slide.

Figure 6.10 - A cropped screenshot inserted on an existing slide.

As can be seen in the previous two images, the effect is quite different, even though the context of what is being shown is the same.

There are advantages and disadvantages for using screenshots that occupy the entire slide. The advantage is obviously readability. More real estate gives you additional space to enlarge the screenshot to make it more readable. The disadvantage is that a full screen view might be jarring for the audience. As there is no continuity with the existing template or theme, it can be difficult to relate the screenshot to the existing section or topic.

My advice is as follows: If you are using a series of screenshots to walk through specific functionality with the audience, full screen captures will likely work best. The audience will be able to view more of the image, and the consecutive screens will likely flow better.

If, however, you are just showing one screenshot, and you are not planning to explore the details of the screen or link it to other screens, you might be able to get away with a cropped screenshot in a slide. An example of this could be a competitor's website, where you want to remind the audience about what it looks like or give a visual cue to the topic, but don't necessarily want to walk through the site in much detail.

Regardless of whether you will be presenting your screenshot as full screen or embedded on an existing slide, the details of the image still have to be readable. On frequent occasions I've seen screen captures that have been taken at too high of a resolution and then pasted into a slide deck. The result is often an unreadable screenshot, and one that has a lot of whitespace on either side of the actual content.

Although you don't need every piece of text in the screenshot to be readable, I would encourage you to experiment with the zoom in/out features of the browser to try and get the best result. Using Google Chrome, this can be done using the zoom in/zoom out options from the view menu.

Browser chrome

When taking screenshots for use in a presentation, another important factor to consider is whether or not to include the chrome (or frame) of the browser with your screenshot. Figures 6.11 and 6.12 show examples of both.

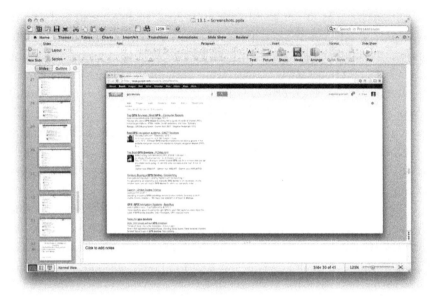

Figure 6.11 - A screenshot with the browser chrome.

Figure 6.12 - A screenshot without the browser chrome.

Again, there are advantages and disadvantages of each. Including the browser chrome with your screenshot looks more real, which can be useful for product-related presentations. A screenshot with the chrome, and potentially a URL, will show the audience that this screenshot was taken from a real production server, so it will look more authentic.

There are disadvantages and caveats, however. Firstly, the URL in the browser chrome can give away more than you had hoped for. If you do have a real URL included in your screenshot you should be prepared for at least some people in the audience to browse to it while you are speaking.

On one occasion, I was presenting to an internal audience about a new website that we were building. The website was in the very early stages of development, and unfortunately I had included the URL in the screenshot of my presentation. Before I knew it, many people were hitting the URL from their machines in the room, and I was getting

261

comments such as, "It's not working in my browser" or "Will it be this slow in production?" which I had to defend halfway during the presentation. It was a good lesson that if you share any type of URL in a screenshot or anywhere else, you should be prepared for the audience to hit it at that point in your presentation.

A second caveat to including the browser chrome is to ensure that you are not sharing more information than you had intended. The audience can be very observant and will notice the titles of other open tabs in the browser as well as anything that might be saved in your browser search bar (if your browser has a separate bar for search queries). As a rule, if you are planning to include the browser chrome as part of your screenshot, you'll want to ensure that everything is clean and you are only showing the tab that you need to.

Showing detail

Taking screenshots that are easy to read for the audience, especially the ones at the back of the room, can be difficult. Even with experimenting with the zoom level in the browser, many fonts and details in the screen will be too hard to read. This can be troublesome if you are planning on including several screenshots or walking the audience through a series of steps that they might need to do. There is, however, a technique that can help.

Let's imagine that we want to show the audience the details of the Google search we've been using in this section. Showing the whole screenshot may not be very effective as the fonts would likely be too small. On the other hand, showing a clipped version doesn't give the audience any context of the search.

To overcome these issues, we can use a combination of both. Firstly, we take a screenshot of the whole image, as shown in Figure 6.13.

Figure 6.13 - Screenshot of complete Google search.

Next, we copy and paste this image twice, creating two additional copies of the same image, as shown in Figure 6.14.

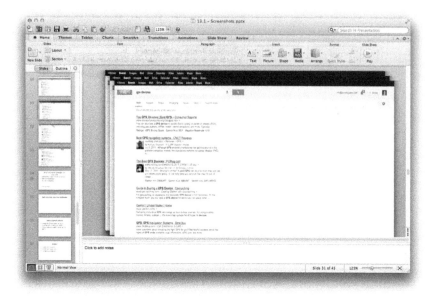

Figure 6.14 - Making an additional two copies of the same image.

Once this is done, we crop each of the duplicates. The first is cropped to show the search input field, while the second is cropped to show the first three results. For the cropped images, we also add a shadow so that they appear to stand out in front of the original image. The result should look something similar to what you see in Figure 6.15.

Figure 6.15 - Cropped images with shadow effect.

If this all seems strange, bear with me as I promise it will make sense very soon! Next, we enlarge the clipped images and place them so that they are roughly over the center of their original location in the first image. The result is shown in Figure 6.16.

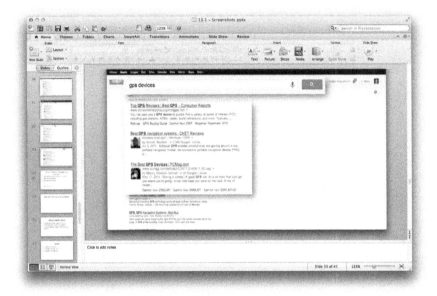

Figure 6.16 - Enlarging the cropped images and placing them over the original content.

The final part is to add both entrance and exit animations to the clipped images. For best effect, the animation should use the "faded zoom" effect, zooming in when the mouse pointer is clicked, and zooming out on the next click.

Although this animation effect can't be shown in a book, the result is that the audience sees the original image, and on additional clicks of the mouse, the various clipped images are "zoomed to the front" for the audience to see in detail. The benefit of this approach is that as a presenter, you can take a complex image, large screenshot, or a set of text that would otherwise be illegible to the audience and highlight pieces of this for the audience by bringing them to the front as part of your presentation.

References and quotes

In additional to diagrams and screenshots, many presentations can also benefit from having references and quotes. This might be a headline from a recent online article, or maybe an anecdotal quote from a customer that you would like to include in your presentation.

Headlines are great as they can provide an independent or third-party perspective for a point that you are trying to make. For example, if you are trying to convince the audience that your product had a successful release, you may choose to include the headline from CNET or another such publication as you emphasize the point.

Rather than just copying and pasting the entire screen or browser when doing this, a more effective way can be to copy and paste an area of the web page and then use a "paper tear" technique to show just the headline. This effect is shown in Figure 6.17.

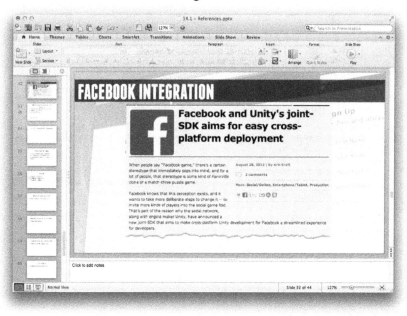

Figure 6.17 - Torn paper effect for headline quote.

As you can see, this technique makes the headline standout and draws the audience's attention more directly to the point that you are trying to make. This technique is also relatively easy to do in both Microsoft PowerPoint and Apple Keynote. For Microsoft PowerPoint, paste your image and use the Freeform Line tool to draw a jagged edge towards the bottom of the image, as shown in Figure 6.17.

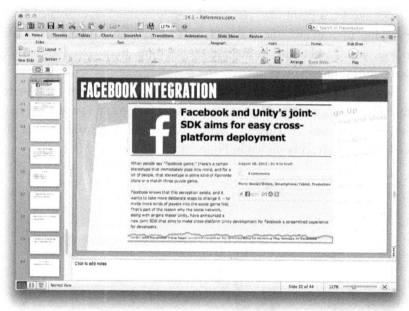

Figure 6.17 - Drawing a jagged line edge in Microsoft PowerPoint.

When this is complete, set the line and fill color to solid white (or whatever your background color is) and add an outer top shadow. This will turn the jagged line into a torn paper effect that appears to blend in with the overlaying image and background. It might take you a couple of attempts to get the perfect look that you are after, but it is fairly effective when it works.

For Apple Keynote, a similar effect can be found in the Stroke menu to the left and below the menu bar. Different stroke patterns can be applied, including a torn paper effect as shown in Figure 6.18.

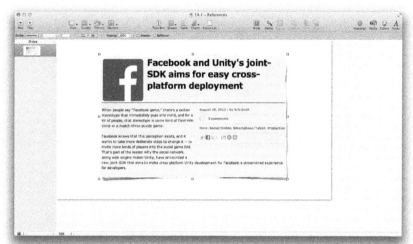

Figure 6.18 - Torn paper stroke effect in Apple Keynote.

If you are using this technique, however, I do recommend inserting the original URL either at the bottom of the slide or in the notes section. This link back to the original article will provide validation, and can also be a useful reference for anyone reading the presentation at a later point in time.

If you don't have official web pages containing headlines, a variation on this technique is to create your own. This can be done in a similar way by creating a text box with the quote, and then selecting an appropriate paper tear border to highlight the content.

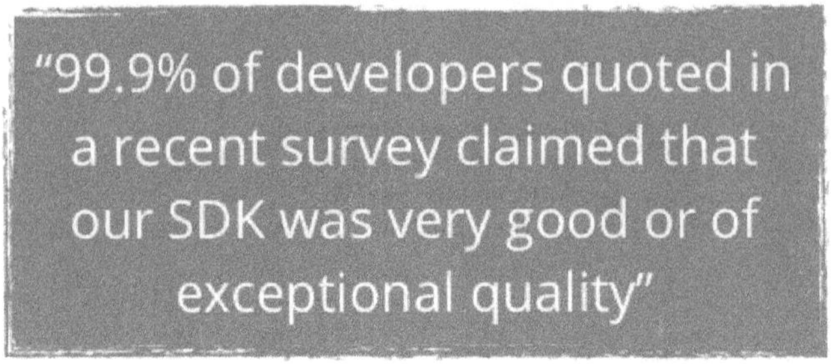

"99.9% of developers quoted in a recent survey claimed that our SDK was very good or of exceptional quality"

Figure 6.19 - Creating a torn paper look for a custom text box

Shown in Figure 6.19 is a simple text box created in Apple Keynote, with white Open Sans font on a black background with 50% opacity. The text box has a crayon-like stroke of 30 pixels applied to give it the rough, painted-look edge. Again, I encourage you to experiment with different effects that match the style you are looking for, but have found this very useful, especially when overlaying quotes and references. Ultimately, I hope you'll agree these much more visually appealing than just placing a plain line of text on the slide.

Animations

Without a doubt, animations are one of the most abused features of many presentations. Over the many years of watching presentations, I've witnessed bouncing text, spinning logos, and bullet points that have visually caught on fire, all of which have done absolutely nothing to enhance the quality of the presentation in any way.

On the flip side, removing all animations can make for a very stark and jarring presentation. Objects that suddenly appear out of nowhere, or text that appears with no animation, can appear subconsciously harsh for the audience.

The key to successful animations is to achieve a balance in between.

Animations should help the audience transition from object to object, and slide to slide, without the audience really noticing, and certainly without any gratuitous pyrotechnics! In this section of adding the fine details to your presentation, I wanted to share some recommendations for doing just this.

What should you be animating?

Even with a subtle set of animations, it can be tempting to animate many of things in your presentation. To support transitions for the audience however, it really is only necessary to animate (or provide a transition for) any new content that the audience will see. This should include the following:

- **New slides.** As new slides are presented to the audience they should support some kind of transition. Again, this transition should be subtle. Your taste might vary, but I would recommend using the Fade transition in Microsoft PowerPoint, as shown in Figure 6.20.

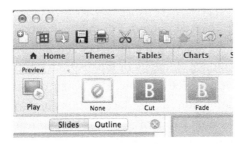

Figure 6.20 - The Fade transition in Microsoft PowerPoint.

This particular transition gradually introduces the upcoming slide, while fading out the current slide. The effect for the audience is subtle enough to indicate something is changing without the animation standing out on its own. With all of the transitions in Microsoft PowerPoint, you can also experiment with the timing of the transition. Personally, I find around 0.75 seconds to be suitable for

271

slide transitions, but your mileage might vary.

- **Lists.** As we discussed in Chapter 4, any list of text, graphics, or other objects you use in your presentation slide deck should also be introduced gradually. This means that each item should be introduced manually as you are speaking to that point, rather than putting them all on screen at once. In Chapter 4, we used the default Appear animation for the sake of time, but this is also a great time to go back and select a different build type to suit your presentation. As with the transition effect, I would again recommend using the Fade entrance effect for introducing text, shapes, and other objects. There is also a Fade exit effect, if you ever have the need to remove text from the slide in the same way.

In terms of timing, you'll likely want individual objects to appear slightly quicker than it would take a slide transition, therefore an animation time of less than 0.75 seconds makes sense here, probably one around 0.5 seconds or less.

- **Diagrams.** We covered diagrams at the beginning of this chapter. To restate, if you are walking the audience through a complex diagram, you should introduce elements of the diagram through animations. As you might have guessed by now, I'm going to recommend that you use the Fade animation to introduce sections or parts of your diagram in sequence. As with list items, I would recommend choosing a build time of around 0.5 seconds to make the animation more subtle for the audience.

If your diagram is overly complex instead of having to apply a build animation for many different parts, you should consider using the Group option by creating groups out of multiple pieces of the diagram, and then applying the build animation on that group.

Being consistent

While I have tried to heavily influence your use of the Fade effect for both slide transitions and object builds in the last section, you are free to use any animation that you think might fit with your presentation style or theme.

If there was one piece of advice I would give, however, it would be to ensure that all of the animation that you choose is consistent throughout your presentation. If you select a particular slide transition, ensure that every slide supports it. If you deviate from the Fade transition for build objects, ensure that every object builds using the same animation.

Finally, please also avoid the cardinal sin of using the Random animation build or transition for any of your deck. Doing so not only means that you'll lose control of your content during your time on stage, but the end result will look scattered and unprofessional.

When should the animation occur?

After you've decided what elements to apply a transition to, and which effects to use, an additional consideration should be as to when you should apply the animation.

In general there are two options for applying an animation—either on the click of a mouse (or presentation remote) or a timed effect where the animation occurs after a preset amount of time.

Both of these have their advantages and disadvantages, but in general I would recommend sticking to enabling animations using your presentation remote. Even though complex slides will often require multiple clicks before they are fully built, by doing so you will gain much more control over your animation and will have the ability to go faster or slower as you might wish. In addition, if someone in the audience asks you a question mid-slide, the last thing you would want is for various parts of the rest of the slide to be animating while you are giving your answer.

There is one exception to this rule, however, and this is if and when you are using information on a slide that is related to what you are showing, but not directly tied to the speaking point. A good example could be the legend of a graph that you are introducing. The legend (representing the colors shown on the graph) might appear slightly behind the actual transition of the graph itself. Unless you are walking through the legend point by point, it can likely be animated after the graph has appeared and while you are still talking.

Multiple slides vs. Single slide with animation

If you have been playing around with slide transitions and animations so far, you may notice that there is little difference between having multiple slides containing information that builds upon each other versus a single slide that uses multiple animations to get to the same point. This is especially true if you use the same animation effect as both will look virtually identical to one another.

Many of the topics covered to date have recommended leaving the content spread across multiple slides as opposed to creating a complex animation on a single slide.

There are of course advantages and disadvantages of both approaches. The advantage of splitting up a conceptual animation across multiple slides is that the animation will be somewhat preserved if the presentation is shared as a PDF afterward. Each page of the PDF will represent a single slide, which in turn represents a single stage of the animation. Splitting animations across slides can also make it easy to find and adjust elements, especially for animations that potentially might be covering other elements in the slide.

Of course, there are disadvantages also. If you make one change to the animation, then this change has to be reflected in all subsequent slides that contain this item. For example, if you added an item to a list, all slides after the new item would need to be modified as well.

It's worth reviewing your own presentation at this point, especially if you have been following along over the course of the previous chapters, to see which of the two options will work best for you.

Path transitions

To close out this section on animations I wanted to introduce one more. Up to this point you might be thinking that I am completely against the majority of animation and build effects that is supplied by Microsoft PowerPoint or Apple Keynote. While this is mostly true (Microsoft PowerPoint ships with dozens of animation effects, and I rarely use all but one), there is an exception to the rule: the path transition.

A path transition is a transition between slides that involves an element or object moving along a path to support the next slide. The path transition can be a very powerful way of taking a concept within one section of your presentation and expanding upon it in another.

The path transition works by creating a copy of the same object on both the before and after slide during a transition. The object can be in the same location and same size—or for a more dramatic effect, can be located elsewhere on the slide and of a different size. To see this in effect, let's take a quick look at how this might work using the Magic Move function in Apple Keynote.

Thinking back to our GPS example, let's look at a slide that we used previously in the chapter, now imported into Apple Keynote, as shown in Figure 6.21.

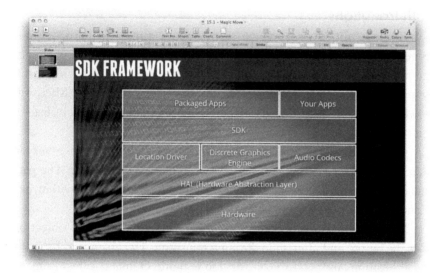

Figure 6.21 - SDK Framework slide in Apple Keynote.

As you can see, the slide shows our conceptual SDK framework. Let's imagine that we were going through the details on the slide, and wanted to dig deeper into the "Packaged Apps" part of the framework. To do this, we create a second slide and copy/paste the "Packaged Apps" text box to a location on the slide, as shown in Figure 6.22.

Figure 6.22 - The "Packaged Apps" text box copied and pasted on a following slide.

Once this is done, we highlight both slides and using the inspector as shown in Figure 6.23, configure the transition to be set as Magic Move.

Figure 6.23 - Using the inspector in Apple Keynote to implement a Magic Move.

Of course, it's impossible to show this in a book, but during the transition, the Magic Move effect fades out the first slide, with the exception of the "Packaged Apps" text box, which gets transformed to match it's new location on the second slide. Not only is the transition subtle, but it also provides a way for the audience to have extended context between slides, especially when digging deeper into a framework or complex subject such as the one shown in the example.

Packaging the deck

Over the past three chapters, we've covered a lot of information and detail for creating a compelling presentation. At this point, I wanted to spend a little time on packaging your presentation. By packaging, I'm referring to the first and last slides, typically the title slide and final slide in your deck, as well as what the audience will experience when they first walk into the room.

Title slide

The title slide is the first slide in your deck, and will contain the information that the audience immediately sees as they walk in the room and start to take their seats. As a result, it should be simple, and contain the necessary information for the audience at that point. In general, a good title slide will have the following elements:

- **Title.** The title of your presentation, as discussed at the end of Chapter 3. If your session is also listed in any agenda slide or handout, it should match word for word to avoid any confusion.

- **Your name.** Your full name should be visible on the slide.

- **Your title.** Including your title is important, especially if you are presenting to an external audience. If you are presenting to an audience who already knows you well, you can consider omitting this.

- **Your company name.** If applicable, the name of your company, organization, or group. If you are presenting to an audience who already knows you well, like the title, you can also consider omitting this.

- **Session code or other details.** If the presentation is part of a track at a conference you may be given a session code. Although it's not as important as the title or your name, you should also include it.

- **Contact details.** You should include at least one method of contact information for the audience to reach you. I would recommend either your email address or twitter handle (if you are active on social networks). Avoid including too much contact information, as you don't want to turn the first slide into a contact card, and I would avoid including any telephone numbers, website addresses, or URLs that the audience can't immediately remember, as these all have the potential to change, and frankly probably aren't that useful for the audience at this point.

Layout and template

The layout of your title slide is important, and you'll want to ensure that the important pieces of your title slide content are displayed in the right way. There are many templates to help, and Figure 6.24 shows one of the sample layouts that you can use.

Figure 6.24 - Slide layout using a sample template.

As shown, the title of the presentation is the most prominent. The contact details are contained within an offset block, right justified.

The reason that I'm using a sample template here is that if you are presenting at a conference or event, there is a good chance that the organizers will have provided a template for you to use. While I strongly rejected the idea of using a supplied template in Chapter 4, the title slide is one exception. Having a custom title slide isn't going to add a tremendous amount of audience value, and including a style that goes against the grain of the template used at the conference will likely be a battle that's not worth fighting. My recommendation is that if you are given a slide template, use it for your title slide, but as soon as you "click" into your opening story, the content should be yours to own.

What will people see when they walk in the room?

Many conferences and events have breaks between sessions. With people moving between rooms and sessions, there's a good chance that you will have people in the audience filing into the room several minutes before you are due to start. While the title slide is confirmation that they are in the right session, it can also serve as a communication vehicle between you and the first people who are just finding their seats.

A good example of this can be found in many sessions presented by a good friend of mine, Miha Kralj. While Miha puts together a fairly standard looking title slide, he often has the title slide on an animation loop with other facts about the subject he is presenting on. Every few seconds the presentation will switch between the standard title slide and one or more new facts for the audience. While I've not tried this myself, and while this will really only work with larger audiences for sessions that have breaks in between them, it can be a great way of touching upon some of the topics that you might be covering in your presentation, as well as providing additional value for the early arrivers to your session.

A variation on this, and something that I have used in the past, is to answer any immediate questions that the audience might have about the session. Before one of my talks, I had noticed that many early arrivers in the audience were coming up to the podium asking the same question, "I'm looking forward to your presentation, but will you be covering X?" The title of my presentation was a little generic, so this was a fair question. To help other early arrivers, I put together a second title slide that answered this question by showing the three things that I would be covering (and not be covering). While this led to some initial dissatisfaction in the audience (I saw a couple of people leave when they realized the answer to the question wasn't what they were looking for), and while this proved to be a good lesson for me in creating more accurate titles, it did guarantee that the expectations of the audience members already in the room were more accurately met.

Final slide

Similar to the opening slide, the final slide should be simple and to the point. The purpose of the final slide is not to conclude the presentation (as you will have already covered this when creating your conclusion section in Chapter 3), but instead provide opportunity for a final thank you and to add your contact details.

As with the title slide, if the conference or event that you are speaking at has provided a template, I would recommend using it. Doing so can help bring the audience "back" into the conference. The final slide should be a single slide that has the following three pieces of information:

- **Thank you.** Preferably in the middle of the slide, in a readable font used previously in the deck, place the words "Thank you" on your final slide. The audience has invested a lot of time listening to your presentation, so the least you can do is thank them for their time. This should also coincide with you verbally thanking the audience, which we will cover in the next chapter.

- **Contact details.** Assuming that you would like your audience to follow up with you if they desire, the final slide is a great place to add your contact information. Similar to the title slide, you should keep this to your email address or twitter handle. If the audience wishes to follow up with you this is enough information.

- **One piece of follow up.** In addition to your contact details, it is nice to have one piece of follow up information. This might be the URL to your website, or some other key location that the audience might want to go visit following your presentation. For example, if you are going to be headed to a particular place after the session (such as the expo hall in a trade show), this could be a great piece of information to share. A good place to start is to look through the "calls to action" that were developed during Chapter 3. Selecting the most important one out of the list can make for a good final URL.

An example of a final slide containing these three elements can be seen in Figure 6.25.

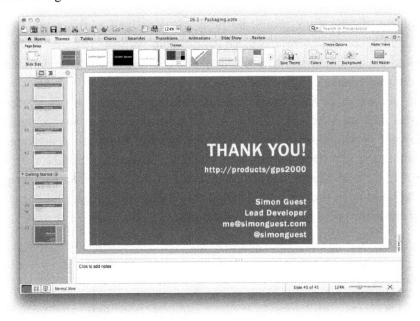

Figure 6.25 - A simple ending slide.

The key with this information, however, is to keep it as brief as possible. You'll have already run through your conclusion by this point, so you should think of the final slide as a way to "sign out" rather than a slide that you are going to speak to.

In addition, and as we've mentioned on a couple of previous occasions, remember to evaluate the length of any URLs that you share with the audience to make sure they are concise and easy to write down!

Where are we?

Over the course of this chapter, we've covered many fine details for your presentation, including creating diagrams, inserting screenshots, clippings and references, dealing with animations, and packaging the deck by adding a title and final slide.

If you have been following along with your own presentation, the content of your deck should be fairly close to final at this stage. You should becoming more and more comfortable with the material at each pass, and the quality of the deck should be of a high enough standard that you would consider using this on stage.

As we've covered at the end of previous chapters, this is another great time for a rehearsal. Doing so will help add another layer of polish to your presentation and will commit to memory some of the diagrams, animations, and transitions that you've added during this chapter.

In the next chapter, we are going to dig a little deeper into rehearsing, and build upon the packaging that we covered in this chapter by starting to create the opening for your presentation.

---

1. Courtesy of: http://thedailywtf.com/Articles/Best_of_2006_0x3a__The_Customer-Friendly_System.aspx

2. The post human font can be downloaded here: http://www.dafont.com/post-human.font

3. If you'd like to see a full presentation that uses this style, you can visit: http://www.slideshare.net/simonguest/patterns-for-cloud-computing (from Slide 44 onward)

CHAPTER 7: Rehearsing

★ ★ ★

If you had skimmed through the table of contents of this book before reading it, you might have thought that this chapter would have been the place where you would be starting to rehearse your presentation. If you've followed each chapter of the book to this stage, however, you'll know that rehearsals can't and don't wait until Chapter 7!

The good news is that you've already gone through four, if not more, rehearsals of your presentation by this stage. Starting with a rough rehearsal of the mind map and going through the pencil sketch, composition, and fine details chapters you've had the opportunity to run through the presentation on many occasions. By this stage, the "muscle memory" for your presentation will be fairly strong, and I suspect that there will be many slides and sections in the deck where you just "know what's coming next" well before you press the button to advance the slide.

In this chapter, we will be adding more polish to your rehearsals. We'll start by covering the opening of your presentation, talk about rehearsing humor (yes, that's possible!), cover rehearsing in the actual room that you will be presenting in, and end by covering different rehearsal types including a final timed and recorded rehearsal.

The goal of this chapter is to give you additional tools to continually improve your presentation through strong rehearsal techniques.

Opening your presentation

As a presenter, the opening of your talk is one of the most crucial parts, if not the most crucial part of your presentation, which is one of the reasons it has been left until this stage in the book. In the first 30 seconds of a presentation, the audience will begin to form an opinion about your skills as a presenter, and ultimately a mental prediction of how good (or bad) the next hour or so will be. Therefore, it is vital that the opening of your talk paints a positive picture that leads into the rest of the presentation.

There are many varied ways of opening a presentation. I find that many presenters, especially those who are new to giving presentations, gravitate towards the "Who am I?" speech in order to create the opening. Often, a speaker will start with something similar to the following:

> Hello. My name is Simon Guest. Welcome to this presentation on Developing for the GPS-2000. I'm the group manager of the product development team at ACME Corporation. I report to David Smith, and my team is responsible for development and tier two and three product support for our medium to large customers, so there is a good chance that you've run into one of us when you have called the call center...

On first read, this might sound good. The speaker has introduced themselves and supplied some factual information to the audience about who they are. While this might be true, let's decompose the opening to investigate the parts individually.

> Hello.

We have an opening word, which is nice, but we need to be careful of two things. Can the audience hear you, and is the audience ready to hear you?

If this conference is like most, there will be a lot of conversation in the audience before you begin. The issue with background conversation is that if you start with "Hello. My name is Simon Guest. Welcome to…", there's a good chance that you could reach the third sentence before the audience is quiet and attentive. Also, if the microphone needs turning up, the audio team in the room might compound the effect. As an audience member, this can be annoying as they would have missed two sentences of the opening, including the presenter's name. Is this Simon speaking?

As a presenter, you need to signal to the audience that you are ready to start. This is also a polite way of asking them to end their conversations. Many presenters just do this by announcing the intent.

OK! I think we are ready to begin.

This works most of the time, but there is a slightly different way of doing this that can create a better connection with everyone in the room.

To start, you'll want to announce the general time of day. Assuming it's morning, this could be as follows:

Good morning!

This should be said in your loudest voice. You want to capture the attention of the room, which includes the folks standing at the very back, so announce this much louder than you normally would. Then pause.

You want to leave about three seconds. In this short pause you are waiting for the audience to reply back to you.

Assuming that everyone has heard you, leaving this pause will help the room become quiet. You may also get a few quiet "Good morning" replies from the front row. Our first objective is complete. The microphone works, and the room is quiet. Our second objective is to now grab the attention of the audience.

To do this, in the same loud voice, repeat the line.

Good morning!

This second line will sound even louder than the first as you are no longer fighting over the audience's conversation. It will also (in 99.9% of cases where I've tried this) generate a positive reaction from the audience, who will reply with an equally loud, "Good morning!" and usually a smile when they realize that you were waiting for a reply. You now have the audio level and audience attention. Let's move on.

My name is Simon Guest.

The speaker is telling the audience their name. This isn't necessarily bad, but if you've been following the previous chapter, you'll know that the speaker's name is on the title slide, in which case it is a little redundant. Also, depending on the audience, the full name is a little formal. You still need to indicate that you are the speaker, but opening with "My name is Simon" can create a friendlier bond with the audience, if that's desired. There is also a variation on this if you happen to know some of the audience. Remember the second question in Chapter 2 where we covered having a personal connection with the audience? If you believe that this might be the case, you can prepend "For those who I haven't yet met" to the opening.

For those who I haven't yet met, my name is Simon.

This can be effective as it supports the shorter name and creates a stronger personal connection with the audience. There are hidden messages, even in this short line. Firstly, it shows the audience that you know some of them. For those in the audience who don't know you, this can be reassuring. Secondly, it indicates that you intend to meet other people in the audience. Don't worry—no one is going to expect you to do personal introductions to a crowd of hundreds after the talk! Finally, it makes you sound more extroverted. It implicitly says that you are a social person that likes to meet and talk to people, even if you are an introvert locked up writing code with no desire for human contact! Let's move on with analyzing the opening.

Welcome to this presentation on Developing for the GPS-2000.

Assuming the title of the talk is "Developing for the GPS-2000," the speaker is introducing the title of the session, which isn't horrible, but as with the name, it's probably redundant. Any good title slide will have the session title on it, and people are generally good about knowing which presentation or session they are attending. In all of my experience presenting and watching others present, I've never seen an audience member realize that they were in the wrong session after the speaker had started.

> I'm the group manager of the product support team at ACME Corporation. I report to David Smith, and my team is responsible for development and tier two and three product support for our medium to large customers, so there is a good chance that you've run into one of us when you have called the call center.

This is where it gets bad. There's no easy way of saying this, so I'm just going to come out with it. No one cares. Really. You may think that it's really important to tell people who you are, or who you report to, or what your team does, or where someone has interacted with you or your team—but it's not. I've seen presenters who go even further with minutes of diatribe about what they or their team has accomplished, organizational charts, and on one occasion I was even horrified with a "speaker bio slide."

This is not an interview. No one in the audience has come to your presentation to find out this information about you. If they wanted to know this, they could catch you at the end of your talk and arrange a coffee. The audience wants to know about the subject of your presentation, and the quicker you get to the subject, the better.

Of course, with this said, there is need for a transition. It would be very strange to have an opening like this one:

> Good morning. My name is Simon. Our previous GPS devices

didn't work that well.

This just sounds bizarre, and although the presentation needs to get to the main topic quickly, there is a need to ease the audience in.

There are two parts to such a transition. The first part gets the audience accustomed to your voice. This is important, as you want everyone to tune in to your particular style of speech. Listing off the name of the session is one way to do this, but a much more effective way is to introduce a positive comment or compliment for the audience. Here's an example:

> Good morning. My name is Simon. I want to say how honored I am to be here today. This developer conference is one of my favorite events in the year, as I really enjoy feedback from audiences like yourselves.

This is the first part of the transition. The audience has the chance to get accustomed to your voice, and they learn some new information—that you are pleased to be here. They also received a compliment. It's a very subtle compliment, but nonetheless it will help create a positive mood in the room.

You can, and should, modify this introductory part to match your own situation. Maybe you are visiting a new city or country, in which case you can use this as a reference.

> Hello. My name is Simon. Thank you for inviting me today to speak. Vienna is one of my favorite cities. I had the chance to spend some time in the city over the weekend, and the architecture is just amazing.

Again, we have a similar construction with the subtle compliment. This time it is not directed at the audience, but instead at the surroundings. Assuming that the audience lives in or around the area, and that you are visiting from out of town, this is also interpreted as a compliment.

As you may do in a regular conversation, be careful not to overdo the compliment piece in the first transition. You certainly don't want to spend five minutes gushing about the audience or introducing one compliment after another, as after a couple of sentences it will become cringe-worthy and the audience will be questioning your motives.

The second part of the transition is where the presentation moves from the opening into the actual content. As you'll recall from Chapter 2, the opening piece of content is going to be your opening story. We'll need something to transition to this opening story, and it can be as simple as this:

> To start, I'd like to tell you a story.

Coming back to our GPS example, here's a line that we could potentially use:

> I'd like to start by sharing a story about Edna.

The key to the second part of the transition is to keep it personal. The speaker is moving from a personal introduction to the story, so the "I" part of the sentence is important. Transitioning with a "we've been doing some research" would technically work, but the ownership has moved away from the speaker, which takes away that personal connection. As the opening story is truly a story, it should be told as one by the speaker.

We've covered several points, so let's recap by looking at where we are. Recall our original opening:

> Hello. My name is Simon Guest. Welcome to this presentation on Developing for the GPS-2000. I'm the group manager of the developer team at ACME Corporation. I report to David Smith, and my team is responsible for development and tier two and three product support for our medium to large customers, so there is a good chance that you've run into one of us when you have called the call center…

Although it wasn't going to take down the presentation in flames, it wasn't a great opening, either. It's full of one-way information that lacks a personal connection with the audience. Now let's compare it with our new opening:

> Good morning! (Pause, waiting for audience to be attentive.) Good morning! For those who I haven't yet met, my name is Simon, and I'd like to thank you for inviting me to speak today. This developer conference is one of my favorite events, as I really value the great conversation with folks like yourselves. Now, I wanted to start by sharing a story of one of our customers, Edna... (Click to the opening slide.)

Much better!

Humor

We've all been impressed, entertained, and amazed at speakers whose humor seems to come naturally to them. We've all wanted to be that person when we present, and many of us have tried on several occasions. Although it might seem to come naturally, doing humor well is a very tough subject. Even the presenters who are the best at humor have spent years crafting the art of being funny. Scott Hanselman, a colleague when I was at Microsoft, has a reputation for delivering lines that are perfectly timed and incredibly funny. Even though I would argue he has a natural gift, what many people don't know about Scott is that he spent a lot of time on the comedy circuit in order to hone his skills.

When humor works in a presentation it can result in great audience feedback. The problem is that when humor is done badly, it is terrible. Bad, poorly timed, or inappropriate humor can leave the audience cringing and will kill any presentation regardless of the quality of content.

There are many other books on learning to be funny, telling jokes, or generally understanding the construction of a humorous comment. While

I won't go into any of the details in this chapter, I wanted to share some recommendations for your own presentation that you might find useful:

- **Be yourself.** The first, and most important, recommendation I can give when considering humor is to simply be yourself. Don't try to be someone else, or try to fool the audience into thinking that they are getting a funnier version of yourself. If you wouldn't have told a similar joke or punchline in conversation, please don't put it in your presentation. Likewise, if you take a lighthearted approach to conversation, ensure that it's the same you during the presentation. Be sure to smile, be sure to enjoy yourself during the presentation, but most importantly, be yourself.

- **Rehearse your humor.** If you have jokes, lines, and other sayings that you want to get out in your presentation, and that you believe will work with the audience, know that timing is everything. Get the timing of your punchline down to the second, and rehearse until you are spot on every time. I've seen great presenters tell the same jokes in the same way with the same timing on multiple presentations and they can pull it off every time.

- **Never laugh at your own jokes.** When you are on stage, avoid laughing at your own jokes or punchlines. Any laughter will be amplified through the microphone, which is a terrible acoustic effect for the audience and any recording, and if your joke doesn't work you'll be left with a deathly silence afterwards. Feel free to smile after delivering punchlines, but never laugh. Good jokes and punchlines let the audience laugh for you. Recently, I've been giving a presentation talking about mobile software development. One of the examples I give is of Angry Birds, a popular game on iOS and Android devices. When it came to the section of my presentation speaking about older Blackberry devices (which were text based), I dropped the punchline "Of course, Angry Birds wasn't so popular on this platform" before showing a screen full of the following text:

"Launch bird. Bird hits rock. Bird bounces." Clicking to the next slide and having the audience read the screen, and subsequently laugh at the joke, was enough. I didn't need to laugh for effect—and after I'd rehearsed this enough times, I knew that this was actually a great place to grab a drink of water.

- **Don't let the humor overtake the content.** If you are naturally funny, and I'm going to wager a guess that you are, feel free to use humor in your presentation—but don't overdo it. Having an hour's worth of jokes, quips, and punchlines might be great entertainment, but if it doesn't have the content to back it up the audience might leave the room a little "empty." I've seen a couple of presentations where the audience feedback was largely positive right after the delivery, yet the next day they couldn't actually remember any content from the deck.

- **If you are stuck…** Finally, a quick tip for if you are ever stuck in the middle of a presentation where you thought a joke would have worked, but it fell flat on it's face. This one I borrowed from Ian Phillips, a colleague of mine from back in the UK. During one of his presentations, he tried a joke that just didn't work. Everyone knew it was a joke, but several factors (including his session coming at the end of a long day) meant that the reaction was less than stellar. After a few seconds of dreaded deathly silence, Ian turned to the audience with a confused look, reached for a nearby piece of paper, and stared at it for a couple of seconds. His comment to the audience went something like, "That's strange. On my script here it says 'wait for the audience to laugh!'" It was of course particular to that situation, but this was very timely, well rehearsed, and a genius move to get the audience laughing and re-engaged with his content.

In-room rehearsal

When thinking about all of your rehearsals, I can't stress enough the importance of doing at least one in the room or area that you will be presenting in. It's not always possible to do this (e.g., if you are traveling to a customer site for the first time), but if you do have the opportunity, you should definitely take advantage. Doing so will give you an opportunity to "feel out" the room, checking audio, lighting, seating, and an array of other factors that you might not have thought about up until now. If you are presenting at a large conference spanning multiple days, you'll likely find that many organizers will be able to give you access to the room ahead of time, possibly during a lunch or other break before your timed slot. You won't need to cover your entire presentation during this slot, so should only need 15 to 30 minutes to run through enough slides to make you feel comfortable.

When you get to your room for this rehearsal, there are two areas that you should be looking to getting accustomed to: the general setup of the room, and the equipment that you'll be using, such as the audio and visual systems. Let's start first by looking at some of the considerations for how your room will be setup.

Room setup

One of the primary reasons for rehearsing in the room or area before is to understand the environmental considerations of the room. This might include the room setup, your position, lighting, and other factors, which can have a major impact on the presentation that you will be giving. To cover these angles, here is a list of questions that I would recommend asking when you reach the room:

- **How will the audience be seated?** Many rooms have particular seating layouts that the conference organizers will set up ahead of time. Such layouts might include a theater style (rows of chairs with or without tables), dining style (multiple round tables with chairs surrounding them), or a U style (a U-shaped arrangement of tables with chairs).

Getting to the rehearsal room early can help you determine what

295

seating arrangement will be used and whether you'll need to factor in any considerations as a result. For example, a U style layout can promote a more relaxed presentation style with the presenter able to walk around the space, whereas this will likely not be possible with a dining style setup.

When you arrive to the room, it's also worth double checking with the organizers to ensure that the seating layout you see during the rehearsal will be the one used for your presentation. As rooms are often used for more than one function, on more than one occasion I've seen the table and chair layout change between a rehearsal and the actual day of the presentation.

- **Where will you be standing?** Understanding your audience seating is useful, but it's equally important to get a feel of where you will be presenting to your audience. It might be behind a podium on the floor, on a raised platform with a lot of table space, or somewhere in between. Either way, having an idea of how you will be presenting to the audience and what will be in front of you will help you become adjusted to the room.

- **Where will your laptop be?** Assuming that you are bringing your own laptop with you (which, as we'll cover later in the anti-patterns in Chapter 10, I thoroughly recommend), you'll want to know where it will be positioned. Is it going to have to be on an angle on a podium? Will this affect your ability to type or use a mouse/trackpad during your demo, if needed? Will it be on a low table that might also make it difficult if you need to switch to it for a demo? Can you see your laptop from the podium? As you will be relying on your laptop to show you what the audience is seeing, you'll want to ensure that it is clearly in view.

Getting these questions answered during the rehearsal as opposed to a few minutes before you start will definitely be less stressful!

- **What is the lighting setup?** One of the things I noticed with my own presentations is that large rooms are often lit with very powerful stage lighting. As a presenter, such lighting means that you may not be able to see anyone in the audience beyond the first couple of rows, and the direct spotlights can make you much warmer on stage.

  Conversely, you might find yourself presenting in a room that is very well lit with natural light. While this can be a pleasure to present in such settings, getting to the room early can also be a good test to see whether this amount of natural light might interfere with the projector, and whether you'll need to block out some of windows as a result.

- **Where will people be coming from?** For most presentations, you'll find that people will be entering from the back of the room or area, opposite from where you are standing, but it can still be worth checking to ensure this is the case. Having latecomers walk in front of you during your presentation can be fairly distracting (to you and the audience!), so checking for other entrance points or ensuring that side doors are locked and well sign-posted can be useful.

  As you do more presentations, you will be surprised by the flow of the audience in and out of various rooms. On one occasion, it wasn't until halfway through the presentation I discovered that the door to the left of the stage was actually the bathroom (I was presenting at the back of one of Microsoft's retail stores). The audience certainly found it amusing when a mother and her two children made their way between me and the projector in order to use the facilities!

Museum of flight

On several occasions I've found myself walking into a room with an image of what the setup will be like, only to find that it was completely different. On one such occasion, I was asked to present at the San Diego Air and Space Museum. The Museum is a beautiful building, home to many great aviation artifacts, and I was looking forward to the opportunity of presenting there.

My experience, however, was vastly different, when I found out that the museum is in the direct flight path of the San Diego airport. Combined with the glass roof of the museum, I had to cope with the roar of jet engines overhead every few minutes during my presentation. Although I couldn't prevent this, having the opportunity to check out the space before my presentation allowed me to make some accommodations for the interruptions (as well as rehearse some well-timed, aviation-related jokes!)

Audio, visual, and equipment checks

While the room setup will give you an understanding of the layout for your presentation, rehearsing in the actual room will give you the opportunity to test audio, video, and any other equipment that you'll be using for your presentation. Testing all of this ahead of time will ensure that the presentation will look its best to the audience, and will often surface some "gotchas" that are much easier to fix during a rehearsal as opposed to in front of a waiting audience.

Following on from the room setup, here are a list of questions that I would recommend asking during your checks:

- **Does the audio work?** Assuming that you are presenting in a large enough room to warrant a microphone, I highly recommend testing the audio ahead of time. Doing so will ensure that you are comfortable with the microphone that you are using, and will also give you a feel for how you sound in the room. If you are in an extremely large room, it's always useful to have someone stand at the back of the room to ensure that they can hear you clearly, understanding that you'll also need to speak a little louder once the room is full. Many conferences will have a dedicated audio/visual (A/V) team that can help you with this, and will likely be adjusting the volumes for you, especially if your presentation is being recorded.

- **What type of microphone will you be using?** There are many types of microphones available for presentations, the most common being lapel based (the main unit will clip to your belt, and a small microphone is placed about six inches under your chin). The device has a small on/off switch normally on the top or side that you can control, if necessary. Many also have a battery indicator—something that I would definitely double check ahead of time also.

If you are presenting at a larger venue, you might be given a headset style microphone that clips to one ear and wraps around your head. You typically won't be able to turn these on and off, but the A/V team will definitely help here. As a presenter, I don't recommend using a handheld microphone unless you are participating in a question and answer session. While convenient to pass around, a handheld microphone is awkward to use for longer periods of time, and almost impossible to use if you have to hold the microphone in one hand while doing a demo using the other.

Again, this rehearsal provides an excellent opportunity to become familiar with the microphone that you are allocated, as well as make any adjustments if necessary. If you don't feel comfortable, you should have ample opportunity to address this before your presentation starts.

- **Does your laptop need audio out?** If you are showing any videos or playing music during your presentation, you'll want to work with the conference organizers to ensure that this works in your rehearsal. Often the A/V system will have a 3.5mm jack that you can plug directly into your machine's headphone slot. Unless you are in a very small room (with no more than five people), please don't try and use the speakers on your laptop. I've witnessed many people go down this path with less than optimal results.

- **Can I connect my laptop to the projector?** One of the most important checks during the in-room rehearsal is to ensure that your laptop can work with the projector provided. Often the first thing is to check that you have the right connections.

Although things are changing, at the time of writing, the standard connection type for many projectors is VGA. While it doesn't offer a phenomenal resolution, it does provide the most compatible interface with the widest range of machines. If you are presenting often, you'll definitely want to ensure that your machine has some kind of VGA-out (for some newer laptops this might mean an additional cable).

Over the past two years, I've also found that HDMI is becoming more widely accepted for projection units, especially for larger conferences or areas where you will be presenting using a large LCD or LED display. While I haven't yet come across any setups that are exclusively HDMI only, having the necessary cables can mean that you can take advantage where possible.

Finally, many organizations are offering the ability for presenters to remotely present through devices such as AppleTV connected to a projector. This can be convenient, allowing multiple presenters to follow each other without having to worry about whether the "cord will reach." While this setup is likely limited today, and the technology is still evolving, it's always a good idea to ensure that your machine could present, if needed.

- **Does the projector force my laptop into a "bulky" resolution?** One of the main issues when connecting to a projector is to ensure that the screen display and resolution are correct. Especially the case with VGA projectors, I've experienced that when connecting to many, the resolution on my laptop will randomly change, often to something that makes everything look very big. While this doesn't affect any Microsoft PowerPoint or Apple Keynote presentation, any demos that you have planned will likely look bulky and things will have to be resized to accommodate. Often the issue can be resolved by experimenting with different resolutions (I've always had the most luck with 1024x768). But again, this is something that is much easier to deal with during the rehearsal.

- **Can the audience read everything?** Even when you have the correct resolution on your machine, it's vitally important to check that the audience is able to read everything on the screen, especially the ones sitting in the back row of the room. This is most important when coming to demos, and something that we'll explore in a lot more detail in Chapter 8. Any fonts (e.g., some code that you are planning to show in an IDE) should be adjusted so that they are easily readable from the back of the room. Your situation will vary, but I've found a font size between 18pt and 22pt seems to work well for large rooms (even though it might look ghastly to write code in). To test, simply adjust the font size, and walk to the back of the room. If you can read the text without squinting, you are probably good.

One caveat to the large font, however, is the inability to show as much information. I've seen several presenters stumble with this, especially when walking the audience through code. They'll adjust their font size and what used to be a couple of paragraphs of code now turns out to be multiple pages, or longer lines go off the end of the screen, requiring the presenter to scroll down and sometimes even get lost! To avoid this, after you've found the correct font size for the projector and room, I would definitely recommend re-rehearsing any demos that you are planning to show. Given that the resolution of your display may have changed, this is also good practice.

- **Does the room meet my network requirements?** We'll again cover this in more detail in Chapter 8, but if you are showing any demo that requires networking I would heavily recommend turning off wireless networking and use a fixed Ethernet point instead. Doing so will greatly reduce your chance of the network dropping out, especially if your audience is hammering the wireless networks with their laptops, tablets, and phones.

Once you have your Ethernet connection, instead of just pulling up a web page to make sure things work, you should definitely re-run through your demo—especially if you have other requirements such as connecting to a VPN. Doing so will test that the quality and performance of the network connection is going to be sufficient. The network speed that you've been accustomed to in your office might not be the same as the one that you are being supplied in the conference room of the hotel!

• **What other needs do I have?** The in-room rehearsal is an excellent opportunity to also check any other extra needs that you might require for your presentation. As I've mentioned on several occasions during this section, finding and fixing issues during the in-room rehearsal will be a lot easier than having to deal with them in front of a packed audience who are waiting for you to start!

Additional rehearsal techniques

As you've likely guessed by this point, the more you rehearse, the better the quality of your presentation delivery will be. To emphasize this, I wanted to end this chapter by covering three types of different rehearsals that you might not have yet considered, but can be very effective for improving the quality of your presentation.

The external rehearsal

With the exception of the first rehearsal of the mind map that we covered in Chapter 3, most of your rehearsals have been solo. While this is useful in helping polish your presentation, by this point your presentation should be in a state where it can be rehearsed in front of a small group of people.

Doing a rehearsal in front of an external group will not only better simulate presenting in front of a larger audience, but you'll also be able to garner feedback from the group about elements of your presentation such as the quality of your slides, your opening, and how you communicate.

If you do go ahead with an external group, you should carefully seek out representatives that closely match the personas that you developed in Chapter 2. It might be easier to convince a couple of your peers to come down to the conference room over lunch, but unless they are representative of your audience, you run the risk of getting feedback that might not be relevant or actionable. You may also get feedback that sends your presentation in the wrong direction!

Accept any and all feedback gracefully, and ensure that the external group sits through your rehearsal and takes notes rather than interrupting you in the middle of each slide. This works out well as the group can compare and share notes at the end, even if the feedback is delivered verbally.

Finally, as a presenter, you should take each piece of feedback with a grain of salt. The best type of feedback are the small actionable points that will enhance the quality of the presentation. For example, pointing out that the font size on the third slide was slightly too small is great feedback that you may not have caught otherwise. Avoid falling into the trap of completely restructuring your presentation or making major changes to the presentation based on feedback from this external group. Not only will it likely be too late to restructure the presentation, but this external group is not a true representation of your audience. Kindly accept the feedback as something you'll think about and move on.

The dreaded recorded rehearsal

Every presenter has one or more speaking habits. It might be speaking too quickly, repeating words often, and commonly beginning sentences with the same word. I have several bad habits, including adding the word "So..." at the beginning of each sentence. I've seen other presenters using the word "...right?" at the end of each statement to give themselves some validation throughout the talk.

Many of these habits are really difficult to pick up on when you are delivering a presentation. Often the audience might notice them, but they will be too polite to mention them to you at the end of your talk. Also, the severity of the habits might not be apparent if someone just mentions it in passing.

To get a handle on your own speaking habits, you need to do a recorded rehearsal. Doing a recorded rehearsal is fairly straightforward, and instead of capturing just video and audio from the laptop, I would recommend setting up a tripod with a physical camera in the room. By using an actual recording device you'll also be able to pick up on other physical habits such as pacing across the stage or other gesticulations that you might be making. Don't get me wrong—most people I know, myself included, hate watching themselves on video. I find nothing worse than hearing myself present and picking up on all of the idiosyncrasies of my dialect or presentation style, but it is a very effective tool to help improve the quality of your delivery.

Addressing these bad habits can, however, be a little more challenging. Just because you are able to recognize them from watching a video doesn't mean that you'll be consciously correcting them when you next present. To start, I recommend picking one habit, preferably the major one that you most want to address, and write one or two words in large text on a piece of paper or a small Post-it note that you can stick on the edge of your laptop screen during your next presentation.

When I first immigrated to the United States, I was finding that I was speaking too quickly for most audiences (especially given that I had a different accent). This was quickly recognized after going through a recorded rehearsal and hearing it for myself. To address this, I simply wrote the words "SLOW DOWN" in large text on a Post-it note that I would make visible during each of my future presentations. As I glanced back at the screen during the presentation my eye would catch the Post-it note, which would be a frequent and conscious reminder to myself to check my speed ("Am I speaking too quickly?") and adjust, as necessary. The results weren't instant, but after applying this technique on several occasions I found that the adjustment became second nature.

The final rehearsal

By this point in the chapter (and possibly in the book), you might be exhausted from all the rehearsing! There is, however, one additional rehearsal that you need to do: a final, timed rehearsal.

With the presentation close to completion, you should add time in your rehearsal schedule for a final, timed rehearsal. This rehearsal will typically be one of the last that you do before you are ready to present. It will also be similar to many of the others that you have done up to this point, except you will be doing all parts of the presentation, and you will be timing yourself with a stopwatch (or other device).

The golden rule to this final rehearsal is that you must go through the entire presentation and any demos without stopping the timer. If you notice any errors or things needing fixing during the presentation have a pen and paper handy to jot them down, but do not fix them until the very end.

This final rehearsal will give you the best guide in terms of timing for an uninterrupted run through of your presentation.

Where are we?

In this chapter, we have built upon the theme of rehearsing found throughout the book, and refined the concept to include your opening, humor, in-room rehearsal, and additional techniques for perfecting your content.

However, with all of this focus on rehearsing, there is one time that I don't rehearse—just before I'm about to go on stage. It might sound strange, but I find that if I rehearse just before my main presentation, I walk in with a mindset of "the audience has already heard this." As a result, I find myself subconsciously omitting details because I just went through the same script a few minutes earlier. Again, your experience might be different, but in general I would recommend avoiding a full rehearsal right before you are taking the stage for this reason.

Finally, many of the rehearsal techniques that we have covered in this chapter have focused on preparing for demos. Given that demos are a major factor for many software developers this is a subject that I wanted to devote an entire chapter to, and something that we'll be covering next.

CHAPTER 8: Demos

✱ ✱ ✱

Many presentations include a demonstration (more affectionately known as a demo) in order to provide validation for the audience, as well as often serving as a natural and often needed break in between slides. For software developers, if slides are the "talk," then the demo is often the "walk."

If you are thinking about including a demo in your presentation, one of the first questions that you should ask yourself is why and what. Why is the demo necessary over showing similar information in slides? What will the audience get out of the demo? What are you hoping to get out of the demo? Well-received demos must have a purpose. Often that purpose falls within one of the following three categories:

1. **To reinforce the speaker's story**. One of the most common uses of a demo is to reinforce a point, or series of points, that the presenter has just made. Here, the presenter will make the point in slides, then break for a demo to visually show this to the audience. This concept provides the presenter a chance to relearn the information, as well as validation that what the presenter said is actually true. It's one thing for the presenter to repeat a few words on a slide. It's another for the same presenter to show how

this will work in front of a live audience.

2. **To reveal something new**. Many presenters will use demos to show something new. This might be a new product, prototype, or something else that has not yet been shown to the world. Here, the presenter wants to make an impact with the demo, and ultimately wants to make the audience feel like they are seeing something special for the first time. This type of reveal is often mostly used in keynote presentations, where a company or organization will be revealing one or more products as part of an annual conference.

3. **To show the audience how to do something**. Finally, demos can also be used to effectively show the audience how to do something. This might be an educational example, where the presenter is demonstrating part of the product in order to teach the audience how to do this for themselves. The goal for the presenter is to impart wisdom and knowledge so that the audience feels empowered to do something after the talk that they wouldn't have been able to do beforehand.

Often, the best demos are a combination of all three. A demo will connect with the audience if it supports the underlying story, reveals something new that the audience didn't know, and empowers the audience to do something that they couldn't do previously.

How many demos should I have?

How many demos should I have? This is a great question, and similar to our discussion in Chapter 4 about how many slides a presentation should have, the number doesn't really matter. In many cases, what's more important is the balance of demos to other content. Let's explore this in a little more detail.

Let's imagine that a presenter has a 75-minute presentation with one demo at the end. Without necessarily going into detail of the presentation content, the ratio of demos to slide content is probably going to be low. The demo might account for 5 or 10 minutes towards the end.

A second example is a speaker with a 75-minute presentation, but with 5 minutes worth of slide content, and then 70 minutes worth of demo. Again, let's not worry about the content for the minute, but just realize that this is of course the other end of the spectrum.

Why is this important? What would happen in the above examples if the demo were to fail? Both presentations would suffer, but there would be a marked difference in the situation. In the first example, the audience would likely be disappointed as the presentation led up to a demo in the end that ended up not working. It's likely that the speaker would have tried for a few minutes to recover the demo, after which they would have apologized to the audience. The audience would go away unhappy, but at least they got some value from the presentation.

In the second scenario, however, things are much different. Here, the audience has 5 minutes of content before everything comes crashing down around them. In this example, if the presenter is unable to recover the demo, they would be forced into a position where they would have to improvise or at least do something to avoid a mass evacuation by the audience.

With both these examples, I'm not saying that one is better over the other. The purpose of this is to show how demos rely on the presenter to have an extra level of preparation. This level of preparation is needed to defeat the one being that can ruin any presentation... The demo god!

Demo gods

The demo gods are cruel, unforgiving, and have a wicked sense of timing. Even when you are confident that you have tested everything, they will come unannounced to introduce issues that you will have never experienced before.

Although they can come in many guises, the demo gods repeatedly strike in three areas:

- **No network found!** Having a demo that relies on an active and relatively fast network connection is one of the finest invitations a demo god can ever receive. I've lost count of the number of demos that I've either presented or seen from others that have failed in some way due to networking. Often the network will just drop out in the middle of the demo, leaving the presenter with a "Page Not Found" error message when they least expect it. Other times, the network will work, but will have the speed and performance equivalent to someone trailing through thick mud. The speaker will be faced with a spinning hourglass or loading bar, forced to interject some conversation as the audience waits for the demo to reach the next stage.

This effect is compounded with wireless networking. Especially true at large conferences, having a demo that relies on the wireless network in the same room as 1,000 people also using the wireless network is generally a bad idea. This has caught many people out, including the late Steve Jobs during the iPhone 4 launch event where he had to ask the audience to turn off Wi-Fi and Bluetooth on their devices in order for the demo to work.

Although a wired (often referred to as Ethernet) connection can help, as a speaker you should never go into a demo that has a dependency on the network without some kind of backup plan.

- **But it worked in my hotel room...** In an effort to be more prepared, it is a good idea to rehearse your demos well ahead of your presentation. Doing so will increase the chances of success.

Despite this, however, I have on multiple occasions experienced a situation where the demo worked flawlessly just before beginning my presentation, only to fall to pieces on stage. I remember vividly one occasion when I was presenting to an important customer. I had spent weeks putting together what I believed would be an incredible demo, and even though it was fairly complex, thought that I had checked and double checked everything.

My presentation was to be held in the same hotel that I was staying in, so my plan was to rehearse the demo up in my hotel room until the last minute possible. After running the demo multiple times successfully in my hotel room, I walked downstairs with my laptop to the presentation room. Just to prove how paranoid I was, I actually kept the laptop open during the walk to avoid the machine going to sleep, and something potentially going wrong!

I plugged in my laptop at the podium, did a quick introduction and a few slides, before launching into the main part of the demo. Despite all of the additional preparation in the hotel room beforehand, the demo failed miserably and I was treated to a selection of error messages that I had never seen before.

The moral of the story is that despite how much preparation you put in, or how much you try to preserve the "working demo environment" before going on stage, things can and will still be affected by the demo gods.

- **The "baked" demo.** Finally, a variation of the previous situation, which can also strike at any time, is the "baked" demo. This is a demo which works fine up until the point that it is left on stage in front of an audience to "bake."

Let me give you an example. On a previous occasion, I was asked to present our group's early prototype to an internal audience of about two hundred. The schedule for the day was fairly packed, and I was following multiple presenters in quick succession. As a result of this, the team had setup a "Demo PC" at the podium, where all demos would be loaded on. The idea was that this dedicated machine would negate the need for speakers to switch laptops between presentations, and theoretically this should move things along quicker.

311

On the day of the presentation, I got to the room early to setup my demo on the podium PC. Installation went without a hitch, and the demo seemed to work well. In order to save time, I left the demo running on the machine, and simply moved it to the background. When it was my turn to speak, my intention was to come up on stage, bring the demo from the background, and I would be set.

It all seemed like a great plan, until it was indeed my turn to speak. I went up on stage, accessed the PC, brought up my demo from the background, and... nothing. The demo sat there, completely unresponsive, and what I had hoped would be an amazing demo of our prototype turned into several minutes of frustration trying to bring the demo back to life. Fortunately, on this occasion, I was able to quickly relaunch the demo to get things back into a working state, but the lesson of leaving demos to "bake" had definitely been learned.

Protecting against the demo gods

As you've hopefully gathered, and may have discovered from your own experience, the demo gods can and will strike at any time. While there is no complete protection against these strange occurrences in your own presentation, there are a few things you can do in order to help mitigate the chances of them striking.

The first, and most important, is to be analytical. Even though you may be very confident that your demo has no chance of failing, admitting that it might is a good thing to do. A great question to ask yourself is, "What could possibly go wrong with this demo, and what would I do if it did?" List off all of the usual suspects that might happen locally such as a dropped network connection, loss of power, and the demo PC rebooting randomly, and then think about some of the non-local things that could go wrong. What would happen if the website that you are showing off is running slower than normal? Would anything happen if someone else from your company is accessing the same part of the demo that you are trying to show?

After you come up with a list of possibilities, the next step is to think about what you would do as a speaker to mitigate, and the potential impact for the audience. For example, you might decide that if the network were to lose connection halfway through, you would switch quickly to a set of screenshots that you had taken earlier. The audience would be disappointed that they couldn't see the live pages, but would be happier than seeing you fumble around with the network settings for ten minutes. In another example, if you find that your website appears to be responding too slowly, you might decide to switch to a copy running as a backup on your local machine. The audience might experience a quick switch in the browser, but the demo would still be functional.

A presentation and demo that I will never forget was one that I did with Kirill Gavrylyuk at a conference at Microsoft's PDC event in 2005. Kirill and I were demonstrating a piece of software that would take heart monitor and other health readings and send them across the network to a set of devices on the other end. The audience would be shown a display of vital signs as proof that the demo was working.

To add a dose of realism to the presentation, Kirill was playing the role of the doctor and had even come dressed on stage in a white coat, and I was playing the role of the patient connected to the heart rate monitor. The demo was fairly complex to put together, but had worked flawlessly in the rehearsals, and we felt very confident.

The big day came, and we were presenting our session to around 400 people in a very hot and packed room. We got to the demo, and playing the patient, I clipped the heart rate monitor to my finger in order to instruct the software to send the data.

Uh oh.

After I saw the first few readings come from the heart rate monitor, I realized that we were in trouble. I faced an issue where the pressure of being on stage, the anticipation of the demo, and the combination of the heat and packed room, had elevated my heart rate up to 134 bpm (beats per minute). The data was still being sent successfully, so the demo was still technically working, except the graph that the audience was viewing on the projector had a scale of 1 to 100, which meant that the data wasn't being plotted. Even though we had tested this numerous times during development and rehearsal, my resting heart rate during normal circumstances had been around 70 bpm. We chose a scale of 1 to 100 thinking that this would give some buffer in case things changed, but had never dreamt that we would be facing such a high number!

Of course, this also had a compounding effect. As soon as I realized that the demo was going wrong, I became nervous. What happens when people become nervous? Their heart rate goes up. Within seconds I was facing a heart rate of 140 bpm, and it seemed to be climbing!

Fortunately, a little bit of humor and a good backup plan helped us prevail. After explaining the situation to the audience, most of whom found it hilarious, I gave them two choices. I joked that I could either lie down on stage and do some deep breathing in order to try and reduce my heart rate to under the 100 bpm or we could switch to a backup plan. In this case, the backup was another piece of software that would simulate the vital signs of a virtual patient within a set of normal parameters. This software was written exclusively as a failsafe for the demo, and I had never thought that we would need to use it—but when the time came in front of so many people, I was very glad we had invested the extra time!

Slide or video backups

While the heart rate monitor example highlights the benefits of mitigating a demo through having a detailed recovery plan, it doesn't have to be as complicated as writing software to get things back on track. One effective way of mitigating demo failure of most kinds is to have either a slide or video backup.

The slide backup is the simplest of the two, and involves taking screenshots of your demo that are then placed in an appendix within your presentation. If you are doing an online demo, taking a screenshot to the clipboard is relatively easy for most machines. When the screenshot is on your clipboard, you can then paste it into your appendix slide. I would recommend having an image for each of the major parts of your demo, and a separate slide for each. You'll likely end up with a fair number of slides, but in case of complete demo failure, it will be relatively easy to skip to the end of the deck and talk through the demo with the static images instead.

A nice side effect of the slide backup is that you'll also end up with something that is reusable. If you happen to share your presentation with others, you'll have the option of including the images for the demo. Folks who receive the deck will be able to experience the demo in some form, even though they didn't attend the presentation in person.

The video backup involves a similar approach, but takes a little more work. Here, you use video recording software in order to create a video of the demo that you are trying to show. Again, this probably works best for online demos, but nothing would stop you recording any video that shows another kind of demo, either. If you are recording a demo from your screen, I recommend TechSmith's Camtasia[1] if you are running Windows, and Telestream's ScreenFlow[2] if you are on a Mac. Note that you are only recording the video portion of the demo, and there is no need to record the audio.

Although it takes a little more work, the experience for the audience is improved over simply showing static images. Here, in the event of a demo catastrophe, you switch to the pre-recorded video and talk over the points as the video rolls. I've tried this a couple of times, and I've found that once I've switched to the video the audience really doesn't seen much difference between that and the actual live demo.

One caveat to this approach is that the video files tend to be large, so you'll be unlikely to share them with the presentation, and you'll need a quick way of getting them to the presentation machine, if needed. I normally keep my video backups on a USB stick, so in the event of need, I can quickly plug in the USB stick, play the video, and resume the demo for the audience.

When to let the demo gods win

Of course, while there are a lot of things that you can do to protect against the wretched demo gods, valiant attempts to recover a demo can also lead you into trouble. While the audience will commend you for trying to fix the demo in order to show it to them, there comes a time where watching the presenter scramble on stage just becomes too awkward and it's time to move on.

To avoid this, I recommend creating a mental time box for recovering your demo of around 50% of what the demo would have taken to show. For example, if your demo takes 5 minutes, it's acceptable to spend up to 2.5 minutes trying various things to recover the demo before it's time to move on. If you don't, you run the risk of losing the audience (as they will start speaking among themselves) which will require extra effort on your part to get things back on track.

The nice thing about this approach is that even if things go wrong, you credit yourself some time at the end of your presentation. For example, if you spent 2.5 minutes trying to recover your 5-minute demo, after you move on you are essentially running 2.5 minutes ahead of time. This credit means that you will likely finish a little earlier, which gives you time at the end to give the demo one last try for the audience. There's an increased likelihood of the demo working, especially if it was network- or performance-related, and the audience members who stick around at the end of the presentation to see if you can recover the demo will definitely be the interested audience members. The rest of the audience will, of course, be free to leave.

Separate demo machine

One common technique for avoiding the demo gods is to create a separate demo machine. This can be done using either a separate laptop or using a virtual machine created using a tool like VMWare Fusion[3] or similar.

A completely separate demo environment definitely has its advantages, especially for repeatable demos, and I know many presenters who swear by using them, especially virtual environments. A separate environment will allow you to cleanly segregate the demo from the environment running the presentation, which greatly reduces the risk of things going wrong. Virtual environments can also be paused or taken back to a snapshot in time, which can be great for when you have to undertake the same demo time and time again for many events. In addition, virtual machines can also be shared with attendees who might be interested in exploring the demo environment after the presentation.

With this said, however, a separate demo environment does come with some caveats. There's an overhead in maintaining a separate environment, such as keeping the hardware running (if it's a separate machine), installing required software twice, and simple things like keeping passwords up to date. If you use the demo machine infrequently then you also have to watch out for updates (if the machine hasn't been used for many months, you'll likely be prompted for a host of operating system and application updates).

Virtual machines can also introduce things to watch out for, especially with networking. On several occasions I've seen presenters struggle getting the virtual machine correctly networking with their local host machine, and the wireless network provided at the conference.

To summarize, if you are doing many scripted demos that are likely to be repeated on frequent occasions, a separate environment makes sense. It will create a sense of stability that is abstracted from the rest of your machine. If, however, you are just creating a single demo for a one-time presentation that you may never redo again, the overhead of setting up a separate environment might be too much and I would likely recommend to combine this with the machine that you are using for your presentation.

Demo script

Regardless of whether or not you use the same machine or a separate demo environment, there is one thing that is an absolute necessity for any demo—the demo script.

The demo script is a set of cues, often handwritten, that you can use on stage during a demo. During the heat of a demo, the script is designed to be a foolproof, repeatable set of steps that can ensure success by prompting you through the sets of tasks that you need to do.

The script has two parts to it: a list of pre-requisites and a list of steps. Let's take a look at an example, by imagining that we were doing a simple demo of how the audience can use Google. It's a little contrived, but a simple example nonetheless. The pre-requisites might include the following:

- Close all windows/applications

- Launch Google Chrome

- Navigate to http://google.com

The above three steps are all required to get the machine into a state where the demo can be run. Of course, for more complicated demos, this list would be a lot longer and might include loading project files in the IDE, starting services, and other tasks. This list of prerequisite steps should be done as part of the setup on the podium, which is something that we'll cover in much more detail in the next chapter.

Next in the script, come the list of steps required to execute the demo.

- Click on search box

- Type in "GPS Devices"

- Explain results to audience

- Click on link to home page

Again, this is just a simple example, but the steps above take you through each of the tasks required to execute the demo. As you can see, it's a simple technique, but one that reliably lays out the steps of the demo to ensure everything goes smoothly—even if you have a thousand people looking at you.

I would recommend creating the script on a single page, with one page for each demo that you are planning to show. The script can either by typed or handwritten, but the text must be big and the instruction must be concise so that you are able to read it quickly under pressure. This is a good example:

• Drag config file to current settings

This, on the other hand, is not so good:

• Drag the configuration settings file to the second window on the left, titled "Current Application Settings"

As you can imagine, the above step is so long that you are less likely to read it under the pressure of a demo, even if it is in big text.

These demo script steps can also work wonders if you need to type code in front of the audience.

• Type: var test = $resource('/api/tasks/:taskId', {}, { query: {method: 'GET'}});

For example, having the above code in a script step in front of you during a demo will mean that you can type it in accurately in front of the audience, ensuring that all of the symbols, closing braces, and capitalization is correct. Also, accurately typing in complex lines of code can make you look like a coding hero in front of a packed room!

If you haven't used it before, I thoroughly encourage you to experiment with creating a script for your own demos. I've personally found that it makes demos more reliable, while at the same time also helping calm the nerves. Everything I need to run the demo successfully is in front of me, which takes the pressure off remembering multiple, complex steps in the right order in the heat of the moment.

I've seen a few presenters avoid using demo scripts as they feel it's like cheating or the audience will see them use the script and this will harm their credibility as a presenter. For the most part, this is untrue, and

319

the audience's attention during a demo is mostly on the screen, not you. As long as you are not fumbling through reams of paper to find the script, the audience will often not see that you are reading any instructions for the demo, and you'll actually gain more credibility from them when the demo runs perfectly.

Secrets to a smooth demo

Up to now we've discussed some generic recommendations for running demos, together with strategies for overcoming the dreaded demo gods and creating a demo script. For the remainder of this chapter, I wanted to share some secrets to running a smooth demo. These are tips and recommendations that I've compiled over the years from various presentations at different conferences.

Many of them might be common sense, but if you do demos on a regular basis, I'm hoping that you also find some new ones that can help improve your demo delivery.

Ensure everyone can see your demo

We covered some of this in Chapter 7 when we spoke about the in-room rehearsal, but ensuring that everyone in the audience can see your demo is critical. All of the attendees, especially the ones hiding out in the back row should be able to see everything that you are showing.

There are a few aspects to this. The first is resolution, and you want to ensure that the resolution of your machine is set to something that is clear for the majority of people in the room without being too bulky that you can't operate the machine correctly. I tend to find that something around 1024x768 (or 1280x768, if you are on a widescreen machine) tends to be a good setting.

Next comes font size. Any text that you wish the audience to read needs to be at a suitable size. You'll need to experiment with the setting that works best for you, but I tend to find a minimum of 18pt font works for medium to large rooms, and possibly 20pt if you are stepping through code in an IDE.

There may be elements of the demo that you would like to show, but can't control the font size of. For example, if you want to highlight some data in a status bar or dialog box. For these, I would recommend a "zoom in" control that will enable you to zoom in to pieces of the UI in order to show the detail for the audience. For Microsoft Windows users, I recommend Mark Russinovich's ZoomIt Utility,[4] a free download from Microsoft's Technet site. For Mac users, similar functionality can be obtained by holding down the Control key and scrolling up/down with the mouse or trackpad.

Finally, if your demo uses any external devices (maybe an iPhone or Android device), then you'll want to work out how to show this to the audience as well. Typically there are two ways of doing this. The first is to use a screen capture tool to display the contents of the device in a window on your laptop (which can then be shown to the audience). For iOS devices, I recommend Reflector,[5] which uses Apple's AirPlay to mirror the devices screens. If you want to mirror the screen of an Android device, you can try Android Screencast,[6] an open source project that captures screens over ADB (Android Debug Bridge).

If you have a need to actually show the device to the audience (e.g., if you are demonstrating some new hardware), one option is to use a USB camera connected to your machine which can relay the image to the audience. To achieve this for a recent presentation, I ended up developing a small utility called QCamera,[7] which is a free download from the Mac AppStore. This application takes the feed from a connected USB camera, displays it in a window on the desktop, and can even be positioned on top on an existing Apple Keynote or Microsoft PowerPoint presentation.

Have a solid backup plan for network failure

As we touched on earlier, demos that rely on network connectivity are an open invitation for the demo gods. Networking that works perfectly beforehand will, for no reason, simply stop or become unusably slow when shown in front on an audience. While slide and video backups work well as a last resort, there are a few techniques that can help ensure a networked demo goes to plan.

The best way of mitigating networking failure is to ensure that your machine is connected to a fixed Ethernet point, and your machine has wireless connectivity turned off. The majority of networking failures I've witnessed in presentations tend to be caused by the wireless network becoming saturated with too many attendees. If you have the option of bypassing wireless and using a fixed line instead, this can work to your favor.

I've seen a few presenters go one step further and mitigate any networking problems by running everything locally. They will pull up the demo web page and announce that they are "signing into the service," when all they are doing is running a pre-canned version of the server on their local machine.

While this certainly avoids the potential of the network going down, I would advise caution with this approach. Firstly, the performance of the server running on your local machine is likely to be screaming quick— which will be great for your demo, but might not match what the audience will experience when they go and hit the real site after your presentation is over. Secondly, many people in the audience will be tech savvy. If you open a browser, navigate to an address starting with http:// localhost, and try to pass it off as hitting the real service, members of the audience will certainly notice. They might question why you are not demoing against the real server. Maybe the site isn't as reliable as it should be? Maybe this is a fake demo? You'll definitely want to make sure that you take these two caveats into account if you do head down the road of running networked demos locally.

Be prepared for the audience to test the demo for you

If you show something to the audience that they can try out during your presentation, there's a very good chance that they will do so—and this applies equally to demos.

During my time at Microsoft, I was demoing an alpha version of a product to an internal audience of around two hundred. The product was still very much in its early stages and I was remotely launching the demo from my development machine. Everything with the demo was going well, but after a couple of minutes I noticed things grinding quickly to a halt. Pages weren't loading and it appeared that everything had frozen. What I quickly realized is that when the demo started, about half of the audience had also opened a browser and typed in the same URL that I was showing to them. As you can imagine, the alpha code running on my development machine didn't stand a chance as it was bombarded by so many requests. I had to login, reset the server, and politely ask that people didn't hit the page so I could get through the demo! While I was able to recover, what this lesson taught me is that if you show a URL to the audience during a demo, you should be prepared for people in the audience (especially a large crowd) to start hitting the service at the same time.

There is another variation of this related to the audience maliciously inserting content into your demo. A good friend of mine, Shy Cohen, was demoing a product he had been working on in mid-2005. The demo showed how a service could take input from multiple users and aggregate them into a single feed—similar to how Twitter works today.

The demo was going great, and the service was running on production hardware, so there was little risk of the audience inadvertently taking down the demo. Despite this, a few bright people in the audience quickly found that they could post anonymous comments to the service which, after a few seconds, would appear on Shy's laptop, and therefore on the projector in front of the whole room. Within a minute or so came some very "colorful" comments from the audience that I won't repeat here, but as you can imagine, led to Shy having to quickly end the demo and move on with the rest of the presentation!

To summarize, if you are planning to show a demo to the audience, it's worth considering the impact of what would happen during your presentation—from the number of people in the audience who might be able to hit the demo at the same time, together with anything they could possibly do to your demo that might affect you mid-flight!

Learn how to code in front of the audience

If you are presenting to other software developers, there's a good chance that you might have to demo code. Maybe you are walking the developers through a new SDK or API that your team has developed.

Demonstrating code in front of an audience can be very difficult. There's a good chance that you might have to enter multiple lines of code in front of the audience accurately, which can be stressful under pressure, plus having to debug if and when that code doesn't compile correctly (although I've found many audiences very helpful for telling me what I've done it wrong on several occasions!). Here are a few tips that might help you write better code in front of your audience:

- **Avoid copy and paste.** I have a strong aversion against demos where the presenter opens an IDE and then simply copies and pastes code— either from a separate window or through some kind of code snippet. While this guarantees that the demo will work, I personally find that there is little to no value for the audience. All the audience is seeing is someone at the front of the room can use CTRL-C and CTRL-V effectively. Even if you paste the code and then step through it with the audience, there is a lack of context.

  The resolution to this is, of course, to write all code from scratch. Starting a new project, writing code from scratch, and running it in front of the audience can be very powerful. In essence, you are taking the audience through the multiple steps they will likely have to go through, which builds up almost like a story to them. If you were ever able to witness Don Box and Chris Sells present together, you'll know how powerful this can be. This is also where the power of the demo script comes in, as you may recall from earlier in the chapter. If you are worried about accurately typing lines of code in front of the audience, simply add it to your demo script. While it's never foolproof, the code that you need to type for the audience will be right in front of you.

324

FILE > NEW > PRESENTATION

Of course, running out of time is always an issue, and it's likely that you won't have time to write 50 lines of code in front of the audience —nor would they appreciate it if you did! Because of this, you'll want to focus on the pieces of code that support your story, and are going to be of most value to the audience. For each line of code, you should be asking yourself the question whether this is of value to the audience.

- **Backup using code snippets.** Before you take an aversion to code snippets, however, they do have a place as a backup for demos. For example, if you have typed in four lines of code and they just won't compile for the audience, it is acceptable to overwrite the code with "something that I did earlier." The audience will still have lived through the story of creating the code from scratch, and copy/pasting working code from another source will likely mean that your code will run and you can move on.

- **Use hidden constants.** There is a chance that the code you want to type in front the audience might have long ID fields or other arbitrary pieces of data. For example, you might need to type in a GUID (Globally Unique ID) to access a service—something like 3a768eea-cbda-4926-a82d-831cb89092aa. Even if this is written down in your demo script, it can be painful for the audience to watch you type this. To overcome this, you can definitely use a code snippet—and this is more effective if you assign a keyboard shortcut to the snippet so you don't have to switch windows and copy/paste the information. I've seen several presenters do this, and then make a quip about how quickly they were able to type this!

There may, however, be situations where you don't want to share this data. Maybe it's a license key to a service, or a unique identifier for your developer account. While the audience is unlikely to write this down, if the presentation is being recorded, there is a chance that others could pause the video at a later point and take a note of this data for their ill-gotten gains. To keep this from happening, I'd recommend creating a demo "constants" file in code. This file contains all of the keys and other data for the demo that you don't want to share, yet is accessible to the demo. During the demo, you can then refer to these constants using "Demo.LICENSE_KEY" or similar, which will still ensure that the data is available to the code, yet the audience will not have the ability to see the value behind this constant.

• **Be wary of typing passwords.** As you can imagine, the constants file explained previously can also work well for passwords. Having a constant of "Demo.PASSWORD" will overcome having to type your password in plain text as part of the code you are showing. With this said, however, there are occasions where you might still need to enter your password in front the audience. For example, you might run your code, which then prompts you for user credentials. While most of this can be done in front of the audience, I want to share a word of caution when doing this on mobile devices. The password field for many mobile devices briefly shows the letter before obfuscating it with a circle. This is different behavior to entering a password on a desktop machine through a browser. Again, while most people in the audience will never see this because it is so quick, if the session is recorded for viewing later, it is definitely possible to pause the video just after the key press to reveal the password letter by letter. If security is top of mind, and you are showing a demo that uses a mobile device that exhibits this behavior, I would recommend either using a temporary account, switching the screen off, or having the password available on the clipboard for these situations.

Don't let the personal stuff get in the way!

Earlier in the chapter, we covered the advantages and disadvantages of using your own machine as opposed to a dedicated demo machine. While it was argued that using your own machine provided benefits for running the occasional demo, there is one more caveat that you need to watch out for: Your personal stuff! If you are using your everyday machine to show a demo, there is a laundry list of personal artifacts and items that you can potentially reveal to the audience. Most of this will likely be harmless, but on more than one occasion I've seen presenters accidentally "leak" things during a demo because they were using a personal machine. Here is a list of a few of these to watch out for:

- **Desktop background.** If you have a custom desktop background on your machine (maybe a picture of your kid's birthday party) you may want to consider the appropriateness of showing this to the audience. On occasion, it can help build a bond with the audience, but if you are aiming for a more professional audience you may want to switch it out with a solid color background instead.

- **Desktop icons.** The same can be said for desktop icons. I'm the worst for using the desktop as a dumping ground for files that I'm working on, and never removing them when I'm done. Showing these files, even though it's just the icon and title, is not necessarily good practice for a demo, though. Having files on the desktop called "Team organizational restructure—July" or "My updated resume" might not be something that you want to share to an internal team!

- **Applications.** When a presenter switches to their desktop to do a demo, one of the things I often look for is what applications they have installed. Most of the time it's curiosity as I'm eager to discover new applications that I've not yet come across, but similar to the desktop icons mentioned previously, applications can also give away more information than you might think. For example, if you are working for company X, and you switch to your demo only to have the audience see that you have software installed from company Y (your competitor), what kind of impression might this leave— especially if you are advocating for your own product?

- **History.** Both desktop icons and applications represent the history of

327

your machine, but there are many other places where history can be obtained. The browser is one example. If your demo involves you having to search for items, there's a good chance that previous searches might be displayed. Again, if you type "D-E-V" and your machine shows several cached results for "developer jobs" it can be somewhat revealing to the audience that you might be looking to move on! A similar side effect of this is to have the last search visible in the search bar and the browser. Although most browsers are now moving to a single field for address bar and search, you should be careful about browsers that have the last search displayed upon opening, as they can instantly reveal to the audience what you were looking for just before the presentation.

- **Interruptions.** Finally, if you are using your everyday machine to do a demo, you need to be wary of anything that could potentially interrupt you. This might include incoming IM (Instant Messenger) conversations, new email alerts, calendar reminders, Skype chats, and anything else that has the potential of popping up at an inopportune moment during the demo. All of this should be turned off just before you go on stage. More recently, I was presenting to a very senior executive at a mortgage company where a calendar alert popped up reminding me that I should take my vitamins. Fortunately it was taken in good light, and it led to a great conversation about healthy living, but it was something that definitely interrupted the flow.

Before we leave the topic of interruptions, there is one potential interruption that you must always check for before starting a demo—the dreaded system update! On many occasions, I've seen presenters be halfway through a demo only to have the machine apply a mandatory system update and then restart in front of a packed audience. Not only does the audience have to wait for the machine to reboot, but then the presenter has to re-setup the demo from the point where things went wrong. Because of this, I highly recommend that you turn off automatic system updates before any demo!

Where are we?

In this chapter on demos we've explored the demo gods, created a demo script, and run through many other tips and techniques for running a demo while you are on stage.

To refine some of the recommendations that you should be thinking about while on stage, the next chapter will cover a series of ideas and thoughts about preparing for your big day. From dress code to handling questions, being prepared while you are on stage will add that additional level of professionalism to your presentation.

---

1. http://www.techsmith.com/camtasia.html
2. http://www.telestream.net/screenflow/
3. http://www.vmware.com/products/fusion
4. http://technet.microsoft.com/en-us/sysinternals/bb897434.aspx
5. http://www.airsquirrels.com/reflector/
6. https://code.google.com/p/androidscreencast/
7. https://itunes.apple.com/us/app/qcamera/id598853070?mt=12

CHAPTER 9: Your Big Day

* * *

Your big day is just around the corner, and everything that we've covered in this book so far has been leading up to it. Before we dig into some of the things that you should be doing on the day, it's worth first taking some time to think about what time and day you will actually be presenting on!

The time and day can have a tremendous impact on how your presentation is received by the audience. This is especially true for conferences that last for the entire week. An audience will be in a very different mood on the first Monday morning directly after the keynote as opposed to the last session on Friday afternoon.

In conferences such as this, it's likely that your time slot will be automatically assigned for you. If, however, you have any flexibility for when you are able to present, there are a few things that you can look out for when selecting the most optimal time.

For a 5-day conference, I would recommend selecting a slot about 60% of the way through (either Wednesday or Thursday). The 60% is important as the audience will have already acclimatized to the conference, and will also have a benchmark for the types of sessions and presenters. In addition, Wednesday and Thursday will likely see the highest number of attendees as quite often attendees will arrive late or leave early to weeklong conferences.

On that Wednesday or Thursday, I would suggest trying to pick a time slot just before lunch. You'll likely find that the audience is most attentive just before the lunchtime break. The session is late enough that even the over-sleepers will make it, and no one has had the chance to be affected by a heavy lunch. I tend to gravitate towards this time slot regardless of whether the conference is a week long or a single day.

Moreover, if possible, I try to look to see who is speaking in the same slot (if the conference has multiple tracks running concurrently), and in addition, who is speaking before me. Understanding the topic and presenter speaking either at the same time or just before you can greatly impact the number of attendees that might come to your session. If the conference has an invited guest or industry luminary who has a session just before you are due to take the stage, it's something that you may or may not want to follow.

When thinking about the most optimal time slot for speaking, there are a few things to watch out for. Sessions that are held directly after a heavy lunch can definitely be a drag. I call these the "lunchtime graveyard shift." After the conference lunch, the audience will likely be feeling sleepy and the presenter will have to redouble their efforts in order to keep everyone engaged, especially if the subject is one that doesn't necessarily apply to everyone in the audience.

Somewhat similar are early morning sessions following a conference party or event the night before. On several occasions I've been given the "gift" of an 8:30 a.m. time slot the day after the attendee party. The audience size will likely be much less than if the session was held later in the day, and the ones who do show up might be feeling a little worse for wear if they overindulged the night before. With that said, the ones who do show will definitely be the ones eager to learn about what you have to say!

As a final note, I would also recommend to watch out for time slots directly after any keynote session in the conference. Keynote sessions involving all of the audience—especially the one kicking off the conference—tend to be the sessions with the company announcements, giveaways, or other pieces of news that have the potential to generate excitement with the audience. If your session is directly after the keynote where 5,000 people have just been told exciting news or given a new product to try, it's going to be a tough act to follow.

Preparation

As you've hopefully gathered from a lot of chapters in this book, for a successful presentation, preparation is everything. Not only does this apply to the actual content, but being prepared mentally and physically on the day of your presentation is equally important. In this section, we'll cover some of the areas of preparation that are vital to a successful day.

What are you going to wear?

Planning what to wear in front of an audience of hundreds or thousands of people can be difficult. Similar to your presentation you should aim to be yourself, but at the same time it's also important to somewhat mirror the members of the audience where possible. Turning up in athletic gear to a dinner banquet might achieve the former, but you would look very out of place compared to the other attendees.

Before we touch on some of these aspects, I wanted to start by covering a pet peeve of mine: The speaker shirt. Many large conferences have branded, colored shirts that all speakers must wear during the conference so that the audience can identify them as, well, speakers. While I can see some rationale behind this when meeting customers, in my view great presentations are about telling stories in a way that is truly unique to the person delivering the talk. Great presentations should be akin to a work of art. If we take this analogy forward, why would we force the artists to wear the same type of clothes? Needless to say, I try to avoid speaker shirts whenever possible. As long as I don't risk being kicked out of the conference, I'll try to come up with a myriad of excuses, the best being that I've accidentally left the speaker shirt in my hotel room (again!).

333

If, like me, you choose to avoid the speaker shirt, you should still plan on dressing appropriately. As I mentioned earlier, mirroring the audience can be a great way of achieving this. If you know that you will be presenting to a room where everyone in the audience will be wearing suits, you should also plan on wearing a suit to come across as a peer of the audience. If on the other hand you are presenting to a developer conference in Hawaii, something a little more relaxed will of course be more appropriate.

If you are in doubt, it can always help to ask the conference organizers, or search online for images of the conference from previous years. There's a good chance that you'll find previous photos posted which should give you an indication of the dress code. If you still have questions, or are debating between more casual or more formal, I would probably lean towards being more formal. It's generally acceptable for a presenter to be overdressed rather than underdressed at most events.

Before we leave this topic, I did want to touch on three other related areas. The first is whether or not you should wear a jacket while presenting, especially at a more formal conference where everyone else is wearing them. Generally, I tend to find that I'm more comfortable with the jacket off, just because I tend to get too hot wearing a jacket in a presentation, but your mileage may vary, especially if you don't own a jacket! Regardless of what you choose, if you do end up wearing a jacket, be very careful of interference with the lapel microphone. If the jacket brushes up against the microphone on your shirt the audience will hear a ruffling sound for most of the presentation.

Second up is shoes. Many people tend to overlook this, but if you are presenting in a very large room you'll likely be placed on a raised platform, which will mean that the first few rows in the audience will be treated to an eye-level glance of your shoes. If you think this is going to be the case, it pays well to make sure that whatever you wear represents the look that you are going for!

Finally, and this applies mostly to male readers, please consider ironing your shirt! I know traveling to conferences is difficult, especially if you are running late on the presentation, but it's not a great first impression if you walk onto the stage with a shirt that was a crumpled ball in your suitcase a few minutes earlier!

Combatting presentation nerves

If someone tells you that they have presented so many times that they no longer get nerves before going up on stage, I can guarantee that it's not true. I have nerves before every presentation that I do. Every presenter that I have seen on stage or have worked with has nerves before every presentation. Getting nervous before delivering any prepared content to a room full of people is just human nature.

With that said, there are several things that can at least help calm down the nerves. Some presentation coaches will focus on breathing and other relaxation techniques before going up on stage. While these might help (and I encourage you to check them out), over the course of the years, I have found five things that help temper the nerves for me. Everyone is different, so your mileage may vary with this list, but hopefully some of these will help you.

Exercise

I've learned this one from many of my favorite presenters, and after trying this before a presentation several years ago, I was sold.

Preparing for a presentation can be very mentally tiring. This is often compounded if preparation is running behind, which means working long nights, and often the morning or day of the presentation as you add the finishing touches. Not only does this way of working take a mental toll, but it can also take a physical toll. You are spending hours in the same position, hunched over your computer staring at the same presentation or demo, and it's easy to feel overwhelmed and exhausted.

For me, exercise has always been a good stress release, but I had never really tried it before a presentation. Of course, the timing here is critical. You want to make sure that you leave adequate time for preparation, as no one will want to see you walk into the room sweating!

335

My rule of thumb is to do what you can, leaving yourself a 90-minute buffer before a presentation. If I have a presentation at 10 a.m., I'll typically plan a workout in the morning before heading to breakfast. If I have a presentation in the early afternoon, I'll see if it's possible to skip out late morning without anyone noticing. Of course, it's not always possible to escape at the right time—but every time I have had the opportunity to put in a good workout before a large presentation, I've felt more relaxed, both physically and mentally, when it's my turn to go up on stage.

Eating

Somewhat related to exercise, eating right a critical part of preparation. Firstly, you don't want to "go all out" before a presentation. Eating a large breakfast or lunch just before you get up on stage will likely make you tired and slow. Conversely, you don't want to be going up on stage with an empty stomach. Although you may be more alert, if your mind is focused on the expenses-paid dinner you've promised yourself after your presentation, it might not be good, either. As you have guessed, the most important thing is to maintain a balance in the middle.

What should you do if you have a presentation right after lunch? If it's a large conference, you'll likely be dining with everyone else, and that will introduce the temptation to eat a hearty lunch with your colleagues before your session. My advice? Don't fall into the trap, and instead fill the plate with half the amount of what you normally eat. I have done this many times, and had people comment, "What's up? On a diet today?" to which I'll make up some excuse that I had a late breakfast —or if I'm traveling between time zones, I'll use jet lag as an excuse. If in doubt, know that delivering a presentation slightly hungry will feel much better than delivering a presentation feeling slightly full.

Sometimes you won't have the option to eat at all. On a couple of occasions, I've turned up expecting that I'll have the chance to eat before my presentation only to find that I'm too late and the kitchen or restaurant has closed, or the conference food has run out (or is just plain inedible!), which means skipping the meal I had planned. Having this happen just before a presentation adds more stress as now I'm likely worried about not eating, and suitably annoyed at the same time. A good backup is to always have some "power food" on hand. For me this means a power bar or chocolate-covered espresso beans, but your food of choice may vary. The important thing is to have some non-perishable food that you can rely on if this ever happens to you.

Finally, we should also touch on a related topic, caffeine. I really enjoy coffee or tea before a presentation. It seems to help take the edge off the nerves, yet give me a small boost at the same time. I've seen other presenters pound cans of Red Bull and Rock Star before going on stage. If that works for you, that's great as well. Use this with caution, however, as I remember one particular presentation a few years back where I ended up drinking a really strong coffee that I had not tried before. The result was being very jittery through the whole presentation, and I swear my heart was pounding towards the end. The moral of the story here is to know what works for you, but discover it well before you are due to go up on stage.

Listening to the previous presentation

In addition to exercise and eating correctly, I also find one way of calming the nerves is to sit through part of the session prior to mine. I try to watch the last 20 minutes of the session, if possible. Not only does this help me acclimatize to the audio and lighting in the room, but it also let's me get an understanding of the level of energy.

Getting an idea of how the previous presenter is doing can help set the frame of mind. For example, if the previous presentation isn't going that well, or I see the presenter is failing to connect with the audience, I might think, "I can do better than this person! I need to put some energy back into the audience!" If, on the other hand, the presenter is doing really well, I try to remain equally motivated, "I know I can be equally good. I can't let the audience down with my session!"

Somewhat related to this is a wonderful TED talk by Amy Cuddy[1] on

"Your body language shapes who you are" where Amy talks about the use of positive body language to alter people's perception of ourselves. While it's not directly tied to presentation skills, it's a great talk and can help reinforce this area as well as helping calm some of those presentation nerves.

Meeting the audience

Before a presentation begins, there's often some spare time for the presenter. This can be as you are walking into the room, or after you have finished setting up at the podium—something that we'll cover in more detail shortly. During any lull, one way of addressing presentation nerves can be just to talk to people in the audience.

You can introduce yourself, and if you haven't met them before, find out a little about where they've come from. If you are brave, you can also try and assess their expectations for the talk. "What are you expecting to hear today?" can be a great ice breaker and can help reaffirm that the topics you will be speaking about are the ones that the audience is interested in.

What can the audience do?

Finally, I've come across a lot of presentation advice that asks the question, "What can the audience do to you?" Many books on the subject try to alleviate the myth that the audience has any power over you as a presenter or position the question, "What's the worst that can go wrong?"

While this might work for some, I've always found that thinking about a more positive outcome is better. Instead of asking the question, "What can the audience do to me?" I tend to lean towards, "What can I do for the audience?" or "How will the audience be better as a result of my talk?" In addition, thinking about the best outcome from the audience can help frame these questions. I always imagine the audience giving me a standing ovation or cheering at the end, which, by the way, has never happened—but we can all dream!

The majority of airline pilots use a written checklist in order to prepare before takeoff. Together with the copilot, they will run through an exhaustive list including flight controls, instruments and radios, and fuel mixture. For a pilot, the written checklist provides a set of safeguards to ensure that items are not overlooked or missed in the heat of getting ready for takeoff.

Similar to the pilot's checklist, a presenter should also have a similar list for preparation at the podium. I definitely recommend having a written checklist that you print out before the presentation and physically mark off each item during your preparation time at the podium. Although it might sound detailed, it's amazing to see how many things you will capture, especially if you are rushed to get ready at the start of the presentation.

Here are a few of the things from my checklist that you can use to build your own:

- **Power.** When using a laptop, it's worth a double check to ensure that you have power. There's nothing worse than the machine going into standby mode halfway through your presentation because it has been on battery since you started!

- **Presentation remote.** Do you have it installed, and is it working correctly?

- **Interruptions.** Email, IM, Skype, Office Reminders. Is there anything that could potentially interrupt you during the presentation? If so, turn it off.

- **Updates.** Have you checked for system updates? Are there any mandatory updates that might install during your presentation?

- **Power mode.** Is the power mode of your laptop set correctly? Are there screen savers or other screen locks that might appear during the presentation, especially if you are using a separate demo machine?

- **Demo scripts.** As discussed in Chapter 8, do you have all of the demo scripts ready? Have all of the prerequisites in the scripts been followed?

- **Networking.** Does all of the networking work as it did in the in-room rehearsal? You don't need an exhaustive run through the demo (unless it's short), but validating that the laptop can see the network is useful.

- **Recording.** Will you be recording the session? If so, is everything set on your laptop to capture the screen and audio correctly? Incidentally, if you are recording the session, it's important that you announce this to the audience just before you begin. While you won't necessarily be capturing video of the audience, it's courtesy to let them know that any questions they might ask will be recorded.

- **Microphone.** Is the microphone working OK? Ensure that you know how to turn it off/on, and that it remains off while you are setting up at the podium.

- **Cell phone.** Is your cell phone off? Not just on silent (as the signal can still interfere with the microphone), but off or in airplane mode.

- **Water.** Do you have enough water for the presentation? Personally, I get through around two bottles or glasses per hour. If you are using bottles, make sure that the cap is unscrewed slightly so that you are not fighting with it when the time comes to open.

- **Speaker badge.** Are you still wearing your speaker badge? Remove it if you think it might interrupt with the microphone.

- **Jacket.** Are you wearing a jacket? Again, remove it if you think it might interrupt with the microphone.

- **Pockets.** Is everything out of your pockets? There's nothing more off-putting than seeing a presenter playing with a bunch of car keys in their pocket as they are walking around on stage!

- **Bag.** Is your bag somewhere safe, preferably somewhere where you won't trip over it during the presentation?

- **Business cards.** If required, do you have a set of business cards with you at the podium? This helps avoid fumbling around in your bag when audience members approach you at the end of your presentation and have follow-up questions.

- **Title slide.** Is your title slide ready to go, and visible for the audience?

- **Music.** If you are considering having music playing as the audience enters the room, do you have this ready?

And you're on!

The lights dim, and you are on! Congratulations for getting this far! While we covered how to open your presentation in Chapter 7, there are a few reminders and speaking tips that I wanted to include in this chapter that might be useful:

- **Speaking volume.** Many software developers and IT professionals are naturally quiet. While it might feel awkward, it's really important to project your loudest voice at all times during the presentation. During presentations that I do, I always imagine having to speak to someone at the back of the room, and occasionally will question myself during the presentation to make sure my current volume is high enough. If you find that you start off loud, but gradually get quieter as the presentation progresses, I would recommend having a small visual cue—something as simple as a Post-it note on your laptop with the word "VOLUME" written in large letters. As we covered in Chapter 7, these small visual cues can be incredibly helpful reminders during a presentation.

If you are using a microphone, you might have a fear of being too loud. Don't be. A loud voice can always be turned down, and if you have an A/V team supporting you, they will do this automatically. A quiet voice will require the microphone to be turned up, however. Not only will you sound less confident, but there is a great chance of background noises being amplified also.

- **Speaking clarity.** We touched on this a little during Chapter 7, but the clarity of your voice is very important. You should enunciate words correctly, especially if you have a broad accent—and more so, if you are speaking to an international audience. Related to this, pausing between sentences can be a very powerful way of enforcing clarity and also giving the audience time to absorb all of the great information that you are delivering. During a rehearsal where you record yourself, try interjecting a 3-second pause within the presentation. Although it might seem like an eternity while you are actually presenting, you'll see how effective it can be when you replay the video back.

- **Posture.** I've seen a lot of presentation advice that recommends that you root yourself in one spot like a tree trunk. While I don't recommend running around the stage like a caged animal, I do believe a little movement is natural and would encourage you to explore this during the rehearsal. A few steps in either direction can help you direct the message to certain parts of the audience which can help increase engagement.

With this said, there are a couple of caveats to moving around on stage. Firstly, watch where you are walking! You want to make sure that you stay within a somewhat confined area in view of all of the audience, and you certainly want to avoid tripping over cables or other objects that might be in your path. Secondly, never turn away from the audience. With a screen in front of you at the podium or on another part of the stage, you should never have an excuse to turn towards the projected screen. Doing so might feel natural at first, but the turning of the back can quickly lead to potential disengagement with the audience.

• **Eye contact.** As a self-prescribed introvert, there are few things I like less than staring at people's faces for close to an hour. Doing so can be incredibly intimidating, and I believe is the underlying reason for many people's fear of speaking in public. Despite this fear, maintaining eye contact with the audience is incredibly important. Stare at the floor or your screen for the entire presentation, and you'll never connect with anyone in the room.

To overcome any fear, you need to learn the art of looking at people without staring at people. One technique that I have found very effective is to imagine a "figure of eight" overlaid on top of the audience. When I'm speaking to the audience, I will try and follow this figure of eight to direct my eye contact to particular sections of the audience. For example, I might start looking at the back left of the audience, before moving to the back right. After a few seconds more my eye contact might move more towards the center of the room, before focusing on the front left of the room, and so forth. When I do this, I tend to pick one particular person at random, look at them for 2–3 seconds before moving on to the next section and finding another person. Doing this not only over takes away from having to stare at one or two people for the entire duration, but if you follow the figure of eight it also guarantees that you share your eye contact and direction somewhat evenly throughout your presentation.

Even with this technique, there are times when you will find a face that you won't necessarily like! It might be someone that you recognize. It might be that someone has a quizzical look on their face. Or worse, the ultimate presenter's fear, it might be that someone is yawning! The yawn from an audience member can be one of the most off-putting things that a presenter ever has to face. As soon as you see

343

that yawn, you start to question your own content. Is this too boring? Am I going too slow? Am I not being interesting enough? And likely as soon as you do this, you start to make corrections such as speeding up or skipping content that you had originally planned to talk about.

Although it's easy to say in a book, don't adjust anything about your presentation if you see someone in the audience yawn. Please, don't let the yawn put you off. Chances are good that they are not even yawning at you! The audience member might have been out too late at the party, or if they've come from a different time zone they might still be suffering with the jet lag. On many occasions, especially international events, I've seen one person yawning while I was speaking only to have the same person greet me at the end of the presentation with high comments about the talk.

Finally, if you think yawning is bad, just wait until you see people falling asleep on you! During many presentations I've given in Japan over the years, I have witnessed people in the room appearing to fall asleep. As I would be speaking, my attention would be drawn to drooping heads and closing eyes. Initially, I was questioning my own content, and at the time was somewhat offended, only to later learn that this is a cultural norm. Many Japanese believe that by closing their eyes they can hear more effectively, because they are screening out the visual stimulus and focusing on the sound.[2] This is especially true in meetings held in English where they need to concentrate harder because of the language barrier. In addition, the action of closing one's eyes when speaking is not regarded as negative in Japanese culture, which adds to the effect. The moral of this story? While it's easy to internalize a potentially negative reaction from the audience as you are trying to maintain eye contact, there is a very good chance that it might not be as negative as you think!

• **Dealing with interruptions.** There will be many times during your presentations when you will be interrupted. Some interruptions are valid (e.g., if you've run 20 minutes over your allotted end time!) where as others will just happen.

For 99.9% of interruptions, the best approach is to ignore it. If you are presenting in a dinner setting, the waitstaff might drop a glass or break a plate while you are talking. If this happens, simply ignore it.

A major interruption is different and might include a loss of power, or some other event that can affect the audience. I had a colleague of mine interrupted by an earthquake during one of his presentations! In these cases, you should definitely recognize the interruption for the benefit of the audience, and quickly decide if there is any further action to be taken. When presenting once in Poland, I was treated to an unexpected fire drill and quickly found that it was my responsibility to lead the room out into the cold! If nothing else, a good interruption can be a great opportunity for some impromptu humor that helps you further build that connection with the audience!

Interacting with the audience

We move on from the topic of interruptions in our last section to the related subject of interacting with the audience. Interacting with the audience can involve engaging them in the conversation as well as handling unplanned and planned questions from the floor. Regardless of the interaction, it's imperative that a good presenter knows how to interact with the audience because when things go wrong it can quickly derail even the best presentation!

Polling the audience

We often think of interaction with the audience being initiated by one or more audience members, and for the most part this is true. It can, however, be useful to prompt the audience for feedback during a session through the use of an audience poll.

An audience poll is where you ask the room a general yes/no question requiring a response that requires the audience to put up their hand if they agree. For example, you might ask the audience, "How many of you use our previous product?" or "How many in the audience have seen this issue before?" These types of questions will result in a number of hands being raised.

While these types of questions won't provide valuable direction for your presentation (as by the time you are on stage, it's difficult to change), they can help reinforce a point that you are trying to make. In addition, they can help form a bond between you and the audience, and also between different audience members. If an audience member raises a hand next to someone, they implicitly are sharing something in common, which can help reinforce parts of the presentation.

However, there are three things to recommend if you plan to use informal polls in your presentation. The first is to avoid using too many polls during the session. One or two during an hour might be fine, but they will lose their effect if the audience is prompted every few minutes.

Secondly, you should always be prepared for the opposite answer to what you were expecting! If you ask the question, "How many people in the audience are using our previous product?" you should be prepared to have some kind of response regardless of whether everyone or no one in the audience raises their hands. The audience poll should never shock you into thinking that the content of your presentation isn't going to apply to them.

Finally, as a courtesy, it's always nice to echo back the result to the audience. If you ask a question and a third of the hands go up, it's nice to say, "That's interesting. We have about a third of the audience using our previous product." This type of feedback will be useful for people in the front rows, and will avoid them having to stretch their necks around to try and see who had the same answer.

Avoiding poll pollution

There are times where an audience's answer will be affected by the people surrounding them or another political motivation. If the manager of a developer team asks the question, "Who likes the direction that we are taking as a company?" there is a good chance that the majority of the audience will raise their hand just because it's the right thing to do. I call this "poll pollution" because the answer from the audience is being polluted by the circumstances.

One technique I've seen to avoid poll pollution is to ask the audience to "hum" instead of raising their hands. As a presenter, you can instruct the audience to hum if they agree with something that you've said or a question that you asked. By doing this, you'll often get a much more fair reaction from the audience as with the level of humming in the room it's virtually impossible to tell who is humming, and who is not.

Creating a backchannel

Informal polls of the audience are one way to get impromptu feedback from the audience, but as mentioned, can only be used a couple of times during a presentation. A way of receiving more feedback from the audience can be to setup a realtime way for the audience to comment on the session as it is happening. This is known as a "backchannel." A backchannel can be a purpose-built website or filtered Twitter stream that enables the audience to share feedback between each other in realtime.

For a number of internal conferences at Microsoft, we implemented a backchannel for the audience based on the session code. Upon entering the room, the audience, the majority of whom had a smartphone or laptop with them, could log into a site, enter the session code, and get access to a feed that was shared with all of the other attendees in the room. The concept was very similar to an IRC chat room or other instant messaging client. The backchannel can provide a way for the attendees to validate concepts with each other. For example, one audience member might ask,

"Did the presenter already cover X?" or "What does the presenter mean when she says Y?" and other audience members can chime in with the answer. The whole conversation can be saved for later use and, if you are really brave, can be displayed on a screen for the audience to see in realtime during the talk.

I recommend this last point with caution, however. As covered in Chapter 8 when talking about demos, if the audience has the ability to put anything up on the screen during a presentation, it can lead to unexpected consequences for the presenter! I witnessed such an example during a keynote presentation in late 2009. I won't reveal the details here, but the presenter in question had a live Twitter feed on one of the screens, showing the tweets from anyone who used a particular hashtag. About 30 minutes into the presentation, things were not going well, and the audience starting reacting by tweeting messages such as, "This is boring" and "I can't believe I paid money for this conference" using the hashtag. Gradually these tweets started to appear onscreen behind the presenter. As you can imagine, other audience members seeing these tweets started to pile on with additional derogatory comments and things quickly snowballed out of control. It didn't take long for the presenter and conference organizer to intervene. The Twitter feed was abruptly stopped, and the presenter decided to move on to a completely new topic!

Handling questions from the audience

Handling questions during a presentation can and should vary depending on audience size. For small audiences, you'll need to be prepared to be much more interactive, handling questions and also being proactive with the attendees. For large audiences, it's important to divert questions until a more formal Q&A session until the end. You may remember from the end of Chapter 3 we introduced a number of different audience sizes. Let's cover these audience sizes in more detail to see how questions should be handled:

• **Small (2–15 attendees).** If you are presenting a small session with between 2 and 15 audience members, it's imperative that you handle ad hoc questions during the presentation. Trying to push such feedback until the end of the session will appear strange, and possibly even condescending. For smaller groups (1–5 audience members) you might also encourage receiving feedback. "Is this useful" or "Is this what you are looking for?" can help create a positive connection with a small audience.

With this said, with any questions from a group of this size, you should be careful not to rathole on topics as these can take away from the core of your presentation. In addition, as a presenter, it's important that you remain engaged in any side conversation that does result from a question. There's nothing worse than a question leading to a conversation that the presenter is not part of. If this happens, politely try to interject back into the conversation by agreeing with everything you've heard and suggesting that to respect everyone's time you should probably all move on with the presentation.

- **Medium (15–40 attendees).** As the audience grows, so does the difficulty of handling questions. The midsize audience (around 15–40 audience members) can be difficult as it can still facilitate impromptu feedback, yet the audience size is such that you risk alienating others in the audience with questions that they might not be interested in hearing. The key with this audience size is to watch out for that one opinionated person who keeps asking questions that no one else in the audience cares about. Again, deal with it professionally and politely, but never let it derail the presentation for the rest of the room.

- **Large (40–150) and Theater (150+).** For larger groups (any number over 40 attendees), handling questions and feedback mid-flight can be problematic. Not only do you risk changing topics that may not apply to the rest of the audience, but the audio in the room might not facilitate others hearing the original question. The result is that you start answering a question that no one else heard, which is a sure recipe for losing the attention of many people in the room.

For audiences of this size, unless the person asking the question is of upmost importance (such as the CEO of your company!), I would recommend responding by saying that you will take questions at the end of the session in a dedicated Q&A session. Again, this should be done in a polite and professional way as to not hurt the feelings of someone who has asked a question in front of the room.

In situations where you do need to direct audience questions until the end, there will be audience members who won't get the hint, and will continue to ask questions or insist that you should answer the question mid-flight. Again you need to be polite, but firm. A standard response might be: "Thanks for the great question. We do have some time allotted for Q&A at the end, and I'll be sure to cover it then."

If you know that you will be answering that question in after a few slides, the following line can also work: "Thanks for the great question. You've read my mind, as I'm actually going to be covering this topic in a few slides. If I don't answer what you are looking for, however, let's definitely connect at the end."

Finally, for the persevering audience member that just won't leave you alone, I've heard this line used to great effect: "Thanks for the great question. Unfortunately (because we are recording the session), the conference organizers won't let me take questions during the session, but I'd be happy to answer this one in the allotted Q&A session at the end."

Conducting a Q&A session

The end of the session is, of course, the perfect time to open up the floor for questions. For an hour-long session, I would probably recommend between 5 and 10 minutes for Q&A, erring towards the lower end if you are unsure. If you do run out of time in a formal Q&A session, you can always direct people to the podium afterwards, something that we'll be covering next. In addition, if you are out of time completely, I would likely recommend skipping the Q&A session and kindly requesting that all questions should be taken at the podium. Unfortunately, if you are out of time at the end of your presentation and you start a Q&A session, there will be audience members who do not feel obliged to stay or have other sessions and commitments that they might need to make. As a presenter you'll be trying to hold a formal Q&A session while half of the audience is leaving the room, which as well as being distracting can make it almost impossible to hear any questions being asked.

If you do have time for an allotted session, there are a few things that you should consider in order to handle questions effectively. The first is to think about how the audience is going to ask the question. If you are in a large room or theater, you will likely need to have some handheld microphones or microphones on stands that the audience can use. This is especially important for an audience member in the back of the room who wants to ask something.

Next, regardless of whether the audience member uses a microphone, you should always repeat the question. Repeating the question does three things: it ensures that everyone in the audience hears the question being asked, it puts the question on any recording of the session that you might be doing, and more importantly it gives you a few valuable extra seconds to think about a good answer! It might not seem like it, but the few seconds while you are repeating the question can help your brain recall bits of information that you'll use to construct your answer. If you find it awkward to repeat the question, or often forget, simply use the following phrase in front of the question: "Just to make sure that everyone heard the question…"

Once you've repeated the question, it's important to acknowledge that it was a good question—even if you think it wasn't! Doing this will validate the person in the audience, will help create an atmosphere where others will be more likely to ask a question, and will give you a few extra seconds more as you are constructing your answer.

Once the preamble is over, it is time to answer the question! Regardless of the topic, conference, or level of interest in the area, I always recommend answering the question as briefly as possible. There might be many in the audience who are not interested in the answer, and while you need to respect the person who asked the question, at the same time you don't want to spend 15 minutes on a lengthy dialogue. Be as brief as you can and, if required, offer more detail afterwards.

As you answer the question, it's also important that you address the whole audience through your eye contact. You should look at the person while they are asking the question, but as you answer go back to the "figure of eight" approach that we covered earlier in the chapter. Doing so will not only keep the engagement with the audience, but you'll also get a sense of the level of interest in the answer being given, which can help determine how long your answer should be.

Finally, after answering the question, it's always polite to affirm the answer with the person who asked the original question. You might use, "Did that help?" or "Is the answer what you were looking for?" You may think that this response might lead to additional questions or feedback, but I've found in 99% of cases you'll receive an affirmative answer that will allow you to move on to other topics.

What if no one asks any questions?

There might be certain scenarios where no one asks you a question. As a presenter this can leave you with an awkward silence between the end of your presentation and officially closing the presentation. While this isn't necessarily bad, often the audience does have questions, but no one wants to be the first one to ask. To overcome this, there are a couple of techniques that can help.

The first is to plant some questions in the audience. If you have colleagues or willing folks in the audience, you can ask them to ask a pre-planned question or two to get the audience started. This can be an effective way of kickstarting others in the audience to ask their own question.

Secondly, you might consider some form of giveaway or freebie to entice audience members to ask questions. The giveaway doesn't have to be high in monetary value, and it's amazing the reaction you can get to "I've got this shiny new notebook and pen for the first question asked" in order to spur some audience participation. An alternative is to randomly give freebies for the "best" questions asked during the Q&A session, which can also help produce additional questions.

Engaging in conflict with the audience

Sometimes you will get a question from the audience intended to cause conflict. It might be a disparaging question about your product or team, or an opinion that puts a competing product in a better light than yours. After working at Microsoft for many years, I definitely saw my fair share of these, especially from existing customers who had something to say about the product they were having trouble with.

Even if you receive the most disparaging or insulting question of feedback, you should never engage in a conflict or argument with the audience member on stage. Every time I have witnessed this, it has been a lose/lose situation for the presenter. If the audience member is right, and especially if the audience agrees with the question from the audience member, the presenter loses. If the audience member is wrong, but there is an exchange of counter arguments for 10 minutes, the presenter still loses. While it might be entertaining for the audience—and might even make headlines if this happens in a public setting—you should always be prepared to take the proverbial high road and move the conflict to after the session. Doing so will avoid others in the audience forming an opinion of you, often a negative one, especially if they consider your response condescending or rude. Using a response such as the following can help in these situations: "I respect your opinion and would love to go deeper after the talk." Bottom line? Engaging in conflict with the audience member is always a lose/lose and you should try to avoid it wherever possible.

Officially closing the presentation

Once the Q&A session is over, it's important that you officially close the presentation. This will signal to the audience that they are free to leave. Ideally the session should be closed before the allotted time is over to avoid audience members leaving during the Q&A session.

Closing a session is relatively straightforward, and something like the following can work: "That brings us to the end of our time. If you do have more questions, I'll be at the podium for the next few minutes. Otherwise, I would just like to thank you for your time today. Thank you." It's important to actually say the words, "Thank you" as you truly do want to thank the audience for the time that they've invested in listening to you. Assuming your session was well received, these two words can also act as a subtle prompt for the audience to applaud.

At the podium after the presentation

Everything is over and you are at the podium! If the presentation went well, there's a good chance that several members of the audience will approach you to ask follow-on questions.

Podium time is interesting because for many presenters it determines whether they are an introvert or extrovert. Even if they are a strong speaker, introverts will just want to pack up and go to the hotel room. The session will have been exhausting and they need time to recharge. Speakers who fall into the extrovert category, however, will naturally feed off the energy at the podium, wanting to continue the conversation long after the presentation is over.

Regardless of whether you fall into the introvert or extrovert category, there are a few important things to remember about your time at the podium.

The first, and most important, is to deal with questions in an effective and concise manner. If you have ten people approach the podium and you take five minutes to answer each question you are going to be there for a long while. Moreover, the tenth person in line to ask his question will be frustrated that he's had to wait for so long before his turn. Keep answers concise, and if there is room for follow-up, arrange a time and place at a later date. If your presentation was especially well received, audience members might just come up to the podium with compliments, such as "That was a great presentation" or "Best presentation of the conference!" While it's always gratifying to receive such comments, again be sure to thank the person appropriately before moving on to others standing in line.

Second, and somewhat related to the first, is to have business cards on hand. This is useful is you are taking questions from audience members who don't know you as it gives an immediate action for follow-up, and a further excuse to keep your answers to the point. Ideally you should have a stack of cards out ahead of time, as we covered earlier in the chapter, to avoid having to dig through your bag while people are waiting.

Finally, if you are at a large conference or event, please be mindful of any presenter wishing to set up for a session held directly after yours. As you are chatting with the audience members and handling all of their gracious comments, there's a good chance that all of your equipment is still taking up room on the podium and needs to be removed. As a presenter, there's nothing worse than trying to set up for a presentation while the previous presenter is still engaged in active conversation about the last topic. Be respectful, and if you see another presenter trying to set up, pack up your equipment at the same time that you are taking questions.

Written feedback from the audience

Many events, large or small, will provide the audience a mechanism to provide written feedback on your session. This can be a paper form that the audience member completes or some way of entering feedback online. Most feedback forms have a scoring system (typically 1 to 10 or 1 to 5) that evaluate presenter effectiveness, technical knowledge, and other such ratings. If you are unlucky, the audience will be asked to rate the session's applicability to their current job or function. (I dislike this one as it penalizes the presenter for audience members who are interested in the topic, but can't necessarily apply what they've heard to their everyday job.) For larger events, the session will be given an overall rating score, normally an average across all the scores, which will enable you and the conference organizers to compare different sessions, speakers, and tracks. Having been both a presenter and track organizer on previous occasions, believe me when I tell you that many people are very competitive about their scores and ranking compared to others!

In addition to the rating scores, and the most important feedback for the presenter, is any written anecdotal feedback. I like anecdotal feedback as it goes beyond a simple scoring system and often offers the presenter a way to improve the session on future occasions. Good written feedback will include topics or subjects that should be addressed as well as ideas or comments to improve the delivery next time.

However, whether it's the rating or written feedback, you should take everything with a pinch of salt. There is going to be feedback that sometimes contradicts other feedback (e.g., where one audience member will give you 10 out of 10 for your session, and another gives you 1 out of 10, or one audience member will rate the session as too technical, while another says it is not technical enough). There will be feedback for elements that were out of your control, such as audience members complaining about the room being too cold, or the chairs being too uncomfortable. There could also be feedback that might be insulting. As a track owner, I once read the following from an audience member: "If I had the choice of watching paint dry or seeing this session again, I'd frankly choose the paint." Humorous, but not very constructive! In all these cases, understand that you can't please everyone and look for patterns and repeating, constructive feedback that you can use to make your presentation better next time.

Finally, if you don't have a mechanism or time to collect feedback from the audience, or if you believe your audience will not complete the form, there is an alternative and quick way to rate a session that I saw being implemented at a recent QCon conference. Simply place a stack of red, yellow, and green cards towards the back of the room (where the audience exits) together with an empty box. Instruct the audience to pick up a card denoting how they felt about the session (red being bad, green being good, and yellow somewhere in the middle) and to place it in the box on their way out. This takes minimum investment from the audience, is anonymous, and while it won't provide anecdotal feedback, you will still get an overall feeling for how the session was received.

Where are we?

In this chapter, we've had the opportunity to cover many of the aspects important to your big day, including preparation, how to interact with the audience, and correctly closing a session.

As a related final note for this chapter, I did want to touch on sharing your presentation. Often the audience, especially those who visit you at the podium, will want to know where they can download the slides. It's good to have something prepared ahead of time, otherwise you could be dealing with copying the deck via USB sticks or emailing links around.

If you are planning to share the session, I would recommend defaulting to PDF as this will retain any custom fonts that you might have used. A PDF file can also prevent people making their own version of the presentation, if this is something that you are worried about. If PDF doesn't work, then of course you'll have to resort to a PPTX or KEY file.

If you are sharing the presentation publicly, I would recommend uploading to a site such as SlideShare.[3] Not only is this easy to share with the audience, but it also gives the audience a way of reviewing the presentation online without having to download the file first. A blog or other site with a memorable URL can also be useful, especially if you have a domain registered for your name (e.g., simonguest.com).

While this brings us to the end of your presentation day, we are going to continue the conversation in the next chapter as we look at some of the variations that you may have to do as a presenter to accommodate differing circumstances and environments.

Chapter 9: Your Big Day

1. http://www.ted.com/talks/amy_cuddy_your_body_language_shapes_who_you_are.html
2. For more information, I would recommend this article: http://www.japanintercultural.com/en/news/default.aspx?newsid=101
3. http://www.slideshare.net

CHAPTER 10: Variations
* * *

Up until this chapter in the book, we have made certain assumptions about your presentation, which include the fact that it is being delivered in person to an audience that understands your native language.

In this chapter, we are going to flip the bit on some of these concepts, and cover three types of variations for presentations that you might have to deliver. These variations will include presenting in other countries (to audiences that don't speak your native language), presenting to remote or online audiences, and presenting 1:1 with executives such as the CTO or CEO of a company. For each variation we'll cover some of the challenges, changes that you may need to make, and where possible, build upon the concepts that you've learned in previous chapters.

Presenting in other countries

Presenting in other countries can be extremely rewarding, yet at the same time very challenging. I've been fortunate to have had the opportunity to present in multiple countries across Asia and Europe as part of my career. While I've been able to visit some magnificent destinations, I've also learned useful tips and techniques for putting together presentations for audiences in their native country.

Learning a new culture

For any presenter delivering a talk in person, the first place to start is to learn some of the the elements of the culture. Not only will this provide an appreciation of some of the cultural differences, but it will also enable you to be proactive by changing some of your terms and gestures as you interact with others. This might range from forming an understanding that the Dutch tend to be very blunt when it comes to questions at the end of presentations, through to my home country, England, where the English will often deliver a padded, polite piece of feedback to avoid hurting your feelings—even if they thought your session was a flop!

To list all of the countries in this book would be near impossible, and as luck would have it, someone else has already done a much better job. If you do not yet have a copy, and you find yourself presenting in multiple countries with differing cultures, I would highly recommend picking up the second edition of Kiss, Bow, or Shake Hands (Morrison and Conaway, 2006). The book takes a snapshot of over 60 countries, providing an abstract but useful view of cultural norms, language differences, and other factors useful for establishing a strong relationship with others.

Where possible, I also recommend reviewing the content of your slides for norms that might work against you in a particular culture. For one presentation that I did many years ago, I had used a picture of a man answering a phone in a call center. While I thought nothing of this, it wasn't until I got to speaking with one of my colleagues in Japan where I found out that this is very rare. While it wouldn't have caused an outrage, it would have been something that would have appeared somewhat strange to the audience.

Presenting in English to a non-English-speaking audience

Given the pervasive use of English in the software and technology industry, there is a good chance that even if you are speaking in a country where English isn't the first language, the audience will still be able to understand you. But I have found three exceptions to this rule being

China, Japan, and Korea, which we will cover shortly.

While the audience might understand English, it's still important to realize that for many in the room, it won't be their native tongue, and for this reason there are a few things that you should modify in your presentation in order to accommodate.

Firstly, for any non-English-speaking audience, you'll want to slow down your talk. Slowing down will allow you more time to enunciate your words more clearly, and will also allow additional time for the audience to fully comprehend everything that you are speaking about. For this to be effective, you don't need to slow down to a crawl or mimic something that you might see on an instant replay. Instead, simply reduce the speed of your conversational tone to around 75% of normal by inserting carefully placed pauses. What should have taken you three minutes to present should now take four, and you can use one of your timed rehearsals as discussed in Chapter 7 to perfect your timing for this. If you are finding that you are naturally speeding up halfway through, placing a small note to yourself on your laptop (as discussed in Chapter 8) can also help immensely.

Secondly, if you have time prior to the presentation, I always recommend trying to do part or all of your introduction in the language of the country that you are visiting. You can typically work out a couple of lines using various translation engines on the Internet, and while you may need some help from a native speaker to perfect the delivery, the impact for the audience can be amazing. Simply translating "Hello, my name is Simon and I'm very pleased to be here" as an opening line in the audience's native language will demonstrate that you've made a special effort (over and above traveling) and will often form an instant connection before you've even started on the main part of your content. If you often travel to various countries as part of your job, I would encourage you to try this and observe the results.

Finally, even if you don't have the time or willingness to learn a couple of lines in the native language, finding out some current events before the presentation can still be useful. Was there a major sporting event recently? What's happening in the news with this country? Is there something about the local food that you liked? While it sounds trivial, having speaking points such as these can also go a long way to help connect with the audience. You may not want to feature all of these in your opening lines, but inserting subtle references in demo data or other slides can make for a positive impact, and (again) one that the audiences feels that you have gone above and beyond for.

Presenting using translation services

Presenting in China, Japan, or Korea is an incredible experience, but can present a unique set of challenges, especially around language. As we discussed, although English is prevalent in the technology industry across much of the world, the adoption rate for technology companies in many countries in Asia is lower. To present effectively in these countries you will need to adapt your style considerably, especially if you are working with a translator.

For many technical presentations, organizations will assign or bring in a translator. A translator will be one person, possibly two people for larger events, who will be translating your session from English into the native language of the audience. They will also be available at the end of the session for handling questions and answers.

For most presentations there are two types of translation techniques: Serial translation and simultaneous translation.

Serial translation is where the translator will listen to a couple of the sentences that you say in English, take some notes, and relay the information in the native tongue while you pause. Serial translation can be effective, but also very time consuming as you will be presenting in English and then having someone else essentially repeat the same information. If you do get offered a translation service, and do discover that they will be doing serial translation, you should be prepared to reduce your presentation content by 50% or more due to this fact. One upside is that while you are covering far less content, serial translation does mean that you have many pauses in your speech, which I have found makes my delivery more concise and to the point, as I have much more time to think about the next few sentences.

Simultaneous translation, as you may have guessed by the name, is where one or more translators will attempt to translate your presentation in near real time. As you start speaking, the translator will listen, often taking copious amounts of notes, and start reading back the notes in the native tongue while at the same time listening for your next sentences. This is an amazing skill, and I only wish that I could do this! For this type of translation you will likely be speaking into a microphone routed to the translators who are situated in an audio booth towards the back of the room. The translators will deliver their version of the presentation to the audience, who will be listening via radio headsets. In this case, although the audience can see you on stage and knows that you are speaking, their main form of audible communication will be coming from the translator via the headset.

Even though the translation is somewhat simultaneous it is still, however, really important that you slow down the delivery of your presentation. It's actually more important than serial translation because if you go too fast with a simultaneous translator, they will skip sentences or other parts of your speech because they can't keep up, which may lead to the audience missing out on vital information that you might be trying to get across. For simultaneous translation, I would recommend aiming towards delivering 60–70% of your normal content and slowing down the delivery in order to accommodate.

For simultaneous translation it is also really important to leave a long pause at the end of each slide. If possible, you should make sure that the translator catches up to you at the end of the slide to prevent the translator speaking about one slide while you have moved on to the next. An effective way of achieving this is to insert a long pause at the end of each slide and wait. If you are lucky enough, you might also be able to hear the faint chatter of the translator through one of the headsets in the front row (or if you are very prepared, you can even request your own headset that you wear in one ear at very low volume). By doing this, you'll know the point at where the translator has finished speaking about a slide and when you can move on to the next. While it might seem and feel a little awkward to have long gaps at the end of each slide, it will come across as perfectly normal for the audience listening.

One final note on simultaneous translation: Be careful with humor! Not only is humor incredibly difficult to stretch across any language barrier, but performing humor via a translation service means that your original intent is often lost. While the translator might understand your words, they might not understand the humor, especially if you are making a subtle or sarcastic point. In addition, even if the humor does work, because the simultaneous translator is relaying information several seconds behind you, you'll hear the audience laugh well after you've told the joke! This itself isn't a bad thing, but can be a little disconcerting to hear the audience laugh right in the middle of one of your sentences!

Regardless of whether the translator is doing serial or simultaneous translation, you'll definitely want to schedule some time with them before your session in order to review the deck. Often, the translator will have their own copy of the deck and will make notes as you go through your presentation giving a rough outline of each of the topics. This is especially useful to help the translator demystify and expand some of the acronyms or technical terms that they might not be familiar with.

Creating a localized presentation

As you may have guessed, one of the drawbacks of any translation is that while the audience is hearing audio in their native tongue, you will still be presenting your slides and content in English. While nonnative speakers of English can often read English better than they can understand, you might find many in your audience "tune out" the slides during your talk, lowering their heads and instead concentrating on the audio coming from the translator. This is especially noticeable if the audience wears the headsets. All of the hard work that you have put into your "canvas" can be lost on an audience because of this language barrier.

One of the answers to this problem is to localize your content into the native language. You may be wondering how you could possibly present something that you don't understand, but if you have gone through all of the rehearsal techniques that we've outlined in this book, there's a good chance that you already know the slide titles and text by heart. As you move forward to a new slide in your deck even though you might not be able to understand the finer points of the text, you'll already know what you should be saying by the time you get to this point, especially if you have a lot of images throughout your presentation.

Localizing any finished presentation deck is relatively easy and cost effective, and there are many Internet-based services that will do this all online. In addition, most services charge by the number of words, so if your deck is light on text and bullets (as it should be by this point in the book!) cost really should not be a barrier.

For me, the pinnacle of a great presenter is one who can not only work effectively with the translators, but can also deliver a deck localized to the language for the country in which they are speaking. Not only does this demonstrate a level of professionalism, but it will also ensure that the audience is fully immersed in the presentation through both the audio translation and everything that you present to them on screen.

Presenting to online audiences

Due to many factors, including the desire to reach a wider audience and the need to reduce travel, lots of organizations are opting towards online presentations as a replacement for in-person meetings. As a presenter, it's important to understand some of the subtle differences between presenting to an online audience as opposed to presenting to an in-person group.

In general, there are many different types of online presentations. For the purposes of this book, an "online presentation" refers to one where the audience will be attending remotely, typically from their computer, and one where the presenter will be sharing both video and audio to the audience. There are many different solutions for online meetings available, including Google Hangouts, GoToMeeting from Citrix, and

Microsoft's Lync.

Regardless of the technology used, there are several tips and techniques you can use to ensure a successful remote presentation.

Technical setup

You may be presenting from the office, from home, or even on the road. Regardless of the location and the software being used, getting the technical setup right is important.

The first thing to often check is the speed and quality of the network connection. I typically find that any connection below 2 Mb per second can result in stuttering or pauses during the presentation, so it's worth checking this beforehand. If I'm unsure of the network speed, a quick check on SpeedTest[1] will often determine whether you will have sufficient bandwidth. In addition, I don't recommend presenting on a machine connected to a tethered wireless hotspot (such as your iPhone) or a MiFi device unless you are sure that you have a strong 4G LTE connection as anything slower will again likely result in a poor experience for the audience.

Once you are happy with the connection, I would definitely recommend investing in a headset. Although echo cancellation technology has improved over the past few years, using the built-in microphone and speakers on your laptop can often result in poor audio quality for the attendees, especially if you have any background noise. A good quality headset[2] will deliver the best audio experience for those listening.

As you can imagine, being comfortable with the software that you are planning to use is also important. Although this sounds obvious, there are many occasions where you might not have used the conference software before, especially if you are presenting to a customer who insists on using their software or presenting to part of an organized online conference.

While you can't cover every feature of the meeting software as you set up, I always look for three things.

1. How do I mute the audience (in case there is a lot of background noise)?

2. How do I share my screen (especially selecting the right screen if you have a multi-monitor setup)?

3. How do I talk to others using an instant message or chat functionality (especially useful if the audience members want to ask questions halfway through)?

With these three things in mind, I usually feel comfortable that the online meeting should be in my control. Of particular note to these, however, is the screen sharing ability. Many online conference solutions will give you the choice of either sharing your screen or uploading your slide deck for conversion for the audience. If you face this, I always recommend going down the path of sharing your screen as I've found the process of "converting" the presentation can strip out animations, fonts, and other parts critical to the presentation. Sharing your screen will ensure that the audience gets to see the presentation in exactly the way it was intended—although the caveats of sharing your desktop, as we discussed at the end of Chapter 8, still apply! One caveat to the screen sharing rule is to realize that there will be a lag for the audience. This isn't so critical when switching between slides, but is good to have in mind for demos, and often rules out the possibility of showing videos.

Finally, in addition to the podium checklist that we covered in detail during Chapter 9, if you are presenting in an office or conference room, I would also suggest placing a Post-it note on the door with "Online presentation in progress" to deter any people who may otherwise interrupt you.

Handling feedback from an online audience

With the technical setup covered, there are a few modifications that you'll likely want to make to your presentation in order to accommodate an online audience. The first is to reduce the overall content to around 80% of what you would have delivered in person. This will cover any late comers, technical issues, and impromptu questions, all of which get magnified during an online meeting.

Next, I would suggest planning a more formal introduction. As you don't have a physical presence for the audience, you may consider using a more formal introduction that includes the name and title of the session, together with any additional information you might think that the audience will need. This is especially important if you are recording the session as it will provide context for anyone who watches the session at a later date.

During the session, it's also really important to prompt the audience for their feedback, especially in 1:1 and small group settings. Because you can't see the audience, it's impossible to pick up on any visual cues that you might be missing out on. Are people yawning or completely disconnected from the conversation? This is difficult to tell if you can't see people. To overcome this, at various points in the presentation, pause and ask for validation. "Is this hitting home?" or "Does this resonate with what you are seeing today?" can be useful to ensure you still have the attention of the audience. The audience can reply by unmuting their phones, or if they want to provide feedback in real time, by using the instant chat window.

Somewhat related to this, if the audience forgets, don't be afraid to put select members of the audience back on mute after you've asked them a question. It might sound rude to put people on mute, but there's nothing worse than dogs barking or someone forgetting that they are not on mute and having a lengthy conversation in the background.

Having a backup plan

Finally, if you are presenting a lot of online presentations, especially to larger audiences, it's important to have a backup plan for when things go wrong. This might include losing audio, video, and having network or screen sharing issues at any point during the session. On a couple of occasions, I've also had my machine mysteriously reboot in the middle of an online presentation. One of the frustrating things about these types of hiccups is that when they happen, the audience is often unable to tell you about them because the connection has been lost!

To overcome this, if the presentation is critical, I always recommend having a colleague or friend participate in the online meeting as an attendee. Not only will they be able to see the same experience that others in the audience are seeing, but if anything goes wrong they can be in a position to alert you (e.g., by sending you a text message). While these types of failures are on the rare side, having someone who can alert you —and at the same time, communicate with the audience as you are scrambling to get back online—can be very useful.

Presenting 1:1 to executives

For the final variation in this chapter, I wanted to cover presenting to executives.

Getting your presentation format right for executives is important as, unlike a large audience where you have the luxury of controlling the pace, a busy executive is more likely to demand that you get to a part of the presentation that they are interested in. For this, I recommend several alterations for your presentation.

Firstly, although I have rejected the idea of an agenda slide up until now, this might be something that you want to consider for an executive presentation. Including one will frame the conversation, and will act as an opportunity for them to direct you to the piece of the presentation that they are most interested in. This will save you time and allows you to focus on the part of the presentation that is going to resonate the most.

Next, somewhat related to the first, you may want to consider tuning the content to the most important points during an executive presentation. This doesn't mean less slides necessarily (as we covered in the start of the book, there is little correlation between the number of slides and the amount of time), but instead I would recommend questioning each part of the presentation to ensure that it will be relevant for the person you are presenting to. An alternative way of doing this can be to create a new persona for the executive and then run through the applicability of each of the sections to that persona, as we described in Chapter 3. This will help you determine the sections that really will provide the most value.

Moreover, if you are asked to forward the presentation to the executive after your meeting, I would recommend creating an executive summary at the beginning of the deck. This summary can be a couple of slides that touch on some of the salient points raised during the meeting, and will help reinforce your presentation without the executive having to flick through all of the slides. This technique is especially useful if your presentation has a lot of slides behind it.

Finally, in addition to the adjustments to the presentation, you should also think about how you are going to deliver your talk—especially if it is to be held in the office of the executive. Many executives don't have a projector in their office, which will mean that you will both be sharing the screen of your laptop. This can be a little uncomfortable, especially if there is a big desk between the both of you! Assuming you don't have any demos, a much better approach is to load the presentation on an iPad (or other tablet device) if you have access to one, and walk the executive through the slides on this device. You may have to use some alternative presentation software to achieve this, but using such a device in this setting will be much more effective and will also come across as being more professional.

Where are we?

Although there are many different types of variations to presentation, in this chapter we have focused on the three most common. Whether you are presenting in other countries, handling online audiences, or dealing with executives, I hope some of the modifications have been useful.

To take the idea of modifications forward, the next and final chapter in this book is designed to talk about anti-patterns: namely, the types of things that you should never do during your presentation!

---

1. http://speedtest.net

2. I'm personally a fan of the range of headsets available from Plantronics: http://www.plantronics.com

CHAPTER 11: Anti-Patterns for Presentations

* * *

As you may know, software development has the concept of patterns and anti-patterns. Patterns are tried and tested methods for writing and structuring code that has been proven to work well. Anti-patterns are exactly the opposite, and are often published as guidance or warnings for what software developers should avoid in their code.

Using this same theme, I wanted to share some anti-patterns for presentations. In no particular order, these are the ten things that I've frequently come across in the many presentations I've either experienced or witnessed, together with stories for many that will hopefully reinforce the point. My hope is that you find them useful, as well as offer a lighter way of concluding the main content in this book.

Never offend the audience

The last thing you want to do in any presentation is alienate the crowd in the room. Lose the audience, and your presentation might as well be over. Ironically, it is possible to offend the audience—both intentionally and unintentionally.

Offending the audience intentionally is often used together with humor, and is very difficult to do. In all of my time watching others present, I've only witnessed one person get away with it—a friend and colleague, Ted Neward. Ted has a particular style and panache, and has this thing rehearsed to a point. Ted has offended developers from different camps, people from different companies, and even dares to bring up the war when he was recently presenting in Poland!

Ted is Ted. Although this makes for a very entertaining presentation, my advice to you is to stay well clear! Like a lot of humor, it's very difficult to pull off and you can easily land yourself in trouble.

Offending the audience unintentionally is a little easier to do. One of the common ways that I've seen software developers do this is to talk down competing or opposing products. During the Q&A session at the end of a talk, I've heard audiences ask a question about a competing product only to be disparaged by the presenter, "Oh, you don't want to use that—it's rubbish!" While it may or may not be true, the presenter has unintentionally offended the person asking the question as well as anyone else in the audience who happens to use that product. By stating such a claim, the presenter is effectively saying that the audience has made a wrong decision, which in turn may cause negativity or resentment towards the presenter.

The moral of this anti-pattern? Whether intentional or unintentional, don't offend the audience!

Never inflate your ego

A lot of presenters have big egos. It's easy to see why. Drawing a crowd of hundreds of followers all eager to hear what you are talking about, being flown around the world, and being put up in the best hotels, eating expenses-paid dinners can be a big power trip.

While it might seem that everyone is just here to make your presentation successful, remember that you are not a rock star! You should treat everyone with respect, from the conference organizers to the A/V team, and especially the audience.

Never over inflate your ego as it can—and likely will—quickly backfire on you.

Never mention politics or religion in your presentation

If you remember anything from this chapter, please remember the two things that you should never mention in a presentation: politics and religion.

Unless the subject of your presentation is about politics or religion, my advice is to keep clear. Mentioning either can inadvertently make you appear like you are taking sides, and as soon as you do that you run the risk of offending the audience.

I've seen presenters fall into this trap on several occasions, and the outcome has never been pretty. One of the most memorable is a presenter who I won't mention here, but who was concluding a presentation to a packed room of about 500 attendees. The talk had been going especially well, and the audience had been engaged throughout many of the speaking points.

Then came the ending. The presenter wanted to highlight the point that "you never know what you might find on the Internet." To demonstrate this, he had selected a video from YouTube of a character representing Jesus set to a particular song ("I Will Survive" by Gloria Gaynor). About halfway through the set, Jesus gets knocked down by a bus and the video promptly ends.

Needless to say, while there were people in the audience who saw the funny side of the video, the majority were in shock—either from the content of the video or the audacity of the presenter who had the guts to show it.

The presenter's point may well have been valid (there is certainly a lot of strange stuff on the Internet!), but there were a million different other pieces of content that he could have selected to make that point and avoid audience outcry and an apology later issued.

The moral of this story? Stay away from anything that might drag you into politics or religion!

Never swear or include profanity

Many strong presenters can get away with swearing or including profanity as part of a talk, but I don't recommend it.

At its best, it will work and it will create a stronger connection with the audience. At its worst, it will create a sense of awkwardness in the room and you'll start to see people cringe. This anti-pattern is especially true when speaking with audiences from countries other than yours who might not have the same tolerance for such terms. I once had to sit through an hour-long talk where the presenter insisted on using the term "intellectual masturbation" repeatedly throughout when discussing hard challenges that he and his product team had to overcome. While the first time was remotely amusing to some in the audience, after hearing this again and again, many people started to walk out.

Bottom line? Swearing or profanity will likely not add anything to your presentation, and I would wholeheartedly recommend avoiding it

Never present someone else's presentation

We touched a little on this in Chapter 3 when we talked about structure, but I would recommend never presenting someone else's presentation.

It can be very tempting to do this. Maybe a colleague has fallen ill, and your boss needs someone to step in at the last minute. Or maybe you are running out of time and you've found another presentation that "has a lot of things that you can reuse."

Please don't do this. You need to make the presentation your own. On a couple of occasions, I've seen presenters regurgitate slide decks from other colleagues and it has always been a mess. There is no story, a complete lack of preparation, and as a result, the presenter ends up reading the slides verbatim, which is horrible for the audience.

Please don't do it!

Never present from someone else's machine

When presenting as part of a team or at a conference, it can be very tempting to present using the same machine (or use the podium machine supplied at the event). Where possible, please try to avoid this. While it might seem convenient to share a machine or simply copy your presentation to a USB stick, the risk often outweighs the reward. Here are a few things that can potentially go wrong:

- **Different versions of Microsoft PowerPoint or Apple Keynote.** While the slide deck might open fine, you can never be sure that it's going to run without issues.

- **Demos.** Demos will not be copied across or won't necessarily be available on the other machine.

- **Videos and other embedded content.** As we learned in Chapter 5, the same applies to video or other embedded content that you might have included.

- **Custom fonts.** Any custom fonts that you've used in your presentation might not be available on the other machine. This is fairly common with "podium presentation" machines and you may not catch this until halfway through the presentation (when PowerPoint defaults to Helvetica and messes up your deck).

- **Other stuff.** Finally, you have no idea what other stuff might be running on the machine. Virus checkers that could slow down your presentation or other software that interferes with your presentation remote, just to name a couple.

Golden rule? If you have never rehearsed from the machine, never use it in front of the audience!

Never let anyone else give your slides a "makeover"

Many large conferences, especially ones in the technology space, have dedicated organizations that help with "presentation preparation." This can include ensuring that the appropriate template is used, and (pardon my sarcasm) that all presentations look uniformly boring.

If I can get away with it, I never use these "presentation makeover" services. They will often apply templates that I don't want applied, change fonts that I don't want changed, and move images around that don't need to be moved.

One of the nice things about everything that you've hopefully learned throughout this book is that your end result is a presentation that is actually very difficult to give a makeover to. These services are normally used to aligning bullet points on a page. If you hand across a slide deck that has very few bullet points, things get interesting.

I remember one occasion vividly. I was presenting at a conference in Seattle in 2007, and as part of the process I had to submit my slide deck to the "presentation team" 48 hours ahead of time. The company in question had hired an outside company who were going to "make sure [my] slide deck conforms with the company template and standards." Ugh! Anyway, I did what they asked and turned up 48 hours ahead of time with my presentation on a USB stick. Sitting with one of the presentation assistants in the review room, I could only witness a look of horror as she opened the deck on her computer and started to skim through 238 slides worth of material, mostly photos. I even believe there was a picture of a farm animal! After she recovered her composure, she turned to me and said, "You do realize that all of these pictures will need to be put into the company template?" I responded somewhat sarcastically that if she'd like to do this—which I'm sure would have taken her most of the next 48 hours—she was more than welcome, but that I wouldn't be presenting anything apart from my original deck.

My stubborn tone got escalated to her manager, and then her

manager's manager. I was starting to doubt whether they were going to let me present. Finally, as the debate grew, the owner of the design company was called into the room. I feared the worst as the owner sat down and started flicking through my slides on the screen. After reaching about the twenty-fifth slide, she paused, looked at me, and said, "This looks amazing. If more people had presentations like this, we would be out of a job!"

Never move room or location

I've seen a few presenters do this, and also experienced it for myself at a large conference in New Orleans. Once you have your room assignment for your presentation, moving locations can cause trouble.

For the New Orleans conference, as part of my in-room rehearsal, I found that the room was very small. My early expectation was that we should get around 200 attendees, yet the room was only capable of holding closer to 50. Realizing this, I contacted the conference organizers who were able to relocate my session to an alternative room. What I didn't realize at the time, however, is that this alternative room was about a 30-minute walk. Yes, the New Orleans conference center is a big place! Attendees who wanted to come to the session went to the original room, only to be told that the session had moved to an alternative location about 30 minutes away. As you can imagine, only the die-hard attendees actually made it to the new location. Ironically, there were only about 50 in total, but they were now seated in a room that could hold five times that amount!

The lesson of this anti-pattern is that unless it's an emergency (such as the room being uninhabitable), I recommend strongly against moving locations. This is especially true for larger technology conferences where the schedule, agenda, and room assignments will have likely been printed in advance, and will be very difficult to change.

Never mess with the A/V equipment

There is a strong correlation between the size of the room and the amount of A/V equipment that is needed to support it. This anti-pattern stresses that no matter how much A/V equipment you have in the room, it's never a good idea to mess with it!

My particular experience reminds me of a conference in 2006 where I was testing some new effects as part of my presentation opening. The session kicked off, and everything seemed to be going well, but the audience wasn't reacting like I'd experienced when presenting the same content on previous occasions.

A couple of slides in, I was starting to get worried. Was the microphone on? Did I have the right room? Was the attendee party the night before? After a while, I figured it out. I had been messing around with the A/V equipment leading up to the start of the presentation, and had accidentally hit the "pause" button on the projector. I didn't even know that that projector had a pause button! The result was that the projector was still showing my title slide, even though my laptop had moved on several slides and animations since. Of course, it took me a few minutes and help from one of the members of the A/V team to figure out that I had hit this button!

While it wasn't a huge failure, it was a great lesson to leave the A/V equipment alone, especially at the last minute.

Never use "Next slide, please!"

The final anti-pattern that I'll leave you with is the one that ironically motivated me to write this book. For the sake of avoiding trouble, I won't mention the conference, speaker, or time, but let's just say this was the opening keynote of a very large software developer conference in San Francisco.

The opening presenter was indeed the CEO of this particular company and was addressing a crowd of well over 5,000 attendees. After a small preamble welcoming everyone to the conference, it suddenly appeared that this CEO had forgotten his presentation remote. Being a very well operated, professional keynote stage layout, there was no podium or machine to turn to. So in panic, the CEO had to shout, "Next slide, please!" to advance to the next slide. While this wasn't initially that bad, the audience quickly realized that there were around a hundred slides, each of which would require calling out to someone in the back room in order to advance the slides.

While it's not an anti-pattern to forget things—we all do this—what makes this worse is that for the closing keynote, the very same thing happened! The CEO turned up on stage again without the presentation remote. I felt the audience give a collective sigh once they realized that we were going to be hearing the same, "Next slide, please!" over and over.

The moral of this anti-pattern? Of course, try not to forget your presentation remote. And if you do, please don't do it twice! And finally, if you are the CEO of a company, it's actually OK to shout, "Can someone bring me a presentation remote, please?" rather than torture your audience for the entire presentation!

Conclusion

This brings us to the end of the book. Similar to the recommendations that I outlined in Chapter 3, I'm a big believer that conclusions should be short and to the point, and you'll be glad to hear that this section is no exception!

Personally, it has been an amazing experience putting together the content for this book. From defining your audience, structuring your presentation, creating your mind map, developing your slide canvas, rehearsing, thinking about demo gods, preparing for your big day, configuring variations, and learning about anti-patterns, my only goal has been to share tips, techniques, and recommendations that help improve the delivery of your technical presentation. Regardless of where your career takes you, the organization that you work for, or the subjects you are presenting on, you'll have a roadmap before you click on File > New > Presentation!